CULTURE SHOCK!

A Survival Guide to Customs and Etiquette

INDIA

Lynelle Seow

Marshall Cavendish
Editions

© 2017 Marshall Cavendish International (Asia) Private Limited

Published by Marshall Cavendish Editions
An imprint of Marshall Cavendish International

A member of the
Times Publishing Group

Other Marshall Cavendish Offices:
Marshall Cavendish Corporation. 99 White Plains Road, Tarrytown NY 10591-9001, USA • Marshall Cavendish International (Thailand) Co Ltd. 253 Asoke, 12th Flr, Sukhumvit 21 Road, Klongtoey Nua, Wattana, Bangkok 10110, Thailand • Marshall Cavendish (Malaysia) Sdn Bhd, Times Subang, Lot 46, Subang Hi-Tech Industrial Park, Batu Tiga, 40000 Shah Alam, Selangor Darul Ehsan, Malaysia

Marshall Cavendish is a registered trademark of Times Publishing Limited

National Library Board, Singapore Cataloguing-in-Publication Data

Name(s): Seow, Lynelle.
Title: CultureShock! India : a survival guide to customs and etiquette / Lynelle Seow.
Other title(s): India : a survival guide to customs and etiquette | Culture shock India
Description: Singapore : Marshall Cavendish Editions, [2017]
Identifier(s): OCN 966299239 | ISBN 978-981-45-6147-1 (paperback)
Subject(s): LCSH: Etiquette--India. | India--Social life and customs. | India--Description and travel.
Classification: DDC 954--dc23

Printed in Singapore by Fabulous Printers Pte Ltd

Photo Credits:
All photos by the author • Cover photo by the author

All illustrations by TRIGG

ABOUT THE SERIES

Culture shock is a state of disorientation that can come over anyone who has been thrust into unknown surroundings, away from one's comfort zone. *CultureShock!* is a series of trusted and reputed guides which has, for decades, been helping expatriates and long-term visitors to cushion the impact of culture shock whenever they move to a new country.

Written by people who have lived in the country and experienced culture shock themselves, the authors share all the information necessary for anyone to cope with these feelings of disorientation more effectively. The guides are written in a style that is easy to read and cover a range of topics that will arm readers with enough advice, hints and tips to make their lives as normal as possible again.

Each book is structured in the same manner. It begins with the first impressions that visitors will have of that city or country. To understand a culture, one must first understand the people—where they came from, who they are, the values and traditions they live by, as well as their customs and etiquette. This is covered in the first half of the book.

Then on with the practical aspects—how to settle in with the greatest of ease. Authors walk readers through how to find accommodation, get the utilities and telecommunications up and running, enrol the children in school and keep in the pink of health. But that's not all. Once the essentials are out of the way, venture out and try the food, enjoy more of the culture and travel to other areas. Then be immersed in the language of the country before discovering more about the business side of things.

To round off, snippets of information are offered before readers are 'tested' on customs and etiquette. Useful words and phrases, a comprehensive resource guide and list of books for further research are also included for easy reference.

ACKNOWLEDGEMENTS

I owe a debt of gratitude to Mr and Mrs Dayal for opening their home to us and providing a nurturing environment from which we could best explore India. I benefitted greatly from their insights and invaluable feedback.

I would have never thought of putting my thoughts on paper if not for the nudging of friends, who I must thank for believing in me when the nights were long and resolve was short: Ee Huang, Patricia, Priyanka, Tammy and Yumi. Thanks must also go to Amita and friends in Delhi, Mumbai and Singapore who lent their experiences and friendship. Huge thanks go to my editors Rachel Heng and She-Reen Wong for their patience and professionalism, and to my family for accommodating my strange writing hours and creative moods. Also not forgetting "Chindians" Andrew and Devi, as well as Murugan and Dhurga, for help with the Tamil phrases. Thanks must also go to my new colleagues for their support and love.

Lastly I have to mention three people to whom I owe a deep personal debt. I am grateful to Melvin for his kindness and encouragement, and to my best friend Shah, whose unwavering encouragement and friendship have been invaluable to the completion of this book. I am especially grateful to my husband Ben, who has held my hand for 15 years and made me smile for just as long. Ben has been my sunshine and my rock, and this book is my love song to him and a story of us.

DEDICATION

For Ben and our "Indian family" —
the Dayals, Madhu and Santosh

CONTENTS

I sat pondering in my seat as the lights came on and the credits rolled. I had just watched *The Best Exotic Marigold Hotel*, a story about seven people who had left the life they had always known in order to continue it in India. As the movie-goers around me walked away from the fiction back to their comfortable lives, I lingered amid the discomfort of what my life may soon become.

My husband Ben had received word that his job would bring us to New Delhi and we had just enough time to let it sink in and watch a movie, the latter being my only effort at cultural preparation (I'm glad you're doing more, such as reading this book). As fear-driven well-wishers plied me with an immodest supply of medicines and packaged food to stave off death by diarrhoea, I knew I had to adopt a better mental model than doom. Death by close-mindedness would be far more tragic. So I changed my starting point from dread and fear (although caution is useful) and decided my time in India would be "not merely to survive, but to thrive", in the words of Maya Angelou. And to do so "with some passion, some compassion, some humour, and some style".

I believe that this is the perfect mantra for anyone embarking on their personal passage to India; not merely to survive but to thrive. Only then can you get the best out of your Indian experience with all its exotic and marigold-fringed possibilities.

It is not difficult at all to see why "Incredible India" was adopted as the slogan for the country that lies beyond the edge of singular description. Nowhere on earth is there a country older, more colourful, more intriguing, more exasperating than India, this grand old dame with a million facets and a billion characters who has seen the tide of times. Having given birth to four world religions and the oldest living civilisation, she now nurtures the world's largest democracy whilst keeping to age-old traditions in an unparalleled example of cultural continuity. Nowhere else can the past and present intertwine like it can in India. She robes herself with complexity and contradictions and wears diversity like a crown. To understand her is to have to piece together a multitude of encounters, views, odes, rants, experiences, fables and stories. This book shares mine.

MAP OF INDIA

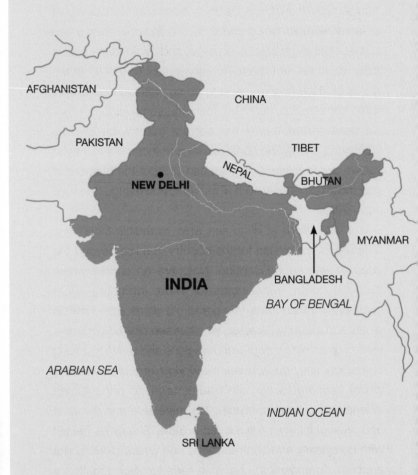

A NOTE TO THE READER

I have tried my best to provide a pan-India perspective but my account comes mainly from my experiences living in New Delhi and Mumbai, and my travels to other Indian cities, such as Amritsar, Bengaluru, Chennai, Jaipur, Hyderabad, Kolkata and Visakhapatnam.

Where generalisations are made, I have tried my best from falling into stereotypes. India is a diverse culture so if I have inadvertently crossed that line and offended anyone, I apologise in advance.

Some terms used in the book are colloquial usage, such as the word "servant" rather than "hired help", "domestic staff" or "housekeeper".

The spellings of Hindi words may differ since there isn't any standard Romanised Hindi spelling. New Delhi and Delhi are also not synonymous, as commonly thought. The country's capital of New Delhi is a district in the city and union territory of Delhi. As for other Indian cities, I have used the most recent names: Mumbai (previously Bombay), Chennai (Madras), Bengaluru (Bangalore) and Kolkata (Calcutta).

And lastly, a personal wish:

Oliver Wendell Holmes, Jr once said, "A mind that is stretched by a new experience can never go back to its old dimensions." I left India with a broader understanding of the world and a keener sense of humanity. May it be the same for you.

FIRST IMPRESSIONS

> *A mind that is stretched by a new experience can never go back to its old dimensions.*

—Oliver Wendell Holmes, Jr

Our destiny with India began as early as 2001 when we were invited by Ben's colleague Shridar to witness his nuptials in his hometown of Vijayawada. With little more than a backpack, youth and naivety, we plunged into India's deep south for a two-week-long lesson in the world at large. I remember emerging from the airport to a swarm of flies and a blur of people in numbers I had not seen before, shouting for my attention above the din of blaring horns and the *put-put-puts* of engines. It was all too much to take in and 14 days later we returned home a little older, thinner (I had food poisoning) and wiser, never expecting that within a decade, we would return once more for another shot at wonder.

In 2009, love brought me back to India. Ben had taken a job in Mumbai whilst I was finishing up my work contract in Manila. I remember emerging from the airport to a swarm of flies and a blur of people... it was the same story but a different self. I was older, more seasoned and yet, despite all I had come to expect, Mumbai served up more permutations of the unexpected. I returned to Manila a little older, fatter (with *tandoori* chicken) and wiser, never dreaming that just three years later we would return yet again—this time to call India home together.

We arrived in Delhi on a crisp November morning to the same blur of people in numbers I *had* seen before and a chilly climate I had not. I will not merely survive but thrive, I thought as an elephant lumbered past our car window. It was a fitting

Overtaking expectations; expect the largely unexpected in India.

beginning that reminded me that no matter how many times I visit India, it remains nothing short of incredible.

On our second day in Delhi, Ben tasked me to go house-hunting whilst he went to work. A few hours into the hunt with what looked like a haunted house and nothing else suitable in sight, my real-estate agent received a text that one house had just come onto the market that very afternoon and we were five minutes from it. The tall metal gate opened up into a neat 1970s double-storey white bungalow with a large garden in which two people sat drinking their afternoon tea. Fate smiled. We smiled. And our kismet found each other. This was my first introduction to the Dayals. Over the course of time, the shared house became a home of shared lives and a sun-filled window into India.

In the next two months Madhu joined us to help me wage the daily battle against dirt, dust and greasy pots and pans. Hailing from the tea estates of Darjeeling, she had the strength of two men and the stamina of 10 so I eventually sat down and let her do the heavy lifting. She swept me off my feet with her common sense and gradually her gentle affection as we grew closer over gossip and grime.

A few months later Santosh joined us as our driver. He came to the interview with a limp from a motorcycle accident a few months before and spoke only a smattering of English, a result of a simple childhood in his village in Nepal and a life unkind. He had moved to Delhi with his mother, brother and wife in search of new beginnings after being abandoned by his father. It could have hardened him, but it made him tender and kind, dependable and loyal to those he cared about. We had all needed each other in some way, initially because of shelter and service and then eventually for comfort and support, which gradually grew over tea and *pakoras* (fritters) into kinship and love. Unexpectedly, India made us a family. Such is her creative spirit in bringing together the unlikely and the improbable.

But I have skipped too quickly to the end. The journey in between is the story, the rocky road of tears and triumphs to which I can only help to provide a crude map to make it a little easier. You will have to forge your own way, whether it's down the well-trodden path or off the beaten track, and determine who and what lies at the end of the road. But first, let's go to the very real frustrating starting point of your journey: culture shock.

CULTURE SHOCK

Settling into a new country is like getting a new pair of shoes. At first, they will cut and bite, and it becomes tempting to rage and cast them angrily aside. But with perseverance you learn to adjust, and with time the shoes become more and more comfortable. You may even like them more than you care to admit. Similarly it is with India. In the beginning, India can seem like a sustained assault to your senses and sensibilities. Nothing is moderate; everything is extreme.

Here are the most common cuts and bites that can wear down even the most prepared.

- **Crowds:** A country with 1.2 billion people is bound to be crowded, but crowds in India also have a tendency to congregate, making the human crush feel much worse.
- **Noise:** White noise in India is chaos and cacophony anywhere else. The everyday onslaught of honks, bells, traffic, and voices blaring in the background, only begins to dull when you learn to turn a deaf ear.
- **Smells:** Spicy curry and incense blended with pungent notes of urine, garbage, sweat and occasionally sewage creates India's most common street scent—Eau d'our. It never fades.

- **Filth:** Overflowing garbage points, litter, clogged drains, spit and urine on Indian streets are overwhelming until they become normal, indicating that you have reached a new threshold.
- **Heat:** This is not the warmth of a sunny day; this is the near burst of the thermometer. Burning, sweltering, oppressive, sticky heat also cruelly intensifies Eau d'our. There is nothing more you can do but cope or escape.
- **Too much attention:** Everybody wants to help you or get you to buy their wares, ride their autos, donate your spare change. "Madam, madam, madam, sir, sir, sir" will be incessant until you get too tired to respond further and coldly walk away. Don't judge me, it can happen.
- **Contrasts:** Rich and poor, old and new, clean and dirty, have and have-nots; the pile-up of paradoxical pairs will be as unimaginable as they are mind-numbing and gut-wrenching. Manage your emotions well.
- **Life:** Nothing will go perfectly the way you planned or in the time you think it will take. It is best to know it now.

It is important to give yourself time to get used to it all. Some say it takes a year to come to some sort of acceptance. To shorten this time, don't fight what you cannot change but do your best to improve what you can. For many, hopes do gradually fade and preconceptions adjust. India is a process. The best way to handle culture shock is to tell yourself that things are not wrong, just different. In the movie *The Best Exotic Marigold Hotel*, Sonny Kapoor gives the best advice on how to handle the frustrations of culture shock: "Everything will be all right in the end, so if it's not all right, then it's not yet the end." It's not the end.

MADAM, YOUR SHOES ARE WELL WORN-IN

Eventually, you will reach the end in shoes well worn by the journey. You might not have found the comforts of your homeland in India, but the end of the road could yield something much more valuable—yourself.

There is some truth in the popular idea that people go to India to find themselves. But personal enlightenment comes not only through meditation in the mountains or other exotic spiritual experiences. It also comes when the environment forces you to face yourself, when it holds up a mirror and reveals your biases and attitudes, and the way you react to challenges. Some change. Others harden and grow cynical. The discovery of India is as much a discovery of yourself. So choose to let India hone a better version of yourself. Novelist Margaret Atwood says: "In the end, we all become stories." What will yours be?

CHAPTER 2

GEOGRAPHY AND HISTORY

> *India has known the innocence and insouciance
> of childhood, the passion and abandon of youth,
> and the ripe wisdom of maturity that comes
> from long experience of pain and pleasure;
> and over and over again she has renewed
> her childhood and youth and age.*

— **Jawaharlal Nehru**, *The Discovery of India*

In the confines and solitude of prison, India's first prime minister Jawaharlal Nehru wrote the book *The Discovery of India*, an ode to his beloved motherland and tribute to her nature. She was born 5,000 years ago, her name derived from Sindhu, the Sanskrit name for the Indus River. Thousands of others have tried to know and understand her, but she slips from the grips of easy definition. She is much too diverse, too faceted, too complex for impatient minds. Instead she reveals her charms slowly to those who wait to discover her, piece by piece, tale by tale. And even so, she is larger than the sum of her parts, greater than all imagination, older, more colourful and more seductive than words can conjure. She will win her way into your heart, if she doesn't crush your spirit first. Love her or loathe her; there is nothing bland and undramatic about Mother India.

THE LAND

A large shapely gal in a colourful patchwork dress, India is the seventh largest country in the world. She spans across a variety of habitats, each with its own distinctive character, customs, colours, climate and wildlife, which together contribute to the visual richness for which India is renowned.

The coastal city of Mumbai enjoys beaches and expanded horizons.

Flying over this vast country allows for a painterly view. The hard grey lines of urban sprawl soon give way to one or a combination of textures and colours in the form of mountains, plains, deserts, hills, and coastlines.

Buttressed in the north by the pristine whites of the Himalayas, the country's craggy greyish character mellows into the fertile greens of the Gangetic plains and Central Highlands that span northern India. To the west, the arid Thar Desert swirls in orange, browns and shades of sand. Further southward, occupying central and southern India, lies the triangular boulder-speckled palette of the Deccan Plateau. This mass is flanked on both sides by the hilly Western and Eastern Ghats, which gradually descend into foam-fringed coastlines bordering the Arabian Sea to the west, and the Indian Ocean and Bay of Bengal to the east.

CLIMATE

She blows hot and cold according to the seasons. India's climate can vary from alpine up in the north to temperate and tropical in the south. It is said there are five seasons in India: winter, summer, monsoon and the almost imperceptible spring and autumn. Depending on where you live, you will feel the seasons literally to various degrees.

From late November, winter in Delhi is a cold, depressing shroud of fog, coats, and bonfires. Coastal Mumbai, in contrast, enjoys a cool respite (20°C) from the heat and humidity that characterises the rest of its year. In February, Delhi's tight winter pall unwraps into bright-blue skies and a profusion of spring blooms until April. Then the mercury rapidly rises and the city braces itself for the punishment that is summer, where temperatures can reach 48°C (118°F). During this time, tempers flare faster than usual and flies thicken the air. There is not much a *delhiwala* (one that lives in Delhi) can do but to find shade and drink *nimbu pani* (lime water). Indeed, Delhi is so hot that cows faint mid-stride (or so I was told). Roads melt—this happened in May 2015 when temperatures neared 50°C! And birds, as if caught in an ornithological disaster, fall out of the sky. The worst hit are the people. Hundreds die every year across the country from sunstroke and dehydration. Thousands more suffer from

Surviving the Delhi Summer

For many people, the best way to deal with the Delhi summer is to spend summer somewhere else. Some head to the hills—Shimla, Mussoorie, Everest—anywhere where the temperature is within human limits of sanity. Some return to their home countries, creating a sudden expatriate vacuum in Delhi. By the end of May, the foreign and the affluent have disappeared, leaving behind those with either no choice or have chosen badly. So if you, like me, tend to make no escape plans and have a penchant for self-punishment, then you are in for an experience as unforgettable as it is regrettable.

I will not mince my words: summer is a subjugation of the spirit. But if you can survive a Delhi summer, you can survive anything. I have weathered three consecutive Delhi summers with open pores and an open mind, and it's been enough to come up with some advice and a brighter sunny-side up to things:

- The first thing you might feel is lonely because your friends have disappeared to their own corners of the globe. Take comfort in the company of those staying behind because the company of the miserable is its own reward. The streets grow quiet and the mood of people, including yours, starts being dictated slowly by degree Celsius.
- The hottest time of the day is usually around 3pm. If you do have to venture out, I find a stole most useful. Not for its sartorial flare, which would be the case in winter. In summer, the stole turns from accessory to necessity. It helps protect your face from the sun, flies (lots of them)

and dust. It also mops up perspiration from your face before the sweat has a chance to burn your eyes. Limp and sweat-drenched is the default style for the season.

- Looking fresh gets all the more daunting when your hair is in a frizz brought upon by the weather. To add to the challenge for women, your makeup melts with you in the sun. I have two sets of makeup to deal with this—one for the winter and one for the summer. At the time of this writing, my summer makeup has lost its will to live and I've stopped using makeup altogether except for sunscreen (SPF 50 or higher).
- To keep hydrated, guzzle down litres of *nimbu pani* as quickly as the air-conditioners guzzle off your electricity and keep your fingers crossed that there is no power failure for today. Thinking short-term is all you can muster with the lethargy the heat brings. Tomorrow is tomorrow's worry.
- Invest in an air cooler. It is cheaper to run than an air-conditioner when you need to cool a small space quickly. As long as the outside air is dry, they work well (April to June).
- If you prefer an air-conditioner, make sure they will work when it's 50°C outside. These are the kind of robust appliances you should invest in. Also make sure the air-conditioners are serviced and topped up with gas before the summer hits. Prices go up with the temperature.
- As much as you are tempted to do so, do not stick your head into the freezer. You don't know when the next power failure will be and you need to keep all that cold air in so that your food doesn't go bad.
- Also, don't leave food out too long because food spoils as fast as you can spell s-a-l-m-o-n-e-l-l-a.
- If you feel thirsty all the time, the animals do too. Leave some water out for birds, cows and stray dogs.
- There isn't such a thing as too many facials. They are necessary to lessen the effects of hours of squinting and scowling that will mark your days and face.
- Laundry dries fast and to a nice crisp. Leave it out in the sun for two hours and you come back with baked goods.
- You will understand relativity. There's no such thing as "cold", just 50 shades of hot. You turn on the tap marked "cold" and hot water pours out. Your vocabulary of words to describe "hot" will expand, largely through experience: scorching, merciless, brutal, sweltering, sizzling, suffocating, stupid.
- You will appreciate ice and pictures of snow-capped mountains like never before. You will eat a disproportionate amount of ice cream.
- You will laugh about this one day or maybe file this in your memory under "never again".

It is 46°C today and there's a power failure. So the last words of advice I have for you are the same that I am now telling myself: Like the tap water, nothing is ever cool, so the best way to cope is to keep yours and think happy thoughts. Now I'm off to get some ice cream.

Monsoon rains annually flood the streets of Mumbai, a reminder of the city's origins as seven islands.

power cuts due to an over-burdened electricity grid. Indeed, hell hath no mercy like a Delhi summer. Its misery also shares the company of the *loo*, a hot, dusty wind that appears suddenly during this season. The sky turns apocalyptically dark as hot winds of dust and fine sand shroud the city. Thankfully, *loos* are few and far between in Delhi, just like the occurrence of its other namesake. But that's another story (see Toilets on page 210).

Far from the animal fainting spells, central and southern India are fanning themselves in the tropical humid air, waiting expectantly for the start of the monsoon rains that will sustain crops and flood cities. Between June and September, the southwest monsoon sweeps its way northward from the southern coast of Kerala, turning roads to rivers, saplings to gold. By September, the rains gradually cover the entire country. Coastal belts and the northeastern states are lashed and the eastern coast is occasionally hit by cyclones. In Delhi, the rains do not come with the same vigour as they do elsewhere, but what they lack in dramatic entry, they make up for in effect: sticky humidity, flooded streets, traffic snarls, disease, damp clothing and acid rain. As November approaches, the moodiness washes away as the air grows crisp with the coming of autumn.

Days then grow shorter, colder and more festive as the calendar eases to winter. For some, it bids the return of frostbite and snowstorms. For others, it means cool happy days and a slew of outdoor events that will eventually fade with the spring flowers to the rising heat of summer. This seasonal cycle of comfort and discomfort continues relentlessly, lending rhythm to life and a timetable to celebration and festivals.

FLORA AND FAUNA

Fauna

Like in Rudyard Kipling's *The Jungle Book*, there are a cast of characters that have become synonymous with India—the Bengal tiger, cobra, and elephant, to name a few. Some

We were once caught in a massive traffic jam in Mumbai that stretched far beyond our patience. We inched forward slowly to finally find the source of the stall—an elephant out for an evening stroll. Deaf to the blaring of car horns, it gave us what we humans equate to the middle finger—its huge swaying rump stubbornly stuck in the middle of the road.

Since then and with lessening surprise, I've seen camels in my neighbourhood, wild boars foraging in dumpsters across the city, and monkeys in more places I can name. My friend's TV cable coverage is dependent on whether the wild peacocks are perched on her satellite dish. She claims she can predict what the peacocks are doing by turning on her TV. They are resting when she loses the sports channels and going to peacock third-base when she gets intermittent reception.

Although most are benign encounters, there is always a risk you might be at the receiving end of some nastiness. Wild boars can get aggressive, and street dogs and monkeys can bite. My encounter, significantly less serious than getting rabies, involved a horse that failed to apply his own brakes and ended up rear-ending my car. (As a gesture of apology, the horse licked the hood clean until the traffic signal turned green, which I must say is a more civil response than some Delhi drivers I've seen.)

are linked specifically to their habitat, like the Asiatic lion of Gujarat and the rhino of Assam. Indeed, there are several national parks and wildlife resorts that bring you closer into their homes but general encounters, more often than not, are found much closer to yours. The Asian elephant, for example, live on the vast stretches of the Gangetic Plains but these pachyderms are also frequently spotted in the streets where you live.

Bovine Sightings

The animal you will encounter the most is the cow. They are everywhere, expected and unexpected. Newcomers to India are usually fascinated by the sight of them strolling calmly through trendy shopping areas or congregating at busy road intersections. To the uninitiated mind, cows are found only on

Cows sauntering through a popular shopping arcade in South Delhi.

farms or at pasture, but like everything else in India, reality here has enough room to encompass the improbable. Within a few months, you will no longer flinch at a bovine sighting. Instead, you would have acquired a view about cows larger than meat and milk.

The Indian cow differs physically from the dairy cow we know by its floppy ears and hump on its back. But it is the way the Indian cow is treated that sets it vastly apart. The cow is respected and honoured by Hindus as sacred, mentioned in Hinduism's major texts. Because of her life-giving milk and gentle nature, she is seen as a symbol of life and a mother figure, as well as an emblem for *ahimsa* (non-violence), a main teaching in Hinduism, Jainism and Buddhism. As a result, the cow is a protected animal in Hinduism (and Jainism) and Hindus generally do not eat beef.

The products of the cow—milk and ghee in particular—are used in worship, penance and rites of passage. Cow dung

The cow is special in India, and it seems not just to man. I live in a very urban neighbourhood that is visited often by a family of seven to 10 cows. They thoughtfully walk in single file following an invisible middle line that separates the two directions of traffic. Sometimes they stop for food and water that have been left out for them or are ambushed by street kids who want to play. At other times, they move steadily along as if solely motivated by the promise of bounty at their destination. I don't know where they go but when the moon is high and the night grows still, they make their way home. On some nights, I awake to their mooing. Then there are other nights where the moos are accompanied by barks in a twisted bovine-canine duet. It is the drill-sergeant bark of the stray dog that lives across the street. As if propelled by a higher reason, the mutt takes it upon himself on occasion to get the herd in order and guide them safely home. This is the story told to me by our night guard, a man whose drink is as strong as his delusions. Who am I to question his sacred cows?

is used as fertiliser in farms and as a disinfectant in homes. When dried and patted into cakes, they are used as fuel for cooking or as building material. It is hard for us to imagine dung being used for anything other than fertiliser so it was with hesitation and a small amount of hysteria that I entered a small hut made of cow-dung. Suffice to say I didn't linger but neither did I balk. I do, however, draw the line at dung-fired BBQs.

The Indian Palm Squirrel

The Indian Palm squirrel is about the size of a chipmunk and is identified by three conspicuous white stripes on its back. This squirrel is considered sacred in India and therefore is left to frolic to its heart's desire. It feeds on a diet of fruit and nuts, but the overweight ones also munch on chips, chapati and other food left behind in parks. In my garden, these squirrels enjoy a diet of mango and custard apple (before the humans do), as well as generous helpings of *channa dal* and rice puffs that Mr Dayal occasionally feeds them.

An Indian Palm squirrel enjoys a grape under the winter's sun.

Unlike other squirrels, the Indian Palm squirrel does not hibernate in winter. Rather, it is up to mischief all year round. In our garden, stealing socks from the laundry line is the number one *timepass* (see Indian English on page 289), followed closely by bathing in the birdbath and swinging in the hanging flowerpots.

Birds and Symbolism in Indian Culture

Birds play an important symbolic role in Indian religion and mythology. In Hinduism, they are the *vahana* or vehicle of

various Hindu gods. There are more than 1,300 species of birds in India. Some are endemic to certain regions whilst some are common across the sub-continent, such as the *tota (*rose-ringed parakeet). Also referred to as the parrot, the *tota* is the *vahana* of Kama, the Indian god of love and desire. Hence, it is also considered to be the messenger of love between two lovers. Look out for them in Indian art.

The owl is the *vahana* of the Hindu goddess Lakshmi, who is worshipped as the goddess of prosperity. Bengalis believe that if a white owl enters your house, wealth will come to the household. Some view owls as bad omens. In the West, the owl is considered wise but in India, it is a symbol of foolishness. It is a gentle derogation to call a foolish person an *uloo* (owl). Often heard is "*tum uloo ho*" which roughly means "you idiot".

The most iconic of these birds is the indigenous peacock, the national bird of India. Its importance in Indian culture is reflected in Indian mythology, folklore, art and architecture. In Islamic culture, the peacock is regarded as the guardian of paradise, its most dazzling expression in the bejewelled Peacock Throne of Mughal Emperor Shah Jahan and in the archways that resemble the open plume of a peacock. The peacock is considered sacred and appears in both mythology and Hindu scripture. Said to have been created from the feathers of the mythical Garuda, the *vahana* of Vishnu, it is also associated with several other gods, such as Karttikeya, the god of war as well as Krishna, who is depicted adorned with peacock feathers on his head. Consequently, peacock feathers are also considered sacred.

It is said that peacock feathers keep away house lizards. I have tested this hypothesis and I can say that since the day I had a few peacock feathers in my living room, I've had no lizard encounters and an unusual gratitude towards all peafowl.

When the squirrel frantically screeches 'chip-chip-chip' and the parakeet echoes its frantic warnings, it usually means danger is lurking above in the form of a hungry black kite. Delhi has the highest density of black kites among the major cities of the world. These brown birds of prey are quite large up close but when you have a few of them sitting atop a

tall bare tree, they collectively look like a scene from a first-grade horror movie. Seeing a few of them circle the air above your head and swoop towards you is equally spine-chilling, especially if you're a squirrel.

Equally plentiful in Delhi and across the sub-continent are the Asian koel, magpie, green bee-eater, brown-headed barbet, common kingfisher, egret, hoopoe, black drongo and rufous treepie, all of which can be found in Delhi's parks, gardens and environs. I am naming them to bring out some curiosity, which might be enough for you to want to find out what they look like. To start, all you need to do is look out (of your house/car), look up and listen. Then tell me if we are not birds of a feather.

From my time in India, I have come to realise that our attitudes past and present are shaped largely by our everydays. Previously I could only identify the crow, mynah and pigeon—city birds that are reason to not park your car under trees. I spent my energy avoiding them. In India, however, I lived in a house with a garden and windows large enough to see beyond my narrow avian prejudices. And so from my new nest, a bird interest hatched. It certainly helps that Delhi's parks, streets and gardens are aplenty with many common birds. I find the best place to start is quite literally in your own backyard.

It wasn't actually the birds I first noticed but the squirrels living in the large mango tree just outside our back window. In the early morning, they would scurry down the tree and congregate at the back of the garden to have their breakfast of birdseed which Mr Dayal scattered dutifully every day. There they would be joined by a motley mix of dove, pigeon, crow, raven, bulbul, parakeet, and the occasional migratory straggler.

At the front end of the house, however, quite the opposite was happening. The battleground was a large bakain tree. Its shady crown and plentiful fruit attract birds of all feathers, but the pretty *tota* (rose-ringed parakeet) seemed to be its most ardent visitor. Each morning and evening, these green birds would come and eat the fruit and play amongst its branches.

The bakain tree was parakeet paradise up to the day when a large house crow built its nest amongst its branches. The parakeets returned that evening only to find themselves unwelcomed and unwanted by a newly installed mother crow. Paradise was lost to the echoes of their retreat. My desk faces the bakain and so it was from this vantage that the pilot episode of Desperate Housebirds found its audience.

I tuned in daily to a script of caw and screech, pecking and chasing as the parakeets tried again and again to reclaim their tree. "Why can't they share and get along," I lamented. But the birds continued to assert their own positions of right and might until there was no resolution but war. It happened on a winter's morning just after dawn. I was awakened by a ruckus of cawing and screeching, like none I had heard before. I pulled open the curtains to find a battle already raging. The parakeets had swooped in with an army of at least 30 to attack the crow occupiers of their beloved bakain. Crows from the neighbourhood also joined the fray until the air was a muddle of green and black wings. But the crows were outnumbered and their aggression no match for the smaller parakeets with their humongous frustration. The battle was over in 20 minutes.

I don't know what happened to the nest and the baby crows that had hatched in it. Young ones tend to be the worst casualty in adult disagreement. Peace returned to the bakain and the regular programming of eat, preen and play resumed. Desperate Housebirds is now a little less exciting but I continued to tune in daily for a view of nature, both bird and human.

Another bird that used to come by was the jungle babbler. These birds are known as *saath bhai* in Hindi, which means "seven brothers". This is because they are always found in groups of seven or so (it's not an exact science). They are easily spotted everywhere; gregarious groups of grey roundish birds with a somewhat grumpy appearance. But what was unusual about the little regular visitor to my garden was that he would come alone. His favourite perch was the side mirror of Mrs Dayal's car and from there he would stare at his own reflection. Perhaps he felt less lonely this way. Or maybe he was a narcissist with introverted tendencies. One could only speculate the reason behind his solitariness, but it must have driven him mad, mad enough to attack his own reflection. This staring and attacking cycle would go on for an entire morning and be repeated for days after. Then one day he ceased to visit. Either death or redemption had freed him. Of course, there is probably a scientific explanation to his behaviour but we can leave that to the ornithologists; I much prefer flights of fancy.

Flora

The flora in India is rich and varied due to a wide range of climatic conditions and environments. In terms of plant diversity, India is considered 10th in the world and fourth in Asia. If you live in a built-up city like Mumbai, you might not notice the greenery because of the density of the urban jungle, but in the wide expanse of Delhi, a garden unmistakably surrounds you. One reason is that Delhi is a planned city (at least the one planned by Edwin Lutyens). Its urban plan specified the type of trees to be planted along the roads, yielding boulevards of neem, avenues of maulsari, streets of jamun and other picturesque images of tree-lined pathways. Urban centres and residential areas nestle between parks, reserves, gardens and the vast Aravalli hills. Delhi is green. And pink and red and yellow and purple. In fact, it always has a colour, from the greys of winter to the springtime spectrum of blooms. Delhi is a city that unfolds colour by colour into summer.

The large orange flowers of the *semal* (cotton) tree is the first floral sign that winter's days are numbered. This is followed by the bright red blooms of the Indian coral tree. As the days warm, more and more trees start to flower like a grand choreography of blooms. Delhi turns from red to purple with the flowering of the jacaranda in March and then to blazing orange with the gulmohar in April. The largest and most spectacular burst of colour comes in May with the flowering of the amalta (*cassia fistula*), whose flowers outnumber its leaves. Thick cascades of these sunshine-yellow flowers hang like floral chandeliers and turn the ground yellow with fallen petals. Seen in the hue of summer's sun, Delhi becomes a city of gold. It blazes with flowers and 40-degree heat, as if nature punishes you but hands you a bouquet to soften the blow at the same time.

Trees such as the ashoka, peepal and neem tree are more than just popular Indian trees; they are highly regarded because of their religious or medicinal significance.

Hindus regard the ashoka tree (*saraca indica*) as sacred. It is often planted in royal compounds and near temples but can be widely seen in parks and gardens. Its name in Sanskrit means "sorrow-less". Therefore it is believed that drinking the water in which its flowers are washed is a protection against grief. The tree is also said to be a symbol of love and is dedicated to the god of love. Because of its mention in mythology, it is used as a decorative motif in Indian sculpture, early Buddhist monuments and in Hindu and Buddhist temples. The ashoka is easily recognisable, being a medium-size tree with leaves hanging downward covering the length of its tree trunk. It reminds me of the flapper dress of the 1920s, especially when the wind blows and the leaves swish about to a Charleston rhythm.

The peepal tree (*ficus religiosa*), also called the bodhi tree, is also considered sacred, having significance in Buddhism, Jainism and Hinduism. Under its branches, the Buddha is believed to have attained enlightenment. Hindu ascetics still meditate beneath its crown. Far more observable is worship of the peepal tree in the form of peepal tree shrines identified by coloured string tied around its trunk and offerings stuffed into its crevices. The tree is considered the embodiment of god or regarded as a wishing tree. It is fairly easy to find such peepal trees in parks and by the roadside.

The neem tree (*azadirachta indica*) features heavily in traditional Indian medicine known as Ayurveda. Known for its medicinal properties, it is used to treat skin and hair disorders. Many Indian households value having a neem tree in their garden because the seeds, leaves, flowers, fruits, oil, roots and bark are good for a wide range of household uses.

The Mughals introduced to India from Persia the cypress, a symbol of eternity. An avenue of cypress trees leads up to the Taj Mahal.

My favourite tree is the saptaparni (*alstonia scholaris*) because I first noticed this tree in Indian miniature paintings. When I saw the real tree in the middle of a park, I half expected to see Radha behind it waiting lovingly for her lover Krishna to arrive, a common context for this tree in Indian art.

Lotus

The lotus is the national flower of India and is considered sacred. Hindu religion and mythology portray the goddess Saraswati seated on a lotus flower and it is used in worship. It represents purity, fertility and the divine.

HISTORY

India is one of the oldest civilisations in the world with a history spanning more than five millennia. It has seen the birth and evolution of four world religions—Buddhism, Jainism, Hinduism and Sikhism—whose developmental imprints have been captured in art and architecture. But perhaps most significant and unique to India is how its past lives very much in its present: in religious practices, art techniques, thought and social patterns—the finest example of cultural continuity. There is a timeless quality to India that bucks the steady movements of the clock. India's history is a living one of unbroken continuity, a 5,000-year-old story set before you, and a key to understanding and appreciating the visual, social and religious character of the India you see today.

The sacred sound Aum is believed to be the cosmic sound at the beginning of creation.

Harappan Civilisation

Considered one of the four cradles of civilisation, the grand narrative of India began in the Indus Valley with the Harappan civilisation, whose sophisticated civic planning and technological feats set them apart from their Bronze Age contemporaries. One of the civilisation's most enduring contributions to culture and religion is revealed in its enigmatic terracotta seals, whose emblems, such as the peepal tree, dewlapped bull, tree spirits (*yakshi*) and a horned diety would make their way through time to be eventually incorporated into the artistic vocabulary of two of the world's foremost religions: Hinduism and Buddhism.

The civilisation's demise around 1,500 BC is shrouded in mystery. Various theories point the cause to the Aryan invasion, ecological change and migration. Regardless of

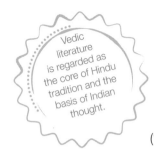

Vedic literature is regarded as the core of Hindu tradition and the basis of Indian thought.

how the civilisation perished, it was regarded as greater and far more advanced than its successors from Central Asia, the self-named Aryans ("nobles").

The Vedic Age

The Aryans entered India through the northwest passes in 1,500 BC and gradually extended their dominion eastward. Their conquest saw the taking of the indigenous people (*adivasi*) as slaves, who were then placed in the lowest rung of Aryan society in what was to become a key social dimension of Indian identity—the caste system.

It was also during this period that the four Sanskrit hymns called the Vedas were created and compiled, the oldest being the Rig Veda. The Vedas, considered the sacred texts of Hinduism, prescribe the worship of Vedic gods and the performance of ritual sacrifices as part of daily life. Each Veda also included treatises called the Upanishads (philosophies), which contain the key concepts of Hindu philosophy.

By 550 BC, the influence of the indigenous peoples on Aryan culture had taken full effect, unifying the subcontinent in a common culture. This synthesis is said to mark the transition from the Vedic civilisation to the Hindu civilisation.

Vedic Gods

Vedic deities were initially nature gods. The most important in the early Vedic pantheon were Indra (god of war, thunder, rain and lightning) and Agni (god of fire). In the late Vedic period, Aryan culture became increasingly influenced by indigenous peoples and, consequently, the Vedic pantheon too became more complex as it incorporated local popular cults and beliefs. Some Vedic gods would later re-emerge in the Hindu pantheon.

The Age of Buddha and Mahariva

The sixth century BC was a time of rapid urbanisation and intellectual ferment. Widespread trade and rising wealth in the region precipitated challenges to the existing social structure. This was the environment in which Gautama Siddhartha (566–486 BC) and Vardhamana Mahavira (540–467 BC) were born as well as the two new religions they founded, Buddhism and Jainism respectively. These religions gained popularity because of the appeal of their simple teachings, such as *ahimsa* (non-violence) and rejection of caste distinctions. They therefore found significant following amongst a growing mercantile class of merchants, affluent urban groups, women, and those who wanted to overcome their low social status. As a result, Buddhism surged in popularity ahead of Vedism, which was evolving into Brahmanism (an early stage in the development of Hinduism).

In 326 BC, Alexander the Great invaded northwestern India, but the famed conqueror stayed only a few months. The Greek withdrawal after his exit produced a period of uncertainty and it was in this political vacuum that the very first empire in India had its beginnings.

The Mauryan Empire

Seizing the opportunity from the Greek withdrawal, an unknown adventurer called Chandragupta Maurya captured the region and established the Mauryan Empire. He implemented the first highly effective imperial administration but it was his grandson, Ashoka (269–232 BC), who had the most profound effect on India's history. Substituting violent suppression of his grandfather's time with a moral political economy, he brought his grandfather's empire to the height of its glory and achieved the first real unification of India.

The bloody battle at Kalinga (modern-day Odisha) was a turning point in Ashoka's life and leadership style. After seeing the carnage of battle, he gave up violence and devoted himself to the Buddhist faith, ordering ethical codes to be inscribed on rocks and pillars (called "Ashokan pillars") across his vast empire, and sending out emissaries of Buddhist monks, which helped to spread Buddhism and Indian culture far beyond the boundaries of his empire. He is credited for establishing a new concept of kingship during his 40 years of benevolent rule, earning him the title of Great and the reputation as one of the best world rulers ever to have reigned.

The Kushan Dynasty

After Ashoka's death, a series of invasions from Central Asia caused the eventual disintegration of his empire. Local kingdoms were established in northern India and gave rise to successive dynasties, such as the Kushans (AD 50–300). Kanishka, the greatest of Kushan rulers (78–110), was a patron of Buddhism, and Mahayana Buddhism developed during his reign and spread to China, Central Asia and Japan. Two great schools of art (the Gandhara and Mathura Schools) supplied the evolving Buddhist faith with the very first sculptural representation of the Buddha.

It was also at this time that the gods Shiva and Vishnu became pre-eminent among the Brahmanical pantheon and Hindu doctrine became codified into texts called Vedanta, thereby marking the beginning of intellectual Hinduism. Key developments in both religion and art made this the most formative period of Indian history before the 19th century and it paved the way for an explosion of art and culture during the reign of the succeeding Guptas.

The Golden Age of the Guptas

The Gupta period (AD 320–500) is commonly referred to as the classical or "golden age" of Indian civilisation and the second such time India was united. It was marked by a highly intellectual climate and a flowering of the arts in the form of the finest sculpture, poetry, drama and literature known to India. Urban society was said to be highly cultivated and sensual, which drove a highly aestheticised culture that many consider never to be matched again in India. It was in the luxury of these times that Vatsyayana penned the most extraordinary treatise on love, the Kamasutra. In science and mathematics, the Indians made their eternal mark with the invention of zero and the decimal system, as well as the calculation of *phi* and

The Kamasutra

It is usually with some discomfort that people hover around part of the bookstore that holds the many versions of the "art of love". Indeed, its varied front covers showing lovers in amorous embrace foretells what lies in between the sheets (of paper). Popular imagination has made it out to be the ancient sex manual, a compendium of (absurdly) acrobatic ways of lovemaking and a trove of oriental erotic wisdom. On all accounts it delivers on its reputation with illustrations so penetrative, it is easy to be caught up in the centrefolds and miss the larger picture; it was a guide on how to live. The Kamasutra was meant to be a book of conduct, offering advice not only on seduction and sexual union (which only makes up 20 per cent of its entirety), but also on friendship, courtship and married life in its seven volumes. Its legacy, on the other hand, extends far more than its tome of advice. Till today, it still holds the unparalleled position as *the* definitive guide to lovemaking in popular understanding. It also has had enduring influence on Indian art, philosophy, architecture and literature.

the length of the solar year. Delhi's famous pillar of pure iron was a metallurgical feat for its time (it remains without a trace of rust till today). Long before any universities in the Western world were established, Nalanda University was already a seat of learning. (It resumed operation in 2014, centuries after its destruction in the 12th century by Muslim invaders).

The Rise of the Southern Kingdoms

With the decline of the Guptas, northern India splintered into warring kingdoms. By then, the ability to create empires had shifted southwards to two key areas: the Deccan and the Tamil plains. Their respective rulers battled constantly for mastery of the region but the individual kingdoms were too equal in power to allow for any of them to have a unitary effect such as that seen in the Mauryan and Gupta ages until the 9th century under the powerful Cholas.

Deccani Kingdoms

We begin at the start of the 1st century AD with the Satavahanas of the Deccan (100 BC–AD 220), who were later referred to as the Andhras. Their renovations of the Sanchi stupa (started by Ashoka) and the building of the Amaravati stupa resulted in the stupa becoming the greatest monument in India of those times. At Sanchi, figures of *yakshi*, first seen in Harappan times, adorn the new gateways and adopt a three-bended pose known as the *tribhunga*m which would go on to characterise Indian sculpture. As Andhra power declined, so did Buddhism in the Deccan.

In AD 250, the Vakatakas (250–550) came into power. Their reign saw the creation of the superb art at Ajanta, the earliest surviving example of Indian painting. In the western Deccan, the Chalukyas (550–757) built the earliest known

The paintings and sculpture of the Ajanta Caves in Maharashtra go as far back as the 2nd century BC and are considered masterpieces of Buddhist religious art.

Hindu temple prototypes at Badami and Aihole. These temples evolved from Buddhist architectural structures and show the earliest manifestation of the *sikhara* (tower), which was to become a defining feature in all subsequent Hindu temples. The succeeding Rashtrakutas (757–973) made their mark as the specialists of excavated architecture in the rock-cut wonder that is the Kailasantha Temple at Ellora.

Tamilian Kingdoms

In the far south, spectacular works of art and architecture were created between the 3rd and 11th centuries alongside new religious doctrine that would go on to define Hindu India.

The Pallavas (3rd–9th centuries) were the first significant Tamil dynasty. Originally Buddhists, they converted to Brahmanism in the 5th century and created the first known purely Dravidian temple form at Mamallapuram.

Towards the end of the 9th century, the Cholas (9th–13th centuries) came into power and established the largest empire in India since the Guptas. They left a lasting legacy in Tamil literature, art and architecture. They spent lavishly on religion, building magnificent temples that were also focal points of their economic, social and cultural life. This concept of a "temple-city", notably in the Chola capital of Tanjore, inspired later temple design in South India and Southeast Asia. The Cholas also took sculpture to new aesthetic heights, particularly bronze sculpture for which they are renowned. In 1216, they were defeated by the Pandyas of Madurai, who were soon to be reminded of a new power from the north so ferocious it shook the peninsula to its foundation; welcome to the age of the Islamic sultans.

Religion

The period from the 7th to the 11th centuries saw great developments in Hindu doctrine in the south, beginning in the 7th century with Tamil-poet saints (the Alvaras and Nayannars) who emphasised a personal union with god through love and devotion (*bhakti*), in what was to develop as the *bhakti* movement two centuries later. In the 400 years, significant developments in doctrine enabled Hinduism to reinvigorate itself and challenge intellectual Buddhism, eventually supplanting it in many parts of India, leaving only Bihar and Bengal as Buddhism's last footholds in India.

Amber Fort, Jaipur.

The Northern Kingdoms

Our story turns back to northern India prior to the coming of the Muslims. At the end of the 8th century, three leading kingdoms—the Rashtrakutas, the Palas of Bihar and Bengal, and the Pratiharas (a Rajput clan) of Rajasthan—were fighting for power. The conflict had weakened their administrative powers, allowing small independent kingdoms to emerge. These were the kingdoms of the Rajput clans, whose names still survive to the present day. Weak, petty and deeply in conflict with one another, they failed to recognise the growing threat of the Muslim Turks at their doorstep.

Religion

After the 7th century, Buddhism and Hinduism became influenced by Tantrism, which sacramentalised the sexual act. This drew sculpture and temple architecture to a new artistic climax. The magnificent temples of Khajuraho (circa AD 950–1050) are masterpieces of erotic sculpture and are considered to be some of the most inimitable achievements in Indian art. The Konarak Temple (circa 1250), one of 4,000 in the Odishan capital of Bhubaneshwar (known as the city of temples) is similarly dominated by writhing *mithuna* (loving couples).

Qutb Complex (AD 1193)

The "Might of Islam" mosque and its victory tower, the Qutb Minar, were built on the site of Delhi's largest Hindu temple to signal the arrival of the age of Muslim rule. It was also the first monument I visited upon my arrival to Delhi. I remember the smell of roasted corn accentuating the puzzlement of seeing carvings of figures and flowers caught in the shadows of awkward arches and it took me a second visit to find out why. Upon the orders of Qutbuddin Aibak, 27 local Hindu and Jain temples were pillaged and their carved stone columns carted over to build the mosque. The carved columns were plastered over in keeping with Islam's injunction against the use of figural representations of living things but over time the plaster fell away, revealing the original Hindu motifs. The Hindu craftsmen employed to build the mosque were unfamiliar with the arch, a Persian construct, and used their technique of building *sikhara* (tower in a Hindu temple) to create an awkward arch-like form. This monument not only marks the start of Islam's hold over India but also the beginning of Indian adaptation to a new aesthetic.

Carved columns frame the view of the Qutb Minar.

By the 12th century, Buddhism's demise in India was inevitable. The syncretic nature of Hinduism had already incorporated the Buddha as an avatar of Vishnu. In Bengal, the Buddhist Pala dynasty (750–1150) was succeeded by the Hindu Senas, who ended the Pala's long patronage of

Buddhist institutions and influenced the rise in the popularity of Shiva. Elsewhere the focus in Indian painting, literature, sculpture, dance and song shifted to Hindu gods, particularly Krishna. However, it would be the Islamic forces that would finish off Buddhism's hold on the land of its birth forever.

The Coming of Islam

Islam first came to India by sea with the Arab merchants in AD 712. Armed intrusion began 300 years later. In 1192, Muhammad Ghuri defeated Prithviraj III of the Rajput Chauhans, ending Hindu rule in Delhi and setting in motion a new era of five successive Muslim dynasties, collectively known as the Delhi Sultanate.

Muhammad Ghuri's slave-general Qutbuddin Aibak (1206–1210) became the first sultan of what came to be known as the Slave Dynasty. To commemorate the victory of Islamic forces, Qutbuddin Aibak erected the Quwwat ul-Islam (Might of Islam) mosque. It was also around this time that another Muslim general conquered the remaining two Buddhist centres of Bengal and Bihar and slaughtered Buddhist monks, thus rendering a final blow that Buddhist India would never recover from. The Slave Dynasty was succeeded by the Khiljis (1290–1320), whose ruler Alauddin Khilji (1296–1316) expanded Muslim imperial rule southward. The Tughluq Dynasty (1320–1414) followed, but their rule was short-lived and independent kingdoms emerged, exacerbated by the savage invasion of northern India in 1398 by Timur (or Tamerlane as he is known in the west). In the south, the last Hindu kingdom, the powerful Vijayanagar Empire (1336–1565) established itself and halted further Islamic expansion until the 16th century. Nobles also broke away from the Sultanate to form their own kingdoms in areas such as the Deccan (Bahmani Sultanate), Bengal and Gujarat. Several Rajput kingdoms also reasserted their sovereignty. After the death of the last Tughluq, an undistinguished line of Sayyids (1413–1451) ruled for another 37 years before the final dynasty of the Lodi kings (1451–1526).

The character of the Delhi Sultanate in 300 years of power had changed from militant power to that of cultural court. Royal ateliers were introduced to produce art, and poetry by esteemed court-poet Amir Khusrau filled the royal halls. Socially, the concept of female seclusion (*purdah*) became further entrenched through the royal harems. But it was to India's visual character, especially that of Delhi, that the Delhi sultans conferred the most. They planted the seeds for a new style of aesthetics that, although initially Persian, became a combined expression of Hindu and Islamic elements that the succeeding Mughals would take to its zenith.

Religion

During this period, Hinduism and Islam also found common ground. Saint-poets of the *bhakti* movement and the mystics of Sufism preached that religion is devotion to god. Kabir (1440–1518), one of the greatest Indian poets, combined Sufi and *bhakti* elements into his poems and songs. His religious message rejected caste, rituals and priestly authority. This was similarly echoed in the teachings of Guru Nanak (1494–1530) who upon the same principles founded the Sikh religion in the 16th century.

The Mughals

In 1526, a Central Asian prince named Babur defeated Ibrahim Lodi at the historic battle of Panipat and founded one of the greatest dynasties in the history of the world — the

The Great Mughals

The Mughals added such richness to the visual and cultural identity of India as well as to its many stories of love, ambition, power and passion. Their names are redolent of both ruthless power and refined cultural achievement in which art, literature and architecture reached an apogee. Of the 15 major Mughal emperors, the first six, from the founder Babur to Aurangzeb, are the most well known. Referred to as "the Great Mughals", they have gone down into legend and continue to animate with timeless appeal the art, music and grand buildings of their times.

Akbar (ruled 1556–1605)

Akbar was a skilled commander, politician and administrator. His court was a place of inquiry, tolerance, culture and sophistication. He abolished discriminating practices on non-Muslims and was a strong patron of music and the arts, founding royal ateliers that produced exquisite jewellery, textiles and miniature paintings that were to reach near perfection under his son Jahangir. It also led to the fusion of Indian and Persian styles (Mughal style) that would come to symbolise the era's achievement in its varied forms and scale. In his long reign, he trebled the dominions he inherited from Humayun and built a strong and cohesive empire, earning him the title "Akbar the Great".

Shah Jahan (ruled 1627–1658)

The third son of Jahangir, Shah Jahan (meaning "king of the world") is remembered most for the love he had for his wife Mumtaz Mahal, who died giving birth to their 14th child. Her death affected him so profoundly that he commissioned a final resting place befitting his beloved, the Taj Mahal towards which his gaze fell in grieving longing until the day he died. Although his death was shrouded in sadness, his life was marked with unprecedented splendour. He commissioned the legendary Peacock Throne to display the most splendid gems in his staggering collection of pearls, emeralds, rubies and other precious stones. The image-conscious Shah Jahan also loved architecture and used it to forge an image of awe and imperial majesty. His reign ushered in the golden age of Mughal architecture in India.

The Maratha Empire

The Maratha Empire (1674–1818) was founded by the warrior-hero Chhatrapati (meaning "lord of the umbrella") Shivaji Bhosle, in response to the increasing Muslim political control over the subcontinent. He is revered by Hindu nationalists for his fight to maintain Hindu freedoms and culture, and for keeping the Mughals at bay. The struggle against the Mughals ended with the death of Aurangzeb in 1707. The weak succeeding Mughal emperors eventually became subordinate to the Marathas, who reinstated Hindu reign in India.

Mughal Empire (1526–1858). Babur ruled for only four years, and upon his death his son Humayun inherited an empire in its infancy. Lethargic in life and combat, he was overthrown in 1540 by an Afghan chieftain, Sher Shah Sur, and sought exile in the desert. Fifteen years later, Humayun regained the throne but died shortly after, leaving his son Akbar to consolidate and expand the empire. Akbar transformed the character of Mughal rule in India from foreign occupation to that of a united Indian empire. Neither his son Jahangir nor his grandson Shah Jahan came close to matching the character and achievements of Akbar. However, they both shared his passion for art, architecture and gardens, and they took these to new heights under their patronage. Their reigns were marked by a sensuality and love for luxury and beauty.

The success of the Mughal Empire prevailed through three successive generations until Aurangzeb's reign. The third son of Shah Jahan, Aurangzeb deposed his father and reinstated strict Islamic orthodoxy. He enlarged Mughal boundaries by military might but his reversal of Akbar's traditions, especially that of religious tolerance, changed the nature of Mughal rule and consequently precipitated its decline.

Following his death in 1707, the empire crumbled, its gradual decay presided over by eight succeeding emperors. The once vast empire shrank to the environs of Delhi. The sacking of Delhi in 1739 by Nadir Shah of Iran and the carting away of treasures, especially the Peacock Throne, was a blow the Mughal Empire never recovered from. The emperor's influence was further diminished by the Marathas and by expanding European control. By 1805, the emperor's role was reduced to a little more than a pensioner to the British East India Company. After an unsuccessful uprising

The Taj Mahal, built in the 17th century, is considered one of the seven wonders of the modern world and the finest example of Mughal architecture.

in 1857 against the British the once glorious Mughal Empire waned into legend.

The Europeans

It was the Portuguese who first landed on Indian soil (even ahead of the Mughals). The Dutch, French and British soon followed and carved out their respective trading settlements along the coast. By the end of the 17th century, the Portuguese had lost all their territories but Goa to the Dutch and British. The Dutch in turn eventually lost theirs to the British, and the French only managed to retain Pondicherry and a few small settlements following the three Carnatic Wars (1740–1763) in which they too eventually lost to the British.

The British

For 150 years, the East India Company (founded in 1600) had been steadily acquiring wealth and land in India by allying themselves with the Mughal emperors and regional Nawabs.

However, British presence took a decisive leap as a result of the pivotal Battle of Plassey in 1757, a major milestone that turned the Company into a military power, allowing the British to consolidate their presence in Calcutta.

This established a new period known as Company Rule (1757–1858), in which the British implemented policies that had a huge impact on Indian society. In 1857 their rule was challenged in a major revolt. It started when the British were accused of greasing bullet cartridges (which had to be bitten before loading) with cow and pig fat, seen as an affront to the Hindu and Muslim sepoys (local soldiers recruited into the Company's army). What began as a soldier's revolt soon escalated into a civilian uprising across much of northern India, particularly in Delhi. Known as the Indian Mutiny of 1857, it was the first challenge to British rule and the final moments of Mughal reign. The British eventually recaptured Delhi at much cost and bloodshed. They exiled the last Mughal emperor Bahadur Shah Zafar to Yangon and executed his young sons. Bankrupted by the conflict, the Company was dissolved and rule transferred directly to the Crown under Queen Victoria. This new period became known as the British Raj (1858–1947), and Indian territories (collectively called British India) became part of the British Empire and were ruled through viceroys with Calcutta as the capital until 1911.

The subcontinent was once again united, the fourth such time in Indian history. But unlike preceding periods, unity came through the proverbial pen and not the sword. The British introduced Western education and replaced Persian with English as the language of government and education. Through English, Western ideas and values were transplanted to the local populace. The British also introduced social reforms in line with Western values, such as prohibiting *sati* (widow immolation) and discouraging female infanticide. They governed via a centralised administrative system, introducing to India what would become one of its more infamous of legacies—Indian bureaucracy. The British also physically united their empire with roads, irrigation canals, postal and telegraph services and a rail network, still chugging along today as a stalwart of public transport.

The Struggle for Freedom

National aspirations began to grow after the Indian Mutiny. In 1885, the seeds of India's nationalist movement were sown through the founding of the Indian National Congress (INC or Congress), which was set up as a platform for Indians to demand self-government. In 1905, the partition of Bengal into a Hindu-majority west and Muslim-majority east was seen as a calculated strike by the British to the epicenter of Indian nationalism, thus mobilising many Indians to join the political arena, and led to the founding of the Muslim League in 1906 to safeguard the political rights of Indian Muslims. A turning point came in 1919 when soldiers under the command of General Dyer fired into an unarmed crowd protesting against suppression of civil liberties in the city of Amritsar. This massacre at Jallianwala Bagh served to awaken and unite Indians of all classes and religions in collective outrage at British cruelty and set the ground for a nationwide movement for independence.

In 1920, Mahatma Gandhi took over the leadership of the INC and transformed the party into a nationalist movement for *swaraj*, political independence from the British, who by then had already stirred considerable resentment. Gandhi rallied hundreds of thousands of common citizens towards the cause of independence, turning the freedom struggle into a mass movement. He launched a strategy of *satyagraha* (a form of non-violent protest) against British law and its institutions. This took the form of the Non-Cooperation movement (1920); Civil Disobedience movement (1930); and finally the Quit India movement (1942). These were met with fierce British resistance until World War II, after which a financially strained Britain lost its will to impose its rule and "quit". A hurried power transference ensued, propelled by horrific communal violence between Hindus and Muslims. The Muslim League, led by Muhammad Ali Jinnah, had also been pressing for an independent state of Pakistan for Muslims. On 15 August 1947, at the stroke of midnight, British rule ended and the independent nations of India and Pakistan came into being. The 550 semi-independent existing princely states were integrated into the India Union (1947–1950), later to become the Republic of India by the promulgation of the Constitution of India on 26 January 1950.

Mahatma Gandhi

Mohandas Karamchand Gandhi (1869–1948), popularly known as Mahatma ("great soul" in Sanskrit), was a Gujarati lawyer, leader and social activist who led India to independence. He is esteemed for his practice of non-violent protest called *satyagraha* (insistence on truth) rooted in the Jain concept of *ahimsa* (non-violence). Recognising his political influence, the British were forced to negotiate various settlements with Gandhi, resulting in the alleviation of poverty, status granted to the "untouchables", rights for women, and eventually independence in August 1947. Less than six months later, the 78-year-old Gandhi was assassinated by a Hindu extremist Nathuram Godse while on his way to a prayer meeting at Birla House in Delhi on 30 January 1948. The road named Tees January Marg (30 January Road) marks where Birla House (now known as Gandhi Smriti) stands and the day an act of violence took away the life of a man who spent his life preaching non-violence. Gandhi's life inspired later human rights leaders such as Martin Luther King Jr. in the United States, Nelson Mandela in South Africa and Aung San Suu Kyi in Myanmar. *Satyagraha* remains one of the most powerful philosophies in freedom struggles in the world today.

Freedom Fighters

It took nearly a century for India to gain independence in her long fight for freedom that began with the Indian Mutiny. During this struggle, hundreds of freedom fighters put their lives on the line to campaign for India's independence, such as Subhash Chandra Bose, Sarojini Naidu and Sardar Vallabhbhai Patel. One such person closer to home is Lala Har Dayal (1884–1939), a revolutionary, scholar (and granduncle to Mr Dayal), who rallied Indians against British rule and helped to spread the freedom movement overseas. In the United States, he founded the Ghadar Party and inspired many overseas Indians to the cause.

Independent India

The communal violence that characterised the final years before Independence did not stop with it. The partition of India and Pakistan led to a massive migration of some five million Hindus and Sikhs eastward out of Pakistan and a similar number of Muslims westwards from India, during which retributive genocide was mutually inflicted under appalling conditions. An estimated half a million lives were lost; 14 million Hindus, Sikhs and Muslims displaced from their homes; thousands of women raped; beautiful buildings pillaged and abandoned; and the high culture of the times decimated. The violence only receded with the shock of Gandhi's assassination in 1948 and Jinnah's death from tuberculosis six months later. Both too quickly left behind for others the tasks of building the nations they birthed.

Through its birth pangs and years after, the brilliant leadership and character of Jawaharlal Nehru steered India into the modern age. Nehru, who had worked closely alongside Gandhi as a key leader in the nationalist movement, became India's first prime minister upon Independence. He established a secular democratic polity, a strong industrial base, a planned economy and a foreign policy stance of non-alignment. He also tackled social issues and modernised India's military. Nehru died in 1964 and his daughter Indira became prime minister in 1966.

Indira Gandhi continued her father's reforms and socialist policies and oversaw the partition of East Pakistan into Bangladesh in 1971. In 1975, she had then-president Fakhruddin Ali Ahmed declare a national State of Emergency under what she perceived was a threat to her power. Her government arrested hundreds of opposition leaders, and people were forcibly displaced from their homes and forced to undergo sterilisation. When the general election took place in 1977, she and her Congress party lost for the first time since Independence but returned to power in 1980. Four years later, she was assassinated by two of her Sikh bodyguards in revenge for sending troops to flush out Sikh militants hiding in the Golden Temple at Amritsar. Her son Rajiv Gandhi was sworn in as prime minster and initiated economic liberalisation but in 1991, he too was assassinated. Economic reforms, however, continued unperturbed, reaching a height under the tenure of then-Finance Minister Manmohan Singh, who introduced a far-reaching comprehensive policy of economic reforms that marked a turning point in Indian economic history. Singh went on to serve as the Prime Minister of India from 2004 to 2014. Since 1996, a series of coalition governments have ruled India, with the Hindu nationalist Bharatiya Janata Party (BJP) emerging as the largest single group and principle opposition party. Gujarat Chief Minister Narendra Modi led the BJP to a landslide victory over Congress in the 2014 general elections.

Since Independence, the life expectancy of Indians has more than doubled and the literacy rate has risen to 71 per cent (2015) from its base of 18 per cent (1951). Its industrial base has expanded and economic reforms have produced a growing middle class. Despite the impressive achievements in the past 60-plus years, poverty remains widespread, with about a third of India's inhabitants living below the poverty line. About two-thirds of Indians still live in villages, some without basic amenities like running water. Social discrimination by caste, religion and gender remains rampant, especially among rural Indians who form the vast majority. India has a rich culture, but swaddles one in every three of the world's poor. She is exceedingly old with a belly of burgeoning youth. The world's largest democracy is also the largest in contradiction and complexity in a story, her-story, still evolving.

CITY PORTRAITS

India has many facets. Each part of her speaks its own story. Here, I provide a snapshot of the six cities in which most expatriates would settle. These are based on my experiences and are listed following their rank in Mercer's Cost of Living Survey 2016, starting with the one that most impacts the wallet—Mumbai.

Mumbai: Dream City

Maharashtra's capital has come a long way from its swampy soggy roots. India's largest and most dynamic cosmopolitan city used to be a group of seven islands that were given by the Portuguese to Britain's Charles II in 1661 as part of the marriage dowry of Catherine of Braganza. Desiring neither, the king leased the land to the East India Company and sowed his seeds in the fertility of other women. Under the avaricious hands of the Company, the small fishing village by the sea saw the tides of its fortune turn. By the 18th century, the city was profit-seeking in design and intent, with opportunity heavy in its salty air. The sea, which had brought the city its name (Bom Bahia is "beautiful bay" in Portuguese), also brought traded goods and people lured by Bombay's promise and port of call. The Gujaratis, Parsis and

The Chhatrapati Shivaji Terminus in Mumbai is one of the city's many buildings that blend traditional Indian elements with Victorian Gothic Revival architecture.

Baghdadi Jews were the first multicultural stock to flavour the city's melting pot. Today the city stews with those from the far reaches of the world as well as Indians from other states, making Mumbai the most populous and popular city in India.

Although Mumbai ranks highest for the cost of living, it ranks a disappointing fifth in India for quality of life according to Mercer's 2016 Quality of Life Survey. Yet it is home to a huge expatriate population and an even larger migrant one. The reason behind its pull is Mumbai's promises of success, and this has given rise to a trait characteristic of its residents: ambition. Ambition cuts across traditional social

Ben and I used to order the subjectively best *tandoori* chicken in Mumbai. It would be delivered to our door (like many other services you can call) by food elves operating some magical machinery that churns out delicious food somewhere over the rainbow. One day, we decided to explore the rainbow's end at the vague address on the menu card. The *masala* brick road led to the edge of a slum and further to a fly-infested kitchen where notions of the "best *tandoori*" went down the dirty open drain beside it. It was a stomach-churning reminder that a slum does not stop dreams from happening, even if it has the equal ability to crush them. Dharavi, Asia's largest slum, is a model of small-scale industry, not squalor. Mumbaikars have a knack for keeping focus on the big break (and sometimes sadly at the expense of the greater good). And they are wired to seize it, tooth and nail and *tandoori* chicken. Like Mumbai's rail system that's built for 5,000 but holds three times more, no one looks at the immediate discomfort because all eyes are on the next destination. And for some, the next station is Bollywood.

Wealth has given the city its sheen but it is its film industry that gives it its sparkle. All come to reach for the stars or become one. It is easy to become star-struck when you know stars are shining in your universe. My evening walks along Bandstand would always include a pause outside Shah Rukh Khan's house Mannat. In this scene, he would be emerging from his large fortress-like gate at the very point of time I cross its driveway. He would see me amidst the cheering crowd. I flick my limp hair (humidity in Mumbai is terrible) and flash a shy but dazzling smile. He returns it, eyes locked on mine and asks me to be in his next movie, *Pagal* ("crazy" in Hindi). City of dreams, indeed.

divides, making Mumbai tolerant, comfortably multicultural, hardworking and entrepreneurial. Thus the city has remained true to its beginnings as a wealth generator for the East India Company till today as India's commercial and financial capital.

The low ranking also reflects another aspect of the city; it delivers life to you raw. Take it or leave it. It offers the dream but nothing greater. So it is up to its citizens to make the most of it and what they can eke out. It produces people with a strong work ethic and a habit of turning setback into opportunity.

Mumbai's glitz is also due in part to it being home to most of the country's billionaires and glitterati, who live lavishly alongside those who make barely enough to survive. The stark contrast exists and makes no apologies. The Four Seasons hotel, for example, is located opposite a large shanty town; its beautiful leafy premises a road and world apart from the *kaca* (makeshift) dwellings opposite. "Garden view or slum view?" I imagine the receptionist asking. No apologies. Mumbai is what it is. And what it is, in some ways, is viewpoint. The slums are indeed a physical crumble of struggling lives but they also embody the spirit of Mumbaikars: striving, resilient, real, restive. This spirit gives the city its unique work culture, pace and hum. The garden view, on the other hand and on the other side, is the world of glitterati, fashion, film premieres and parties.

Glamour is Mumbai's other currency. It trades on who's who and who knows who. It gives Mumbai a cultural and social cache such that any association with the city is instantly contemporary, hip and desirable. It also seems to buy freedom. Mumbai women, or Bombabes as I've heard them called, exude a confidence not found in other Indian cities and they strut it with the latest of hemlines.

I felt as comfortable wearing a *kurta* as I did short dresses in Mumbai (not advisable in many other cities)—only because it is acceptable for women to wear liberalism, filling the catwalks and sidewalks with modern female role models.

Whatever the view and viewpoint of the city, in the city of Bollywood, everyone is IN view. Lives are lived on print, on screen and on your window-TV, the latter streaming a 24/7 telecast of Neighbour. The city is densely packed and crowded with one of the highest real-estate prices in the world because of limited land (heavy monsoon rains remind you that it was once a disconnected clump of swampy islands). So people build closer and higher and into each other's living rooms.

The Mumbai script essentially is the same as everywhere else—that of hard work, hard life in a hardened city driven by hard-earned wealth. But the Mumbaikar also plays hard with full-on *masti* (fun or good time). This is seen on weekends, in the abundance of restaurants and clubs, in parties till dawn, in newspapers that report it, at the beaches of Juhu and Chowpatty, and during festivals. People know how to let loose and give in to fun and romance, worthy of the all-India audience that looks to its glamorous image for inspiration. Like New York City, it has become the global image for the country in which it is situated. Similarly, it is filled with a cast of characters: the good, the bad, the worst (usually reserved for a politician or a mobster). We've encountered warm welcoming people like the auntie-jis who feed us and pinch our cheeks as they offer us *laddoo* (an Indian sweet). But we have also seen its corrupted side (in all senses of the word) and the likes of what you see in *goonda* (gangster) movies. Therefore to live in this city is to star in a mesh of Bollywood scenes, both tragic and hopeful, sometimes funny, always dramatic, like the hero who gets beaten up every step of the way but gets his girl by luck, volition and street-smarts. It means to live with a song in your step to a beat that can't be beat and perfecting the art of keeping it reel.

Ben lived in an old apartment building with a small view of the Arabian Sea and a large one of an abandoned stable, part of an old Parsi mansion whose land the apartment was built on. No state of decrepit remains ignored for long in pricey Mumbai and like hermit crabs, a family soon moved in. Each time I visited, I noticed they had encroached a bit more until they had a fully functioning home with electricity (probably tapped from our building). Every day the wife would see me brush my teeth by the kitchen sink and I would see her prepare meals as her family engaged in other mundane happenings. At first it felt uncomfortable to be watched but I realised it was a give and take, either an open acknowledgement of proximity or a closed window to air and light. I soon embraced my little stardom as easily as I had become addicted to the daily episodes of Hermit Crab family. Real life is reel life.

Bombay or Mumbai?

In 1508, Portuguese adventurer Francis Almeida exclaimed "Bom Bahia!" (beautiful bay) and gave Bombay its Portuguese name of Bombaim. The British anglicised it into Bombay. In 1995, the city reverted to its local name Mumbai, which refers to the Hindu goddess Mumbadevi who was worshipped by the city's original inhabitants, the Kolis. The name change back to its vernacular was part of a larger movement to strengthen Marathi identity in Maharashtra. However, Bombay still sticks out of habit or pride. To a certain generation, "Bombay" is synonymous with commercial and social savvy as well as cosmopolitan cool as opposed to the provincialism that "Mumbai" suggests. For others, the original name had always been used in the local vernaculars of Gujarati and Marathi. Some see it simply as a name change. The term Bombay remains despite the political pressure within the state to fully rid itself of its British moniker. There is too much cultural cachet in Bombay and not enough time for Mumbai to take hold (yet). So for now Bollywood stays (Mumblywood?), Bombayites are officially known as Mumbaikars, and private institutions such as Bombay Gymkhana debate on whether a name change equates a loss of heritage. What's in a name? Apparently in this city, everything.

Delhi: Eternal City

Delhi is a city of cities, layered over one another, strewn in the streets and curling around each other like weeds fighting for a spot in the sun that never quite set on India's perpetual capital. The *dil* (love) for this favoured city by its rulers are entombed in the monuments they built, still standing, still crumbling, defiant to time yet subordinate to its effects. A drive through Delhi is a blur of the clock of horrible traffic snarls and transitioning back and forth between eras and epochs like a time machine gone mad. It is also the spinning of the compass needle unable to find its bearing. Delhi comprises seven (ancient) cities and then some more as embassies take up space and place to further fill Delhi with nodes of different times and nodes of different places. Its many rotaries and roundabouts physically manifest this mental confusion. The city has a dizzying effect and a more dazzling one—power.

Delhi was born into continual greatness first as the royal seat of power for the Delhi Sultanate and subsequently the Mughal Empire and the British Raj. Today a new royalty has moved in—the bureaucrats of modern India—and they work and live in a modern-day citadel designed by English architect Edward Lutyens—New Delhi.

In 1911, the capital of British India shifted from Calcutta to New Delhi. Sir Lutyens (1869–1944) was commissioned to design a grand imperial capital capable of holding its own against Washington D.C. or Paris. He created a city with a long axis flanked by lawns and government buildings, and crowned at its far end by the presidential palace of Rashtrapati Bhavan. From this centre, politics and power ripple outward in the physical form of state houses (*bhavans*), government offices and white government bungalows. Built for its colonial administrators, the white bungalows today with their verandas and spacious grounds are home to politicians. The pleasure gardens of the Mughal citadel have become broad avenues of neem, arjuna, jacaranda and maulsari trees

A modern cricket stadium lies adjacent to the ruins of Feroz Shah Kotla, the "city of djinns" and fortress built by Sultan Feroz Shah Tughlaq in 1345. It was called Firozabad and is considered to be the fifth ancient city of Delhi.

branching out from the city axis and converging and diverging rhythmically at rotaries like a beating heart.

Despite Delhi's reputation for being remarkably polluted, it is remarkably green and expansive—until it joins with the clogged arteries and chokeholds where the rest of the city dwells. The stone walls of the old citadels are now invisible socio-economic ones, tall and insurmountable that separate the privileged from the underprivileged. These social walls wind their way around neighbourhoods, professions, nationalities, separating the in- from the out-caste that live beyond the borders or in its interstices.

This Delhi is hard and tough and large enough to have influenced the city's character and also its crime rate. It may be partly due to the city's very nature; Delhi is a city of migrants, from its diplomatic population to the scores of workers that come from neighbouring states to find work, bringing with them the hope for a future and the baggage of rural patriarchy. There is always the thought of home elsewhere and the easy escape to it, be it from the summer weather or from the short arm of the law. Yet Delhi remains arresting for old-souled romantics like me who can't get enough of its charm amidst its seeming crudity. Indeed, among the six major cities mentioned here, Delhi ranks the lowest in terms of the quality of living due to concerns over pollution, access to clean water, traffic congestion and personal safety. For many residents, the list is subjectively longer and more jarring.

Perhaps it was different in the past. The long-staying generation of *Delhiwalas* speak of the city's younger self before flaunted wealth and greed tarnished its innocence and seeped into its blood. They speak of an ethos of austere sensibility and buzzing intellectual energy, of moonlit gardens in Old Delhi and dinner at Karim's, the poetry of Amir Khusrau and Sufi music, of refinement and elegance. Squinting under rose-tinted glasses, you can still see this Delhi amidst the tangles of wires, open drains and din, as well as in the manners of that generation who grieves for its lost innocence. But the city grew up; it had to because of modernisation. Like in the four Hindu stages of life, it moved on to the *grihasthi* phase, where the accumulation of wealth and wants are a justified preoccupation.

In spite of its image in the media or in minds around the country and the very real challenges of living in Delhi, I would say it is a comfortable place to live in for expatriates. It has malls and all manner in which money can be spent and earned. Because of its large expatriate population, there is also a good variety of international food in addition to the plethora of local cuisine. In November, *Delhiwalas* emerge from their monsoon malaise to play in parks, dance at weddings and let happiness overcome them at festivals and events held throughout the city.

Delhi is a city of power and indeed I fell under its spell. It has been good to me. It is the Indian city I love the most — for its monuments, its colours in spring, its culture in spite of and despite all the things it is accused of. It rises again and again from its ashes and accusations like the rise and fall of India's empires, which crowned it. There is a unique rhythm to Delhi, an ebb and flow of time and people like the *prana* (breath) that fills my *dil* for *dilli* (the Hindi name for Delhi).

Chennai: Twin City

Chennai is the capital city of Tamil Nadu and the gateway to South India. It is India's fifth largest city and ranks ahead of Mumbai and New Delhi for quality of life. It is also the safest

Indian city, according to Mercer's 2016 Quality of Living Survey. Thus Chennai has emerged as an attractive city for expatriates because of its relatively lower crime rate and air pollution, as well as its richness in arts and culture.

My first trip to Chennai in 2001 left me with the lingering memory of curry and jasmine aromas clinging to the air. Twelve years later, with my nose accustomed (or deadened) by Delhi air, Chennai's warm, humid breezes were a respite, as were its clean, shady streets and friendly auto drivers who wouldn't take you for a ride when they take you for a ride. I wandered around the city at ease, prompted by the genuine warmth of strangers and the old-town feel, which could not be shaken off as Chennai developed into a modern metropolis. This sort of city schizophrenia was echoed at a café at Nungambakkam where I overheard an old man talking to his equally old friend at the next table. "I love Chennai, but it will always be Madras to me," he said, before they both proceeded to sigh, pause and sip their coffee. The silence that followed set me thinking and I joined the old men secretly in the delight of lost thoughts. Chennai, it seemed, was two cities: the one of nostalgia languidly moving within a big, modern youthful one.

In 1996, Chennai became the official name of the city, in assertion of its vernacular identity. Before that and since the 17th century, it was Madras, the name encompassing the colonial memory of the city and, for the likes of the old men, their childhood. Madras can still be felt in the stately colonial buildings of Fort St. George and George Town but most of it lives on the edge of consciousness, in afternoon conversations on a veranda or walks along the Esplanade by a generation whose memories keep old Madras alive.

Going to the temple is part of the daily life of many South Indians.

Chennai is often described as traditional compared to other Indian cities. While that is a generalisation, tradition is undoubtedly part of Chennai's character. It is heard in the rustle of Kanchipuram *saris* and the chants from temple priests. It lingers like the scent of jasmine flowers tucked in braided hair. Tradition beats like the rhythmic tapping of nubile classical dancers and it comforts like *idli-sambar-rasam* with a heaped serving of curd rice on a hot and hungry day. But it is the way it smells that invokes Chennai wherever I am: curry and flowers and subsequently, the deep dark note of its most famous intoxicant—filtered coffee.

I was introduced to Chennai's coffee-drinking culture (I had ordered *masala chai* and was given a look of disbelief) when a friend took me to a local coffee shop in Mylapore. The brew was served in a metal tumbler that came with a wide saucer, a *dabara*. "Raise the tumbler and pour the coffee into the *dabara* to cool it," she instructed. She demonstrated, skillfully pouring coffee waterfalls back and forth until her coffee cooled to a nice frothy mix. She told me to drink it without touching the rim of the tumbler and sharply threw a large shot of coffee into her mouth. It went in neatly like those toss-the-ball-into-a-basket carnival games. She won my admiration as coffee dribbled down my novice chin and into my consciousness. Chennai was just like its coffee, a rich, stimulating experience made when tradition percolates through the filters of time to render a still authentic brew.

Hyderabad: Prized City

The spotlight shines on Hyderabad as the top Indian city for the best quality of life and then the lights go out. Hyderabad is often dimmed by electricity outages, but it blazes in many other aspects that support its top-placed ranking in 2015 and 2016. Favourable weather, less pollution (than the northern cities), a tolerant society, an increasing number of good English-speaking schools, and a relatively reliable infrastructure are some of the reasons why expatriates and visitors enjoy their stay in India's seventh largest city. It is also a burgeoning IT-hub, which has given this old city a fresher, younger image and the nickname Cyberabad.

For me, I was captured by the old lustre of the once "city of pearls". Hyderabad used to be the centre of India's pearl and diamond trade, largely due to patronage from its last dynastic rulers known as the Nizams. The fabled wealth and love for gems of the Nizam court created a precious jewellery industry that involved fabled hoards of diamonds, emeralds and pearls, which continue to garland Hyderabad's jewellery workshops and centuries-old bazaars thriving around the 16th-century Charminar, the iconic tower that marks the heart of the city's old beat.

Built in 1591, the iconic Charminar (Four Minarets) is located in the heart of Hyderabad.

The landscape of the city similarly resembles pearls in their poorest version: round boulders and rocks strewn across the land looking like they snapped from God's necklace as he created Hyderabad. A few broken boulder strands away from Charminar is the hill fort of Golconda, the citadel and capital of the preceding Qutb Shahi dynasty (1518–1687). The fort and its surrounding areas are an upward expanse of rock and ruin in all senses of the words, for Golconda was renowned for the most desired of rocks—diamonds. On the coveted list of Golconda diamonds are the fabled Hope diamond and the legendary Koh-i-Noor.

Koh-i-Noor

The Koh-i-Noor (Mountain of Light) is one of the most valuable diamonds in the world. This 186-carat stone was believed to have come from the Golconda mines in the 13th century. Its legacy, however, is far heftier in its long and bloody history that saw it pass through the hands of Mughal emperors, Afghan warriors and Punjabi princes. Shah Jahan used it in the fabled Peacock Throne. Its possessors then and now have fought over it, some having lived lives of terrible misfortune marked by murder, torture and treachery. Some say it is because of the curse that befalls any male who possesses it: "Only God, or a woman, can wear it with impunity." Perhaps it is because of this that when the diamond came into the possession of the British crown in 1850, it was passed down only to the wives or female heirs of the throne. The diamond is currently set into the Queen's crown.

The city's culinary diamond is Hyderabadi *biryani*, once a royal dish for the Nizams. The secret, some say, lies in the unique way in which it is cooked. Served hot and heaped, it is ruin to waistlines everywhere. Hyderabad has long been the place where fortunes are made and diets are broken. Like its past fame, it is an unearthed gem that has been polished by time and politics, and is set brilliantly into today's world of technology.

Bengaluru: Wired City

Bengaluru (Bangalore until 2014) is the state capital of Karnataka and is known as the "Silicon Valley of India". Being India's third largest city, its vibe is young, techy and cosmopolitan due to the mix of people from outside and inside India who are drawn to its buzzy reputation and ample job opportunities. The city feels both large and small, and its surge of development in the last decade has added more girth to the city as well as grit in the form of traffic and pollution. Nevertheless, the city ranks third in India for both the best quality of life as well as personal safety in Mercer's 2016 Quality of Living Survey. One point of pride is the city's constant cool weather throughout the year, making for an eternal springtime when the rest of the country is soaked, sweaty or shivering. (Recent laments, however, have been on how it is losing its cool, temperature-wise and in frayed tempers at worsening gridlock.)

To the year-round pleasant weather, Bengaluru adds its reputation as a "Garden City". Although urbanisation is chipping away at its green roots, the colonial heart of the city remains green and intact. I remember the city for its colour. Painted murals on city walls added the rainbow to the green of shady streets and the reflected blues of modern glass facades. But it was pink that I would associate most with Bengaluru. I had visited when the poui trees (*tabebuia rosea*) were in bloom, cradling the streets in a soft blanket of the baby hue as its warm, friendly people went about their way.

It just takes a look at the many pubs and restaurants and Café Coffee Days (a chain of cafes) around town to realise the city has grown up and outgrown its small colonial boots. Although the contrasts exist, they do so in peaceful coexistence, perhaps as a testament to its inclusive residents.

It is a city that has a place and pace for everyone. Large parks for strolling old men, shaded lanes for ladies returning from market, movies and malls for the young and upwardly mobile phone-in-hand, as well as theatre and dance for the art-inclined. For me, Bengaluru's appeal lies in its pink pace of health amidst a wired-up, stripped-down city culture.

Kolkata: Genteel City

If Mumbai is India's financial capital and Delhi its administrative one, then Kolkata is the country's cultural capital. It and its state of West Bengal are regarded as the crucible from which India's artistic, literary and scholastic heritage sprang, along with the seeds of India's Independence movement.

The city was the headquarters of the East India Company and subsequently the capital of the British Empire before it was moved to Delhi. As such, it was the first to be touched by Western influence, particularly English education, giving rise to a formidable intelligentsia who led a movement that helped transition India into the modern era. Known as the Bengal Renaissance, this movement produced socio-religious reform and an efflorescence of literary and artistic output.

This creative and intellectual climate continues today in the form of Kolkata's cultural and literary festivals and the pastime of *adda*, lively intellectual debates seen widely in the city's cafés. I experienced this first-hand when I met Sushmita, a bright and beautiful lady from Kolkata who lit up as she contradicted my every sentence and seemed to like me even more thereafter. She would quote both Indian and Western literary giants to assert her points and when at peace, she wrote prose and stood behind the rights of humans and animals. She was to me a daughter of Kolkata as Rabindranath Tagore was its most famous son.

In 1912, Kolkata lost its affluence and influence to Delhi. The city today seems to be living in the shadow of its former glory and quite literally so. It is a city in decay, its beautiful colonial buildings covered in grime and rust and ooze, its people living in a hand-me-down city from prettier times. There have been spanking new residential developments south of the city but overall not enough of the right qualities to make it to India's top five in Mercer's Quality of Living Survey 2016. With the loss of its special central place, past political upheavals and a decline in manufacturing activities, Kolkata has the pace of an old *burra sahib*, one that mumbles in monologue as he sits in his wicker chair on the veranda of one of the city's "Calcutta" clubs.

One cannot deny that there is a genteel air to the city, a colonial pace and charm that mask the present and keep it safely under wraps lest the full reality provide too great a shock to romantic hearts. I am such a heart with a literary bent and thus it was easy to relive old Calcutta surrounded by the grandness of Victoria Memorial and the grit and grime of the "city of joy". It was not that much of a stretch of imagination as it was a stretch of time. At Mrs Dayal's suggestion, I visited her favourite cake shop, Flurry's (still situated) along the iconic Park Street. There I sat, surrounded by the characters from yesteryears sharing in the ritual of afternoon tea, the same indulgence that Mrs Dayal had enjoyed decades before. Time repeated itself or perhaps it ticked by so slowly in Kolkata that it had not really moved.

In 2001, Calcutta became Kolkata, the Bengali pronunciation of its name. In my opinion, it allows the book-loving, cinema-watching city to arise from its glory days to write its own city's future. It will be a story not quite old because the past is still steeped in the present; not quite new because the city remains much too obsessed with the old to leave it all behind; not quite borrowed because Kolkata prides itself too much on its creative leanings to be a follower; but definitely blue in a marriage of art and infrastructure. It was strange when I first saw it. The stop signs, traffic cones, lampposts, barricades, curbs and other public infrastructure were painted blue and white. My local driver said it was in honour of Mother Teresa, whose work serving the poor in Kolkata earned her a Nobel Peace Prize in 1979 and sainthood in 2016. Others say these are the *sari* colours of West Bengal chief minister Mamata Banerjee, whose Trinamool Congress came to power in 2011. Whatever the reason, Kolkata is undoubtedly trying to paint itself as India's cultural centre and is doing so with masterful strokes upon the same canvas that had birthed the Indian renaissance and some of India's greatest personalities.

> *A nation's culture resides in the hearts and in the soul of its people.*
>
> **—Mahatma Gandhi**

Winston Churchill once said India was no more a single country than the equator. Indeed, its diversity of religion, practice, tongue, and ethnicity makes the country the elephant in the parable of the blind men and the elephant: Six blind men are asked to describe what an elephant looks like by feeling different parts of an elephant's body. They then come together but cannot agree on what an elephant is. Seeing their squabble, the king interjects and tells them they are all correct because each was feeling a different part of the animal.

This well-known parable illustrates that one viewpoint is no less truer than another and that it takes many such viewpoints to put together a more accurate reality. Like the

The elephant plays a large role in popular imagination and cultural mythology.

elephant, India is far too nuanced for simplification. However beneath the disparate parts beats one common heart. Here this heart is presumed to be the Hindu way of life, which has assimilated diverse beliefs and cultures over centuries to provide the psychological basis for Indian behaviour. The results are common observable traits and similarities that together constitute Indian-*ness*.

Indians too don't fall easily into facile compartments, although they do sometimes fall into simplistic generalisations, which are helpful when used as a starting point for understanding rather than being applied indiscriminately, as in the case of stereotyping. How then does one describe the nature of a billion people? Referencing the parable, perhaps from the inside.

ETHNIC GROUPS

Indians are said to come from two main ethnic groups, Indo-Aryan (72%) and Dravidian (25%), terms commonly used to describe the ancestry of North and South Indians respectively. A common belief is that Dravidian-speaking people were spread throughout the Indian subcontinent before the series of Indo-Aryan migrations. Anthropologists, however, are still largely at odds on theories supporting this ethnic distinction. "Dravidian" in today's context refers to the native speakers of languages in the Dravidian language family who live mainly in South India, Sri Lanka, Pakistan and Bangladesh. Dravidian languages include Tamil, Kannada, Telugu and Malayalam.

DEFINING INDIAN IDENTITY

Central to an Indian's identity is the concept of hierarchy and how it is applied to three defining social structures: religion, caste and family. Who an Indian is depends on where he stands in these social structures, which together define him and give him his sense of self as well as his expected behaviours. Therefore, to begin to understand Indians is to recognise the combined effects of religious and social constructs.

Religious Identity

Although India gave birth to four of the world's religions— Hinduism, Buddhism, Jainism and Sikhism—it is officially secular. Yet religion remains deeply ingrained in Indian society. It permeates both the family and personal life of almost every Indian, be it in the predominantly Hindu majority (79.8%) to Muslims (14.2%), Christians (2.3%), Sikhs (1.7%) and the small number of Jains, Buddhists, Zoroastrians and tribal religions. More than just theological beliefs, religion is a way communities organise and define themselves in India. Therefore, one way to understand Indians is to be acquainted with the different religions that dictate and govern social behaviour and community identity.

Hindus

Hindus form the majority (79.8%) in most of India's 29 states and seven Union Territories. Hinduism, unlike the other religions, has no singular founder, doctrine or scripture and no central governing body. Rather, historians have described it as a convergence of spiritual and cultural influences over five millennia, making it not only the world's oldest living religion, but also one that is tolerant by nature. Many consider Hinduism as a way of life. Because of its syncretic nature, there is a wide spectrum of teachings and practices that fit into the "Hindu" mould. Although behaviours vary by region and community, the most common are the avoidance of beef, the importance placed on religion in a Hindu's daily life, and celebrating festivals and visiting temples.

Muslims

Muslims make up 14.2 per cent of India's 1.2 billion population, making India a country with one of the largest Muslim populations in the world. Kashmir has a Muslim majority, but Muslims are also populous in the states of Assam, Kerala, West Bengal, Uttar Pradesh and Bihar. Sizeable numbers contribute to the rich multi-ethnic culture of Indian cities such as Mumbai, Hyderabad, Kolkata and Lucknow.

Islam came to the subcontinent in AD 712 through traders and was further entrenched through a succession of Muslim conquerors. Islam's impact on Indian history and culture is undeniable, and can be seen today in India's food, architecture, literature, music and art, to which the Mughals were its finest contributors. Islamic customs also influenced Indian social norms, one of which some believe

Haji Ali Mosque is one of Mumbai's most recognisable landmarks and receives thousands of pilgrims and tourists every week.

was the increased isolation of women from the public sphere (*purdah*). Across India, Muslims can be identified by their abstinence from pork and alcohol, the practice of ritual prayers performed five times a day, and sometimes in their clothes: head coverings for women and caps for men. Variations in practice are usually region-based and are also dependent on degree of urbanisation.

Sufism

Sufism is the mystical practice of Islam that began to be more visible in India in the 10th and 11th centuries during the reign of the Delhi Sultanate. It was influenced by Hinduism's *bhakti* movement, which similarly stressed on devotional worship and was propagated by Sufi saints through music and song. Legendary musical poet Amir Khusrau (d. 1325) is considered the founder of Indo-Muslim devotional music traditions. The Sufi Christi Order, known for its emphasis on love, tolerance and openness, has a following in India. Shrines of venerated Sufi saints are places where devotees go to obtain blessings.

Christians

Christianity has a strong presence in India's northeastern states. Christians form the majority in Nagaland, Mizoram and Meghalaya, and have sizeable presence in Manipur and Arunachal Pradesh. Indian Christians are also found in South India, particularly in Goa where they form a third of the population, and also in Kerala, where they form a quarter of the population.

Christianity is said to have come to India with St. Thomas ("Doubting Thomas", one of the 12 apostles) in AD 52. He spent his remaining years preaching the gospel and establishing churches in Kerala and Tamil Nadu before his death in AD 72. In the 16th century, Roman Catholicism arrived with the European Jesuits, followed by waves of missionaries who established hospitals, care centres as well

San Thome Basilica in Chennai was built in the 16th century over what is believed to be the tomb of St Thomas, an apostle of Jesus.

as schools, some of which are still considered the finest in the country. The works of those Christians who protested injustice and engaged in philanthropic works influenced and attracted many Indians.

There are many Christian denominations today but Roman Catholics form the largest group. Christian Indians are identified easily by their names and their behaviour is similar to that of Christians around the world: attending church on Sundays and observing festivals like Easter and Christmas.

Sikhs

About 75 per cent of India's Sikhs live in the state of Punjab. There are sizeable populations in Haryana, Delhi, Uttaranchal, Jammu and Kashmir. Although they are a small minority overall, their impact outweighs their numbers. Sikhs are prominent in the Indian armed forces, politics, sports and businesses across India and throughout its history.

The Sikh religion is a reformist faith that opposes idol

The Golden Temple in the city of Amritsar is the holiest shrine of the Sikh religion.

worship, rituals and the caste system. It was founded in the 15th century by Guru Nanak, the first of 10 gurus. Guru Gobind Singh, the 10th guru, organised the community into a military order called the Khalsa to combat religious persecution. In doing so, he gave the community a religious identity that includes the wearing of long hair. With their turbans and long beards, Sikhs are therefore easy to identify. Men take the surname or middle name Singh (lion) and women, Kaur (princess). The Golden Temple at Amritsar is the spiritual centre of the religion and is where the Sikh holy book, the Guru Granth Sahib, is kept.

Buddhists

India is the birthplace of the Buddha and Buddhism, but Buddhists today make up only 0.8 per cent of the total population. Numbering about 8 million, nearly 6 million alone live in Maharashtra and the rest are in Uttar Pradesh and in the northeastern states bordering the Himalayas, particularly in Sikkim and Arunachal Pradesh. Maharashtra saw a Buddhist revival in 1956 due to Dalit leader and author of the Indian constitution, B.R. Ambedkar, who embraced Buddhism along with half a million of his followers. Every year Dalit Buddhists rally at Nagpur (in Maharashtra) at the site of the original conversion.

Buddhism is based on the teachings of Siddhartha Gautama (566–486 BC), who became the Buddha. It reached its peak during the reign of Mauryan emperor Ashoka in the 3rd century BC and then steadily declined from the 1st millennium onward when its practices were absorbed into the rising popularity of Hinduism. It disappeared with the Muslim conquests of the subcontinent and only began to see a small revival in the 1950s.

Jains

Jains make up 0.4 per cent of India's total population. Numbering about 4.5 million, they are mostly concentrated in northern India, particularly in Maharashtra, Rajasthan, Delhi and Gujarat. Jainism, like Buddhism, is an ancient Indian religion. Its founder, Vardhamana Mahavira (540–467 BC) was a contemporary of the Buddha, and both religions gained popularity because they were egalitarian and open to all regardless of caste. The core ethic in Jainism is non-violence (*ahimsa*), which demands that no living being should be hurt. Jains therefore follow a strict vegetarian diet including abstaining from root vegetables like potato and garlic as it is believed harvesting them would destroy the plant. Because of this belief, many Jains could not become farmers or warriors and turned to commerce. As a result, Jains are some of the wealthiest businessmen in India today, engaging in such businesses as diamonds and precious stones trading.

Zoroastrians

Zoroastrians are more commonly known in India as Parsis. They are a well-defined ethnic community descended from Persian Zoroastrians who emigrated to India in the 8th century to avoid religious persecution in Persia. They first settled in Gujarat but most of them now live in Mumbai, where buildings and places reflect their glorious past as wealthy traders, administrators and successful industrialists (such as the Tata and Godrej families, whose names have become household brands). Their numbers have been in steady decline, with about only 61,000 today, half as many as there were in 1940 because of the strict rules that prohibit marrying out of the community. Despite their small declining numbers they have contributed significantly to Indian society, particularly in the area of philanthropy.

Names

Names are the first indication of the religious community a person comes from. Nirmal Kaur is a Sikh whilst Lorraine Esteves is most likely Christian. Ali Khan is a Muslim and Amita Mehta is a Hindu. There are, of course, exceptions to the rule but in general names indicate religious affiliation.

Social Identity

The concept of the "individual" in the Western notion is not widely found in India. Instead, most Indians develop their sense of identity from the groups to which they belong. Apart from religion, cities and regions also help define them to a certain extent, such as the known rivalry between Mumbaikars and Delhiites. But the two groups that make the most impact to an Indian's sense of self are family and caste, although the latter has its share of controversy. A person's identity is therefore first and foremost the group identity of his family followed by the collective identity of his caste, resulting in the unique way in which Indians perceive others and themselves.

Much Ado About Hierarchy

Indian society is profoundly hierarchical. Indians are always conscious of a social order in all relationships, as well as their status relative to family, friends and strangers since it is believed a person's self-esteem is drawn from the position he occupies in the social hierarchy. It also informs his behaviours and he will adjust his body language, form of address and tone accordingly. Therefore there is always a subconscious need to first determine rank in every interpersonal encounter.

In the past, one's status was a consequence of one's birth according to the prescriptions of the caste system. Today, esteem can be acquired by other means opened up by education, blurring the traditional boundaries and definitions and making it more difficult to ascertain each other's social status.

When two Indians meet as strangers, it often begins with both trying to determine the social status of the other. Without asking the obvious direct questions, Indians have learnt to fish out the information by asking seemingly intrusive indirect ones. Where do you live? Who is your father? Which school did you go to? Where do you work? How much do you earn? Where are your children studying? Most foreigners are taken aback by such intimate questions at the first shake of the hand but for Indians, it is understood that this is a needed prelude to establish the social equation, which will consequently determine behaviours.

With the hierarchical antennae on alert, Indians can infer social background even in a simple answer. For example, we live in Vasant Vihar in Delhi, considered to be an upscale residential neighbourhood and a foreigner would think nothing more of it. But to an Indian, it reveals that we (or rather our landlord, the Dayals) are relatively well-to-do. Vasant Vihar also used to be a housing cooperative for Delhi's senior civil servants, which further suggests that Mr Dayal came from such a family.

Senior government officials, known businessmen, and media and sports personalities are pre-eminent in the social hierarchy, and therefore one's status can also be elevated by association. So when an Indian tells you he knows so-and-so or is related to so-and-so, he is trying to establish his status and awaiting your comeback on your own network. You should be conscious about how you would want to respond to these scenarios. This being said, intimate questions addressed at foreigners could be nothing more than natural curiosity. Nevertheless, be prepared for questions about your father. If you are a diplomat, your father is your country and you can draw from its relative power. Therefore in India business cards go a long way.

Caste Identity

Caste is a way of social organisation in Indian society that comes with its own prescribed identity and beliefs. Each caste will have its corresponding values, traditions and prejudices, which will colour an individual's view of reality and become the conscience by which he lives. For him, it is these internalised caste norms that define who he is and what the right conduct for him is (*dharma*). Caste to a certain extent also determines his spouses, friends and occupation although caste consciousness has been decreasing in modern times.

Caste System

The caste system began several thousand years ago as a functional means of ordering society. The word derives from the Portuguese word *casta* ("pure") and refers to the two institutions of social organisation: *varna* and *jaati*. *Varna* (Sanskrit for "colour") allocates members to one of four social classes in the traditional Hindu hierarchy mentioned in Vedic literature. Each *varna* has its own duties and privileges. At the top of the pecking order are the Brahmins who were

the traditional priests, teachers and intellectuals, followed by the Kshatriyas (warriors), Vaishyas (merchants) and Shudras, who perform a wide range of tasks. At the lowest rung of society are the "untouchables", otherwise known as Dalits ("oppressed"). Each *varna* is further subdivided into subgroups called *jaatis*.

In ancient times, the system allowed upward and downward social mobility between castes but at some stage, the system became inflexible and hereditary, where a person's caste is determined by birth and explained by the deeds and sins of his past life (*karma*). Over the course of centuries, caste practice further degenerated to become a rigid, oppressive institution that led to economic and social exploitation, particularly of the Dalits.

Dalits

Underpinning the caste system is the doctrine of pollution and purity. The Brahmin is considered spiritually the purest. Occupations and even skin colour and diet are said to reflect the degree of purity. Dalits invariably do jobs in society such as clearing human waste (called manual scavenging), removing dead animals, tanning leather or washing clothes. The Dalit touch was believed to be so polluting by high caste members that they were deemed "untouchable".

India's 165 million Dalits have faced disturbing socio-economic discrimination and injustices. In villages, they are denied access to temples and schools, their housing is segregated and their women are not allowed to draw water from the common well. They have endured discrimination in education, healthcare, housing, employment and legal treatment, and have also suffered violence in caste-motivated abuses.

Mahatma Gandhi regarded untouchability as the biggest blot on Hindu society and passionately fought against it, as did other social and political movements after him. The 1950 Constitution of India legally makes the practice of untouchability a punishable offense, but the law is seldom strictly enforced.

For the nearly 70 per cent of India's population living in rural areas, caste dynamics are still part of their daily lives. Throughout India's history, one of the means to improve one's social status was to adopt another religion whose followers seemed better off.

Today this oppression is officially frowned upon as the Indian Constitution has made all citizens equal before the law and also extended protection and opportunity for advancement to Dalits. However, a stratified society still exists in practice. In middle-class India, caste plays a decreasing or negligible role in friendships and marriages but hierarchical thinking continues to impinge on the Indian psyche regardless of background.

THE JOINT FAMILY

The Indian child learns about concepts of identity and the hierarchical ordering of society from his family. The extended family is considered the basic building block of Hindu society where ideally grandparents, parents, children, aunts, uncles and cousins live together under one roof (or near enough). In this unit, members are emotionally and functionally supported within a web of relationships and dependencies.

Family Identity and Values

From an early age, an Indian child learns that the family reputation, the product and expression of the collective efforts of every member, becomes the over-riding identity against which an individual is seen or judged. Therefore, every member knows the roles and obligations expected of him and each of his kin towards the preservation of the family's reputation.

Filial piety, loyalty and fraternal solidarity are the family values often highly upheld in Indian families and there is good reason why. In Indian society, the family is the principle source of satisfaction and dependability, as much as it is about identity. Indeed, family is the safety net in tough times, especially in rural areas where the extended family traditionally

provides practical support such as shelter for the elderly.

The central role of family in the Indian psychology results in a strong obligation to preserve and serve family needs first, sometimes to the exclusion of other considerations. This obligation can be so strong that it is often used to justify ethical breaches such as an aunt hiring her nephew for a job despite having better-qualified candidates, or an uncle peddling influence to get his niece enrolled in a popular school, or a rich man paying off his son's criminal deeds. The behaviours are not celebrated but they are understood, albeit tacitly. Even in today's reality where nuclear families are on the rise, a psychological "jointness" continues to operate with its concomitant family obligations.

Family Hierarchy

You can piece together a picture of a family by listening to how its members address each other. Different relatives are allocated specific terms to reflect their relationship with each other and to the patriarch. The Indian system differentiates between the paternal and maternal relationships because family descent (*gotra*) is patriarchal. Also, there are different obligations and duties for the mother's side and the father's side. Each member is expected to know and perform his/her role to keep the family machinery running smoothly.

Since the family is a strong social element, it is polite to enquire about each other's family. Also, when you marry an Indian man or woman, you are also marrying the family and similar family obligations may be placed on you.

Family Nomenclature (Hindi)

- Father's parents: *daada* (m), *daadi* (f)
- Mother's parents: *naana* (m), *naani* (f)
- Father's sister: *bua* and her husband is *phuphaa*
- Father's elder brother: *thaya* and his wife is *thayi*
- Father's younger brother: *chaachaa* and his wife *chaachi*
- Mother's brother: *maama* and his wife *maami*
- Mother's sister: *mausi* and her husband *mausaa*

When it comes to the individual's generation, however, there is a sudden dearth of titles and it falls back to age. Younger siblings or cousins call their older counterparts (in Hindi) *bhaiya* or *didi*. Someone who is younger or of the same age are called by their names. Terms can vary state to state and by language.

Roles and Relationships

Knowing the dynamics of family relations will help you understand Indian behaviours. The extended family comprises a cast of characters whose roles and obligations are almost stereotypical, further dramatised and entrenched into the big screens of life by Bollywood movies. Some of these roles have become social models, reflecting ideas of identity and duty underpinned by Hindu values and beliefs. Strain appears when these values are confronted with "modern" ideologies, as in the case of the contemporary Indian family. The family structure nonetheless conditions Indians to value connections as the dominant mode of social relations and to look for mentorship and guidance in authority figures.

The Father

The traditional Indian father is seen as aloof, strict, restrained and formal in his dealings with his children. The father figure is also a leadership archetype, where authority figures are looked upon as nurturing patriarchs. One of the more striking changes in modern times is the active and consultative involvement an Indian father has in bringing up his children, which are consequently influencing contemporary attitudes towards leadership.

The Wife and Mother

If the prevalent worship of mother-goddesses is anything to go by, a mother holds an exalted position in Indian society. She defines the family as much as she does the Indian nation. The traditional vision of womanhood puts being a mother as the highest ideal of a fulfilled life. The thinking continues its hold even on many middle-class women, who continue to view maternal obligations as central to a woman's identity regardless of her occupation and education level.

A girl's training to become a "good" wife and "good" mother (by society standards) starts in late childhood through the conscious inculcation of culturally designed feminine roles and values, such as obedience, selflessness and conformity towards her husband and his family. In middle-class homes, these values are tempered with "modern" ideas of educational achievement, equality and independence. The modern Indian woman thus struggles to find the balance between traditional ideologies of womanhood and its expected behaviours, and the modern narrative that frees her to define her own identity.

> ### The Mark of a Woman
>
> The *bindi* is the mark on the forehead worn by Hindu women. It is placed between the eyebrows, which is believed to be the sixth *chakra* and the seat of concealed wisdom. It also symbolises auspiciousness and good fortune. A Hindu woman indicates her married status by wearing a red *bindi* or by dusting *sindoor* (vermillion) in the parting of her hair.

Sons and Daughters

There is a marked cultural preference for a son that goes back to Vedic times, when prayers were said for sons, grandsons and male offspring, but never for a daughter. Hence the birth of a son in some parts of the country is feted by spontaneous celebrations whilst the birth of a daughter is markedly quieter. Although the preference for sons is widespread, it is not uniform. In the northeast and some southwestern states that have matrilineal systems, the birth of a girl is a welcomed event.

Traditional Hindu society prefers sons because male offspring are said to continue the family lineage and are also required for the performance of the last rites for parents. Daughters, on the other hand, are traditionally seen as an expense, someone who cannot contribute to the family income and who will one day take a considerable part of the family's savings for her dowry, which is an illegal practice today but one difficult to control. As a result, rural India has seen high rates of female infanticide, and gender discrimination remains widespread although it has improved with rising affluence and education. Modern parents take equal delight in both their sons and daughters.

Childhood is taken as a time of affectionate indulgence, following a proverb which advises parents to treat a son like a king for the first five years, like a slave for the next 10, and like a friend thereafter. Therefore it is common to see parents indulging their young ones and giving in to their whims at the first sign of a cry. If there is any difference in bringing up sons and daughters, it shows up in restrictions that may be placed on a daughter's freedom of movement after she reaches puberty.

Mother and Son

The mother-son relationship is an idealised bond that is sentimentally depicted in Indian art, legend, folklore and literature. It is helped along by the powerful role played by mother goddesses in Indian culture, but it is the Hindu tradition that lends it its strength. It is traditionally believed that a wife's duty is to bear a son for the family and through him her status is raised in her husband's family. Sons therefore hold a special place in an Indian mother's heart.

The mother-son relationship is often portrayed as a source of intense emotional gratification for both. As a result, Indian men are said to have difficulty in psychologically separating themselves from their mothers. Even educated modern men can show deference and dependence on their mothers for key decisions throughout their adult lives, which can consequently lead to tensions in the household upon their marriage.

> The Sanskrit word for "son" is *putra*, which means "one who delivers from hell".

The mother-daughter relationship can be equally as strong but it does not seem to have the same idealised sentimentality as that of the mother-son bond.

Saas and Bahu

The cruel *saas* (mother-in-law) and long-suffering *bahu* (daughter-in-law) story is the infamous staple of many folktales and soap operas. The *bahu* eventually wins the heart of her *saas* through dogged obedience and steadfastness or more conveniently through the birth of a grandson. Peace and order is restored in the family with the reconciliation of the *saas-bahu* relationship and the husband/son who was conveniently absent during the conflict returns to the scene to embrace them both. In reality, *saas-bahu* relationships in any culture can be tense but can be especially so within the dynamics of the traditional Indian joint family.

In the family hierarchy, the new bride enters at a low position and is viewed as a threat to her new family's unity because of her potential to disrupt established bonds. She may assert herself, which may force her husband to choose between loyalty to his wife and to his mother, which tradition dictates should be unyielding. Or she may cause her husband to neglect his obligations to the family. If family stability is threatened, the *saas* might take it upon herself to restore balance to the family power structure and to make sure her son remains a son of the house.

Whilst suffering at the hands of their mothers-in-law continues to be a bitter reality for many rural Indian women today, it is significantly less so (or not at all) for the modern middle-class woman who marries later and enters her husband's family with more education and maturity. Rather, it is the *saas* of today that sees herself as a victim of a cruel turnaround whereby when it reaches her turn to be the matriarch of the house, she can no longer be assured that she will be getting the reverence of her better-educated *bahu* or the unwavering loyalty of her son. This could be a melodramatic account, but it does suggest that traditional dynamics are changing with the times.

Brothers and Sisters

The bond between brother and sister is considered special and is celebrated in a Hindu festival called Raksha Bandhan. It is now popularly extended to include any sibling-like relationship between men and women who may or may not be biologically related. On Raksha Bandhan, a sister ties a *rakhi* (sacred thread) on her brother's wrist to symbolise her love for him and offers prayers for his wellbeing. In return, he vows to protect her. Brothers thus have an obligation to care for their sisters. This is especially so in a patriarchal society where the woman marries into her husband's family. Should anything happen to her husband and she is rendered

Women buy or make their own *rakhi* (sacred thread) days before the festival of Raksha Bandhan.

destitute, her brother is expected to step in to care for her and her children. Hence, an uncle also shares special bonds with his sister's children throughout their lifetime.

THE INDIAN WORLDVIEW

There will be many instances when Indian behaviour may baffle you, and may sometimes even frustrate you as in the case of the seemingly callous attitude towards the weak and underprivileged in Indian society. It is important to understand that this comes from a difference in worldviews. The Indian worldview is undergirded by cultural and religious concepts that colour the emotional and intellectual responses of Indians. Since nearly 80 per cent of the population is Hindu, the Indian worldview is largely interpreted through the lens of Hinduism and its key laws of *karma* and *dharma*.

Karma, as it is commonly understood, implies that a man's destiny is linked to his deeds in a previous life. It refers to the universal law of accountability where good deeds bring good consequences and bad deeds, bad ones. Therefore people suffer or prosper in accordance with their previous *karma*. The destitute man then is seen as repaying his dues from past transgressions as a form of cosmic justice. Redemption from his suffering can await his next birth with little need of outside intervention in this life. *Karma* also explains why Indians are able to accept setbacks and disappointments in life with amazing stoicism, or conversely to regard wealth and status as an earned entitlement.

Dharma refers to moral duty or right action. It is the Hindu concept of ethics that is dependent on one's caste and one's stage of life (*ashrama*) in the context of the culture, era and innate character of the person. In other words, right or wrong is not absolute. For example, turning the other cheek is right

for a priest but detrimental for a warrior. Therefore, the "right action" in the Indian mind operates in a grey area of ethical relativism. Since Hinduism does not have any one founder, or a Bible or a Qur'an to refer to for resolution, personal judgements must often be guided by the ethical lessons propounded in Hindu holy texts. The right action is a result of taking into consideration the circumstances and context of the decision at that point in time.

As a consequence, Indians may seem inconsistent in their responses, saying or doing one thing this time and another at a different time. This is likely because the context has changed and therefore the position taken would likewise need to be recalibrated. What is the right course of action in one instance can be wrong in another in light of new circumstances. Decisions are therefore flexible and context-sensitive, which does not imply an absence of a moral code, but rather the propensity to change the rules if there is a new larger "right" to be served.

Being aware of the effect of *dharma* in the sense of "moral duty" on a person's behaviour will help you adjust your expectations of others and clearly bring to the fore your own biases. For instance, I always wondered why our gifts to our driver Santosh were never reciprocated until I realised that he viewed gift-giving as our *dharma* as the boss, not his. Rather he saw his service as what was right for his *dharma* and therefore reciprocated through loyalty. But if we've learnt

Hindu Philosophy in Brief

Hindus believe that the real self (*atman*) is eternal and made of spirit (*brahman*). The soul takes on a material body and lives in an illusionary reality (*maya*). Because of human failings, the soul has to endure the repeated cycle of birth and rebirth (*samsara*) but is able to create its own unique destiny by the law of *karma*. It is given the opportunity for liberation (*moksha*) from *samsara* through different paths and through performing one's specified duty (*dharma*), which is revealed through holy books and spiritual mentors (*gurus*).

anything about India, we've found that for every example, there is always a counter-example, a sort of reality relativism that refuses to put India into a neat predictable box. Thus, in contrast, our maid Madhu used to bring flowers on our birthdays and tea after every visit to her village.

The key thing to note here is to be aware that your staff judge their actions against the context of their *dharma*, even if it contravenes what you deem as universally polite or right. They are operating from a different worldview. To prevent misunderstanding or frustration, you should communicate your expectations (your worldview) regarding issues such as punctuality, integrity and other non-negotiable behaviours you expect from them from the outset. Similarly this is a caution to be mindful of acting within *your dharma*. Your servants may see you at the top of their social hierarchy, and therefore when you try to be a friend and blur those lines too quickly, you may confuse them and cause them to unintentionally overstep boundaries. If deeper engagement and a strong trusting relationship are what your conscience desires, it is better to build your role as a family member in their lives rather than as a friend, leveraging on the strong values associated with family on the Indian psyche.

You will also likely interact with many educated Indians who have had various degrees of exposure to Western (and Eastern) notions of ethics and values, and who therefore are able to put on multiple lenses. They will adjust to your worldview as you adjust to theirs. They are also likely to have a more in-depth view of *karma* and *dharma* within the larger context of Hindu philosophy. I have only provided a rudimentary rendering of these concepts and specifically to address the more puzzling questions foreigners have about Indian behaviour.

It's All Relative(s)

Karma and *dharma* combine in such a way to make an Indian self-focussed on his own inward spiritual journey and his personal obligations to kith and kin. This justifies the inward-looking perspective and *relative-ly* favourable actions towards family, sometimes to the detriment of the concept of collective good. This can breed indifference towards poverty, injustice, corruption, ineptitude and even a filthy public environment, unless they start to directly impact self and the family.

HINDU SOCIETY

The family is the heart of Hindu society, and significant life events are marked and celebrated together. These rites of passages are called *samskaras*, which are performed during the various *ashrama* (stages) in a Hindu's life. There are 16 *samskaras* but the ones that you are likely to be invited to are births, marriages and deaths. Thus a brief understanding of family celebrations is useful.

The Four Stages of Life

A Hindu sees his life in four broad *ashramas* that determine his priorities. The early years of the Student life should be devoted to the acquisition of knowledge; the next phase is the Householder stage of life when he pursues material gain and experiences the joys of physical pleasure; the third stage is a transition Retired life where he ceases his responsibilities as a householder and prepares himself for the final stage of the Renounced life, when he devotes his energies to *moksha* (liberation).

It should be noted that the *ashramas* apply to men. Women follow a different system of three stages, which are each dependent on a male in her life: as a child protected by her father, as a wife protected by her husband, and as an elder, protected by her eldest son.

Birth and Birthdays

The birth ceremony welcomes the reincarnated soul back into the world and into the new family, and is marked by purification rituals. Most Indians place emphasis on only the first birthday but in cities, many affluent families celebrate their children's birthdays annually. Opposite to Western culture, it is the birthday child that gives the gifts, and it is common for parents to prepare a bag of sweets to be distributed to classmates and friends. Urban families, however, adopt both practices. For Indian adults, the 60th and 80th birthdays are significant milestones.

Evil Eye (*buri nazar*)

Young children are often seen with a large black dot drawn somewhere near their foreheads. This intentional imperfection is said to ward off the evil eye, which is said to be a curse cast out of jealousy and envy and is believed to cause misfortune to fall on its victim. Babies and children are believed to be especially susceptible to harm from the evil eye and may have their eyes lined with black kohl as additional protection. In many countries, including India, praising a child publicly is sometimes thought to also draw the attention of the evil eye.

Marriage

The most important *samskara* is marriage and great emphasis is placed on it in Hindu society. I was initially surprised when I was asked if my marriage was a love marriage. "Could it be anything else?" was my response until I realised that the majority of marriages in India are *still* arranged to ensure matches are "good". In fact, love marriages suffer under a negative image, implying that the couple was ruled by reckless emotion rather than by rationality. Indeed, many love marriages flounder and fail as if living up to society's self-fulfilling prophecy, but not because of the lack of love but rather because of the social attitudes that put unnecessary stress on the union. Often it comes from the families themselves, who may have been reluctant to accept the new in-law for any number of reasons.

Even in this day, young Indians regardless of education, social class, religion or region, still overwhelmingly prefer arranged marriages partly due to the acceptance of the cultural definition of marriage as an alliance between two families rather than a relationship between two individuals. With family support for the couple, marriages stand a better chance of survival. Love, it is believed, can come after the fact, and the wedding rites. Hence the well-educated modern Indian working overseas will return to India and marry the bride of his family's choice. Or, like in the case of an 18-year-old boy I met on a train, a partner had already been selected for him since he was a child and his filial obligation was to

Love in the Time of Bollywood

Indians have every right to claim the hold on Love with the loin-warming Kamasutra, but despite the eroticism on pages and temple walls, the fires of Love today burn brightest on the big screen. The love stories of Bollywood remain a rain-filled tree-romping fantasy for most Indians. Here, love is pure desire between two individuals, free of social restrictions that characterise an Indian's reality. On screen, love conquers all. When the lovers are threatened by the keepers of tradition, the shackles of family obligations, Bollywood gives love another chance at resurrection through death. Reel life cannot be dampened by real life. And so the enchantment lies locked on screen, giving Indians a chance to feel unfettered romance and love at the price of a ticket.

turn up for his wedding. The stakes are high at losing the support of family for those who choose love over duty. It is even higher if his partner is from a different caste. My previous driver eloped with his girlfriend whom his parents disapproved of because she was from a lower caste. As a result, he was expelled from his family and has not seen his parents since the day he broke his father's heart and expectations.

A hybrid sort of arranged marriage is becoming more commonplace in urban families where the parents may shortlist a suitable partner and the children decide if they would like to take the relationship further. Another variation some consider to be closer to a love marriage is when the couple comes to know each other independently and then seek the approval of their families to proceed with the relationship with marriage as the goal.

Regardless of how the couple come together, families would commonly judge whether a match is good in terms of the socio-economic, educational and reputational qualities of the prospective spouse and his/her family.

Nothing shows the family "values" more than Indian matrimonial ads. Whether online or in print, these ads can sound anywhere between a family search to wed another family to an auction for their offspring. The father's status (the family reputation) is often spelt out in greater detail than the children's. Or if the children can stand on their own qualifications, it will be enumerated with a list of their academic achievements and places of work, augmented with shamelessly immodest descriptions: "Very fair, tall, handsome only son from affluent high-caste Hindu industrial family, MBA from Berkeley, H1B (a US visa, implying a specialty occupation and high salary), vegetarian ... seeks slim, beautiful, fair, educated bride from high-status family." When you can have such a man, how can love compete?

Traditionally, the bride undergoes the all-important "seeing the girl" process that involves her being scrutinised by parents and nosey relatives of the groom's family to see if she has the desired wife qualities—beauty and grace for some, the ability to make round *chapatis* for others. If she passes this show-pony round, the couple's horoscopes are then checked to ensure that the match is also made in heaven. When stars align, then an auspicious date is set for the celebration of celebrations—the great Indian (Hindu) wedding. In the south, it is a serious, simple religious affair; in the north, it is a week-long party to literally display the family jewels.

Dowry

According to ancient custom, the dowry was seen as an expression of affection by the bride's father and the dowry was her personal property. However, it came to be viewed as payment to the groom's family. Widespread dowry-related violence led to its criminalisation in 1961 but the practice continues. Appliances, money, jewellery, property and vehicles are masked as gifts rather than dowry. When a bride's family is unable to accede to the demands, the young bride may in some cases be abused to extort more "gifts" from her family. Because enforcement is weak, dowry deaths (euphemistically called "kitchen accidents") continue to take place in many parts of India.

The Great Indian Wedding

The Hindu wedding is said to mark the start of the Householder phase of life for the couple, with raising children as the purpose of marriage. There is usually a succession of celebrations before and after the actual ceremony, which in itself can last a few days. A wedding therefore can be an expansive and expensive affair.

You could be invited to one or more pre- and post-wedding celebrations, which are combinations of prayers and party. One common pre-wedding ceremony is the *sangeet*, which is held for the bride by her female relatives and friends. It is an all-girls get-together marked by dancing and music, much like a family-friendly hen's night. Sometimes the *sangeet* is combined with the *mehendi* (henna) ceremony in which the

A Delhi bride and groom walk around the sacred fire seven times as part of the marriage ritual.

A priest takes centre stage at a South Indian wedding.

bride and her friends have *mehendi* applied to their arms and feet. According to popular belief, the darker the colour of the *mehendi* on the bride, the more her husband will love her. Many brides also get the *mehendi* artist to draw in the groom's name into the design. This is meant to be an intimate teaser for the groom who has to search for his name hidden somewhere on his bride's limbs.

The actual day of the Hindu wedding ceremony itself can stretch to any length of time depending on the auspicious time chosen for the ritual vows to begin, and these could be times beyond Western expectations. We attended an evening wedding celebration and at midnight had not yet seen the bride. She emerged at the auspicious hour of 2.30am by which many guests were already numbed by sleepiness to consciously witness the bride become wife.

There are many rituals in a Hindu wedding ceremony and they vary widely according to region and denomination. In the north, the three common rituals are the giving away of the daughter by her father to the groom (*kanyadaan*); the groom seizing the bride's hands symbolising their impending union (*panigrahana*); and the circumambulation of the sacred fire (*saptapadi*). After *saptapadi*, the couple are considered husband and wife. In the south, the sacred fire is not a wedding practice, except in some Brahmin communities; instead, a mixture of water and turmeric is used to anoint the clasped hands of the bride and groom. Garlands are then exchanged and the marriage is marked by the groom tying a sacred thread (*tali*) around the bride's neck.

A Typical Delhi Wedding

The popular wedding season in Delhi spans November till February. During this time, you will see a higher than usual number of horses and elephants on the road mounted by a happy groom swaying to the music and drums of the *baraat*, the singing-dancing wedding procession of the groom and his family as they make their way to the wedding venue.

Upon his (usually late) arrival, he will be received by the bride's parents. The bride and groom are then each given flower garlands and it is said that whoever can put the garland on the other first will have an upper hand in the marriage. Gifts are then exchanged between the two families. Traditionally, this was the dowry that the bride's family gifts to the groom's family. Many urban families now reciprocate the gift giving.

The *kanyadaan*, *panigrahana* and *saptapadi* rituals follow and take place around the sacred fire, which is an invocation to the fire deity Agni. In the *saptapadi* ceremony, the couple makes seven rounds around the fire, and each round (*phera*) corresponds to a particular vow. After the *saptapadi*, the husband marks the hair-parting of his newly-minted wife with vermillion (*sindoor*), the sign of a married Hindu woman. He also ties a beaded necklace called a *mangalsutra* around her neck as a symbol of their marriage (similar to a wedding ring). The elders' blessings mark the end of the ceremony.

Karva Chauth

Ten days before Diwali, Hindu wives in North India undergo a one-day ritual fast from dawn till night for the longevity and safety of their husbands. The fast requires total abstinence from food and water until the moon is sighted. In the evening, balconies and rooftops across the city fill with wives decked in fine *saris*, jewellery and *mehendi* on the lookout for the moon. Once the moon is visible, the wife must view its reflection in water or through a sieve. She then views her husband in the same manner after which he feeds her water and some food to break her fast. He then reciprocates by giving her lavish gifts. Karva Chauth is considered to be a romantic festival, symbolising the love between a husband and wife. In modern times some husbands fast together with their wives.

Death and Funerals

Death is not seen as a finality but as an interval between lives. It is the end of the physical body but not the soul. The funeral and rites are therefore aimed at assisting the soul to *moksha* (liberation). Most Hindus cremate the dead within hours of death to enable the departed soul to move quickly and unimpeded into the next life. The eldest son is required by tradition to do the last rites. Three days after the funeral, the ashes are collected and scattered into the Ganges or another sacred river followed by a period of mourning. What is striking about death in the Hindu tradition is how the family continues to play a role. Rites are performed daily for 10 days immediately after the death to help the soul completely break the bonds with its former life. It is believed the soul's new astral body is complete on the 13th day.

If attending a Hindu funeral, wear simple, white casual clothes since white (not black) is the colour of mourning. You can send flowers ahead to the family but you should not bring flowers or any gift with you to the funeral. Superstition dictates that you should shower immediately after returning from a funeral. Women generally do not attend cremations apart from those of immediate family members. At Varanasi and other places, you may witness funeral processions and cremations. Such occasions should be treated with respect and photographs should not be taken.

Widows

The death of a husband signals a social death for many traditional Indian women. Regardless of age, a widow must leave behind her colourful clothes and jewellery, and don white clothing. She can no longer wear the red *bindi* on her forehead, a symbol of marriage, and is expected to mourn and remain chaste.

Elders

Most Indians spend most of their lives in the Householder stage and are only said to be able to move on to the Retired stage upon seeing their first grandson. Although many Indians no longer live by this rule, many do enter some form of mental retirement by retreating from social life and handing over their household responsibilities to the next generation. In the case of Mr Dayal, his unannounced jaunts to the "hills" (of Darjeeling), he claims, are in keeping with the Sanskrit name for this stage—*vanaprastha* or "retreating to a forest"— even as Mrs Dayal wishes his forest to be on home ground, especially when the gardener disappears, leaving the grass to grow thin and high. As Indian women grow older, they also become closer in equality to men, asserting themselves more or being more outspoken if they choose. Elders regardless of gender are treated with a lot of respect in Indian society.

Ascetics

The final stage of life is a time to renounce material desires with a focus on peace, *moksha* and a simple life. This stage can be entered directly from the first stage without completing the Householder and Retired stages. A person who adopts this stage tends to be itinerant with no material or emotional attachments. They are typically characterised as the wandering saffron-clad ascetics with matted locks and meditation beads or the semi-naked *sadhus* (holy men). Some of these professed holy men have become tourist attractions, performing levitation tricks and asking for money in return for a photograph.

My friend once attended a Kumbh Mela, a regular Hindu pilgrimage in which Hindus gather to bathe in a sacred river. She was shocked to see a few *naga babas* (literally 'naked yogis') not because of their nakedness but because of the way they could do incredible things with their body parts, specifically their penises. One rolled his onto a stick just as a baker rolls dough. Another had an Eiffel Tower pinned to the tip of his tower, making one wonder if it is not just clothes that he had lost.

Women

Indian women are aware of their traditionally defined roles as daughter, wife, mother, mother-in-law, grandmother but, with increasing education, they are also more confident in redefining them. Women, led by the urban middle class, have stepped out of their homes to embrace leadership positions

in the previously male-dominated arenas of business and politics, amidst a growing sense of accomplishment and independence. No longer are women confined to child rearing, unless by choice. Even husband-wife relationships have become more egalitarian, thereby changing the form of the traditional family.

However, despite the progress urban Indian women have made, many of their rural sisters still suffer from gender discrimination, sexual violence, and prejudice, where the expectations of the patriarchal tradition limit them to predefined roles and punish them for wanting to step out. Therefore equality in education, at home and at the workplace is still an individual rather than a universal achievement.

Nevertheless, educated women are leading the charge to change attitudes and empower themselves. If this is a cause you can get behind, there are many organisations aimed at uplifting the status of women such as helping rural women become financially independent or providing education for girls. Change is happening, albeit very slowly, hampered by gnawing poverty and deep-seated mindsets. Mother India may still need to weep for her daughters for a long time more to come.

HINDU SPIRITUAL PRACTICE

Spirituality is the world image of India and indeed, religion seems to pervade almost every aspect of Indian life. From the many temples and shrines that punctuate the public space to the religious symbols and icons revered in the privacy of homes, vehicles and stores, the observable signs of the faith mark a Hindu's inward devotion and hope in the rewards that rituals and faith can confer. However interesting it is to observe, the more immediate impact on you is how religious practices affect your staff. There will be days when they will ask for time off to celebrate a religious festival or to go on a pilgrimage. They may return to work with vermillion smeared on their foreheads after a temple visit. It is therefore important to know some basic terms to have a better appreciation of the spiritual commitments that structure a Hindu's life.

Worship

The main acts of worship include meditation, the chanting of mantras and *puja*, the ritualistic worship to a deity or its sacred image. Although communal worship does exist, worship is usually performed individually, with an emphasis on one's personal experience with the divine. It can take place at home, at a temple or outdoors, and there are certain days associated with particular deities and their specific *pujas*. *Pujas* can be accompanied by *arati*, the offering of incense, water, lamps and flowers, and singing of *bhajan* (devotional hymns).

Almost all Hindu families have a home shrine, which could comprise a few pictures or small statues propped up on a shelf. Those who can afford it have a separate shrine room for worship and meditation. Shrines can also be found on the dashboards of cars and auto-rickshaws (for luck) as well as on the streets. Some are obvious, such as a village shrine sheltering a deity, and others are in the less obvious form of rocks, trees, rivers and mountains. The streets of many communities are punctuated with many such shrines: makeshift outdoor ones, black stones daubed with vermillion or a tree decorated with strips of coloured cloth. Places of worship are also connected to sacred sites, which are considered gateways to a higher world.

Temples are considered the homes of god or a particular deity, and people visit to take *darshana* (sacred sight), as it is believed that the deity is present in its *murti* (statue) and can see the devotee. Temple visitors conclude their visit by accepting morsels of *prasada* (sacred food) offered to the deities since it is believed to purify the soul. My maid Madhu returned from her pilgrimage and proudly gifted me a small packet of *prasada* in the form of some white rice puffs and three whole walnuts. I could not understand her enthusiasm for what I had mistakenly thought was a very dry snack.

Jasmine and marigold flowers strung into garlands for use in worship are commonly sold outside temples.

Fortunately for me, she had the vocabulary and patience to explain what it was, and that was her way of passing on a blessing. If you are at a temple and are offered *prasada*, accept it graciously and only with your right hand.

Three and 330 Million Gods

The three main Hindu deities (called the Trimurthi) are Brahma, Vishnu and Shiva. Together they are responsible for the cosmic cycle of creation, preservation and destruction respectively. Each is accompanied by a female consort— Brahma with Saraswati, the goddess of Learning; Vishnu with Lakshmi, the goddess of Wealth; and Shiva with Shakti, who personifies Mother Nature (she is also called Parvati, Durga and Kali). Although the goddesses are often worshipped together with their husbands as a divine couple, they can also be venerated individually.

Gods also have avatars (incarnations), which are believed to be a visible form of that particular god sent to earth at a specific time and for a specific purpose. Most avatars are connected to the god Vishnu. Out of his 10 incarnations, Rama (7th) and Krishna (8th) are worshipped as gods in their own right, while Vishnu's 9th avatar is the Buddha, underscoring Hinduism's historical ability to adapt and incorporate into itself other ideas and concepts. Following the tradition of the divine couple, Rama is paired with his wife Sita and Krishna with Radha.

Joining these main gods are the other legendary 330 million deities that make up the Hindu pantheon. Some are pan-Hindu such as Hanuman and Ganesha while others are region or village-specific, or minor deities with jurisdiction over rivers, forests or natural phenomena such as rain and fire. They could also be deified persons.

Hindus also believe in a single supreme being called Brahman, which all Hindu gods either are subordinate to or are considered representations of his different aspects. It is said that the more educated Hindus of the scholastic tradition tend to adopt the monotheistic view and the less educated Hindus are more likely to view Hindu gods in a polytheistic way. I asked a few Hindus why there are so many gods, and their tongue-in-cheek answer was that if one fails you, you have another 299 million or so to call upon!

Details of a South Indian *gopuram* (tower) reflect Hinduism's plethora of gods.

Superstitions

I was en route to an appointment following "Indian Standard Time" (i.e. late) when suddenly Santosh stopped the car. "What's wrong?" I asked. He points to the side of the road. "Black cat," he says with a shudder. As we sat still for a full minute, his suspected feline phobia revealed itself to be superstition-induced.

Because of the syncretic nature of Hinduism, many beliefs are taken under its fold, resulting in superstitious practices being regarded as religious ones, making it hard to differentiate between the two. Here are a few common superstitions you might observe:

- **Black cats:** A black cat crossing your path is considered a bad omen. Stop and wait for a minute or until someone passes you to absorb the bad luck. I also checked for good measure: black dogs are okay.
- **Garland of lemon and chillies:** Alakshmi, the goddess of misfortune, is said to like sour and hot things, so shop owners in India hang a garland of lemon and seven green chillies at their door so that she will satisfy her hunger and leave without entering their shop.
- **An extra 1 rupee:** When Indians gift money on weddings and special occasions, there will be an extra 1 rupee added to the sum to ensure it is indivisible and does not end in zero, which means the end.
- **Not sweeping the house after sunset:** It is believed that the goddess of wealth Lakshmi visits homes after dusk and will not come in if the house is being swept.
- **Groups of three:** Do not step out of your house or go for an important business meeting in a group of three because it is believed that the work will not get done, which is just one of many other possible reasons.

- **Not leaving your handbag on the floor:** It is believed money will be spent soon if you do so. Good excuse during sale season.
- **Taking care of your bangles:** Breaking them is a bad omen. Bangles are broken when a woman becomes a widow.
- **Listening to the gecko:** If you hate these little house lizards (*chipkali*) as much as I do, it might add a little comfort to know that if their chirping is coming from the east, whatever you are thinking at the moment will come true. "Keep happy thoughts" must be the motivational message from these icky sticky creatures.
- **Breaking mirrors:** You might already know this one since it is also a common Western superstition. Seven years of bad luck will befall the clumsy.

"Don't Touch the Pickle"

One of the most rampant taboos in India is the notion of impurity attached to women and menstruation. Women are considered impure, sick or even cursed when they menstruate. They are told to keep out of the kitchen, as it is believed that whatever food they touch will spoil, even spoil-resistant pickles, which are at risk from even her shadow. Women should also not water plants or wash their hair in the first two days of their period. Many rural women are kept in seclusion for the first three days and have their own separate utensils. Menstruating women are also not allowed in temples and mosques.

The shame associated with menstruation means that shopkeepers commonly wrap sanitary napkins in newspapers and place the offending brick-like packages in black polythene bags to mask their existence. For the whopping 88 per cent of Indian women, however, sanitary pads remain non-existent because of poverty or ignorance. Women in these instances resort to using rags or even ashes and leaves. The whole process of keeping stained rags discreet, from wearing them to washing them, puts immense psychological strain on all rural women. About 20 per cent of rural girls end up dropping out of school after they reach puberty. Fortunately there are initiatives that are trying to break the taboos around menstruation and making sanitary napkins affordable so that women can lead normal lives. If this is a cause you can get behind, check out the initiatives in your city.

- **The sign of the times:** Before making life-altering decisions, many Indians consult an almanac to determine auspicious days and times to begin new things, such as a business, opening ceremonies, journeys and weddings. Even in the everyday, there are auspicious timings around which to arrange your life. Some people may rely on fortune-tellers or fortune-reading birds for a bird's-eye view on fate.

DEFINING TRAITS

At the risk of generalising, I think there is nothing moderate about Indians. They inhabit the space between restrained pensiveness and unbridled emotion, often in just one person. They are expressive, explosive, exuberant and colourful like the country that birthed them, but also quiet, contemplative and other-worldly. But even within this diversity of tone and temperament, there are some visible commonalities. I have identified a handful of traits I have observed and the possible reasons behind them.

Hopeful and Resilient

Indians seem to be able to withstand adversity that would make any other person give up on life. This may be due to the Hindu worldview that allows the average Indian to see beyond the *maya* (illusion) of his circumstances in the belief that his destiny can change at any time by divine intervention. Hindu mythology is full of such stories, of metal turning to gold, and huts into palaces. So as troubles threaten to bury a man, he will fervently propitiate his chosen god(s), obtain the blessings of gurus or do whatever it takes to cajole the universe to change its mind and smile upon him. Maybe this is why Indian society, which sees so much injustice and inequality, has kept afloat, buoyed by the hope offered by unfailing religious belief.

Sensitive to Power

The obsession with hierarchy also reflects an underlying sensitivity to power. Many Indians are adept at finding and adapting to power sources, not only as a means of establishing identity but also in the hope of personal gain. As a result, Indians may act overly obsequious to the powerful, then immediately turn around and be dismissive to anyone seen as inferior.

The powerful are also *expected* to project power since this is a visible way to establish status and so there is little modesty or restraint in both demeanour and display. Strong leaders are often venerated because of the power they exude, even if and despite falling short in other areas. Being aware of the power play in relationships helps you read and react more adeptly to anyone's personal chorus of "I've got the power".

Creative

I am not talking about creative expression, in which Indians also excel, but the everyday creativity of the man on the street to make the most out of a bad situation. It has its own word—*jugaad*—that translates somewhat inadequately to "creative improvisation, ingenuity, quick thinking, resourcefulness, the ability to turn adversity into opportunity". It demonstrates the flexibility and inventiveness of the Indian mind to capitalise on or salvage any situation with the limited resources and tools available. We had a friend who worked as a hotel manager and he said that Indians, as opposed to other nationalities, are usually the cause of his hotel irons spoiling. Not because Indians do not know how to use an iron, but because they

A man uses his bicycle to transport and sell his wares door to door.

use the irons as griddles to make *chapati*. This is *jugaad*: low on cost, high on creativity. But lest you underestimate its application to just solving everyday bread-and-butter (or rather *roti*-and-ghee) issues, the spirit of *jugaad* also powers Indian innovation and entrepreneurship.

Argumentative

According to Nobel laureate Amartya Sen, Indians are argumentative in that they love a good debate. It could be due to an inductive approach to learning that translates to a wellspring of viewpoints and opinions, which may not necessarily result in any conclusion. Those from cultures more prone to listening or taking turns to speak should not be alarmed and debating is not meant as disrespect.

This is especially important for foreign managers who will

need to have meetings with their Indian colleagues. Prepare yourself by watching the evening news, in which there is a particular forum hosted by the news anchor, involving a panel of people invited to give their views on a topic. Shortly after the topic is seeded, the conversation quickly descends into chaos, with several if not all panellists talking (shouting) at the same time. To foreign ears, it is unintelligible, yet Indians watch this daily, making sense of the arguments within the chorus of raised voices. You will eventually get attuned to this way of discussion, which grooms the accompanying skill of quickly sieving out information whilst simultaneously adding your own. To balance debate with productivity in meetings, you should also pick up techniques on how to focus the group's attention so that your own meetings do not resemble reality TV.

Emotional and Expressive

In India, actions, or rather, emotions, speak louder than words. It makes sense that in a society still struggling with rural literacy the heart and the lungs are used to doing the communicative lifting. It only takes watching Indian cinema to know that everyone is permitted to feel, including muscle-bound heroes. Big boys do cry, even if they had broken out into dance about 10 minutes earlier. Whilst some of the emotions on screen are exaggerated, art does imitate life; Indians are an expressive lot. In joy, in sorrow, in wrath and in talking on the phone. So suspend any decibel disbelief and judgement. You have cultural licence to let loose the drama queen when all the world's a stage.

Patient

Indians are patient, perhaps by acquired habit after years of accepting that time has left the building and is not coming back. Meetings start late, parties start later, events start when they are supposed to end. Blame the traffic, the driver, the weather, the alignment of the stars; blame anything but the obvious: culture. Although traffic and weather are indeed significant factors, the habit of tardiness is much more constant. And so Indians have stopped expecting punctuality and learnt to just wait, for it comes when it comes, whether "it" is a dinner guest, bus or pizza. All follow the unique ticking of "Indian Standard Time". Although the term refers to the country's official time, it has taken on the meaning of time's seemingly stretchable quality in India. So wait and let wait. It must be mentioned, however, that trains are surprisingly on time, rather than somewhere in time.

Indians According to Compass Points

Even Indians themselves have generalisations about their fellow Indians in other parts of the country. It is illustrated in this story, which ends differently depending on where the storyteller is from:

There was once a poor (add the location adjective) rickshaw driver who rushed his very ill child to the doctor.

Bihari (north): The child died. The driver beat his chest, gathered a mob and staged a protest.

Tamilian (south): The driver lectured the doctor on medical ethics whilst his wife prayed at home. The gods would heal the boy.

Bengali (east): The child died, as all things do eventually. The driver pondered the purpose of life and wrote a moving eulogy to honour the death of his offspring.

Punjabi (west): The driver decided to set up a hospital because medical care was expensive.

Generally North Indians are seen as ostentatious, boisterous, emotional and confident. South Indians are perceived as the opposite: religious, friendly, cultured, civil, peace-loving, if a little simple at times. Indians in the east, particularly in West Bengal, are regarded as artistic, soft-spoken, intelligent and cultured, while the desert regions of the west produce cool, stoic, enterprising Indians.

Curious

If curiosity killed the cat, it could explain why there are hardly any cats to be seen in India. Rather, the streets are filled with curiosity-fuelled people who make out of anything a spectator sport around which a crowd will form. Onlookers will be aplenty, although helping hands less so. The habit of taking a visual interest also comes in the form of staring. It is not the quick furtive glance, but a long-drawn gaze that follows the foreigner. It will take some getting used to before the discomfort wears off. Dressing modestly can reduce the amount of attention you get, but anything can attract the gaze, from your skin colour to your frizzy hair to just the fact that people have not seen someone like you in their area. Curiosity's cousin, inquisitiveness, will come in the form of seemingly intimate questions about your background when you meet Indians. This is usually benign friendliness and you can seek the same information in return.

Colour Conscious

There is a brand of cosmetics called "Fair n Lovely" which sums up the Indian obsession with skin colour. Fair is lovely, according to commonplace Indian standards of beauty. This stems from the doctrine of pollution and purity in which white is seen as pure and by extension, high status. Matrimonial ads therefore seek "wheaten" complexioned brides for their "fair sons", leading women all over India to smear whitening products on their skin in the hopes that white will make them right for love or for some narrow definition of beauty.

CHAPTER 4

FITTING IN

> ‘The best part of your story is when it changes.’
>
> **— Bella Bloom**

To transit gracefully into Indian society, knowing some of the social norms will keep you from falling on your face, committing embarrassing mistakes or worse, unintentionally stepping on toes. It can also keep you safe. However, even though your best efforts will be recognised and appreciated, you may still be considered an outsider at the end of it all. It is all too easy then to shrug and decide to stick to your own cultural bubble. Don't.

In my experience, the process of learning to fit in forced me to consciously observe others and through this, a common humanity is revealed—underneath it all, we are more the same than different. Therefore fitting in is not just simply integrating well but also allowing our worldview to expand, learning to replace any judging attitude with a more embracing one. In fact, many of my friends have returned home changed by India to various degrees. It is not appropriation, but letting India seep in. And it starts with the desire to fit in well and be open to the different.

GREETINGS

The standard greeting for hello and goodbye in North India is to put your palms together, bend your head and shoulders slightly and say "*namaste*" or "*namaskar*". *Namaste* is a beautiful greeting. It translates as "I bow to you" or more profoundly to mean that the spirit within me salutes the spirit in you, acknowledging the spirituality inherent in each person in Hindu belief. In the south, use "*vanakkam*" for hello and "*poi varukiren*" (I will go and come back) upon departing. Generally *namaste* is understood across India. If all else fails, fold your hands together in greeting and say hello/goodbye.

The Western greeting of shaking hands is also acceptable and widespread, especially in cities and in the context of business. If unsure which greeting to apply, wait and see if the other person puts out their hands first. Even so, do not expect bear-claw grips; handshakes tend to be limp, almost like a hand-touch. Do note that religion, education and social class influence the order of greetings in India. This is a hierarchical culture, so greet the eldest or most senior person first.

Traditionally, a greeting showing respect and subservience is the touching of feet. This is usually reserved for elders or persons highly respected in the community. That is why it came as such a surprise when Santosh touched our feet as we said our final goodbyes at the airport. Ben and I were moved by the gesture because it is unusual for it to occur among people of the same age and we never thought we would be at the receiving end of such an honour. Foreigners are not expected to perform this greeting, except perhaps when meeting those of an extremely high status like a religious leader or guru.

Name-calling

Indians have various terms to respectfully and politely address people (and a number to similarly insult them, but that is beyond the propriety of this book). A suffix of –*ji* is added as a marker of age or importance. Elders are generally called aunty and uncle, but one with considerable years would require the addition of *-ji*. For example, if you were to be introduced to someone's elderly mother, a "*Namaste* aunty-ji" would be a fine greeting to trigger a warm smile and a nod of approval.

You might however find the tables turned and your youthful name *ji*-ised, perhaps as a result of India's ability to quickly age anyone.

Possible geriatric leanings aside, first names connote intimacy and closeness, and therefore a *-ji* is added to normalise it. In the case where an Indian lady might introduce herself with her first name, adding *-ji* to her name when addressing her implies that you are maintaining a respectful distance.

Men are commonly referred to as sir, *sahib* (boss), and uncle. Referring to the latter, Indians are one big family when it comes to names. Younger men are called *bhaiya* (brother) and women *bahenji* (sister-respectful) or *didi* (elder sister-informal). I have been called anywhere from madam, mam, *memsahib* (mam boss) to aunty, *bahenji*, *didi* and *beta* (child). It reflects how the greeter sees me, regardless of how I wish to see myself. Madam is the most common respectful greeting for ladies. *Memsahib* seems to be holdover from the British Raj, and I do feel like donning a gown and having afternoon tea on a veranda when people refer to me as such. Old uncle-jis call me *beta* and young children call me aunty. For any man your age or younger, *bhaiya* is the appropriate term. It is also commonly used to get someone's attention before an instruction or request, helping to soften it.

For more formal situations in which you know the name, Mr or Mrs will be fine. The Indian equivalent of Mr and Mrs is *Sri* and *Srimati*, but the English terms are accepted widely. In some families, a wife will refer to her husband as Mr, even if he is sitting right next to her. Traditionally husbands are referred to in the third person and not by first name out of respect. My previous driver told me that his wife called him *sono*, meaning "listen", which is purportedly another respectful address even if it sounds a tad bit bossy (incidentally, she was).

As much as how you are greeted is telling of how the greeter sees you, Indian surnames are equally telling of a person's roots in most cases. Indian names generally reveal where a person (or his ancestors) hails from, his religious affiliation, caste and mother tongue. It's therefore useful to learn a few common surnames as a way of getting to know a person. Banerjee, Das, Roy, and Mukherjee are Bengali surnames whilst Goan names reflect Portuguese influence, such as D'Costa and D'Souza. Menon and Nair are common Malayalam (Kerala) names, and Tamil ones tend to be multi-syllabic. Sometimes it is the suffix that is defining. Marathi surnames (Maharashtra) end in –kar, such as Kelkar and Tendulkar. These of course are generalisations and there are also an equal number of exceptions. Therefore treat the names as good conversation starters. You should also be ready to give the background to yours if you want to begin with such an approach.

COMMUNICATING
Lost in Translation
There are more English speakers in India than there are in the UK, indicating just how widespread English is on the subcontinent. In the main Indian cities, most people can speak English to varying degrees, and English is more prevalent in the south than in the north.

I made the mistake of speaking Hindi in Chennai and the reply from the shopkeeper came in perfect English, which took me aback since shopkeepers in Delhi tend to speak in broken English or a version that makes its own grammar rules. (Incidentally, speaking Hindi in the south is akin to speaking English to the French. Just don't.) On the other side of the proficiency spectrum are the likes of Mr Dayal, the English-educated elite who displays great mastery over the language and a great love for books. (He is often seen reading in the garden with a cup of *chai* as company).

The English spoken in India is British English (or Queen's English) with its associated spelling and vocabulary, thus Americanisms may not be understood quite so easily. There might also be words that sound English but are used in a different way (see Indian English on page 289). These "Indianisms" add a unique flavour to the English spoken in India. For example, a meeting can be *preponed* to an earlier date. You *click* a picture. Your driver was late for work because his leg was *paining* (hurting). (I know, it hurts to hear.) Watching the world go by is an enjoyable *timepass* for many people. (It is, judging by the scores of people just milling around in the middle of a workday). One of my favourites is *too good*, as in extremely—but not excessively—good. How was your vacation? Too good.

The most common tense you will hear is the present continuous tense: I am not having time. I am not knowing this person. You too might be having this way of speaking by the time you leave India. Because, sometimes, communication is about how accurately the other person understands you rather than how grammatically correct it is. If you speak in the way that people are used to, you have a higher chance of being understood.

At other times, understanding and being understood boil down to accent. It helps to speak *slowly-slowly* (another term) and in short clear sentences when speaking to those less proficient. The Indian accent when thick can similarly be hard to understand. An appropriate reply would be "Sorry, you were saying?"

The Indian Headshake

"Can my dress be ready by Tuesday?"

The tailor shakes his head.

"No?"

He shakes his head again.

"Yes?"

He shakes his head one more time.

"Maybe?"

And the head shaking continues. Welcome to the dilemma of the infamous Indian headshake, the most confusing non-verbal cue that means yes, no, AND maybe.

The important thing to understand is that Indians do not like to express "no", be it verbally or non-verbally. Rather than disappoint you, for example, by saying something cannot be done, Indians will give you a response that they think you want. This behaviour should not be seen as dishonest because an Indian would consider himself rude if he did not try to accede to your request. So he will likely give you an affirmative answer but will be deliberately vague about the details. You must then look at the non-verbal cues, such as reluctance to commit to a time, being overly enthusiastic or the mystifying yet affirming Indian headshake.

In this case, the head shaking may be interpreted as, "I'm hearing you. Tuesday." But that does not mean he intends to do the task by Tuesday; it will be done when it is done. Or he could mean that he can get it done by Tuesday but it all depends on the circumstances and this could be anything from traffic to whether his wife quarrelled with him that day. Practice makes patience so you will learn how to take it easy on specifics like date and time and not shake your head too hard when things don't go as promised.

The Indian headshake is also a signal that your listener is following your words or empathising with you. I am shaking my head now as I tell you of the frustrations ahead of you when it comes to tying down simple commitments. Is it a reality common to all who stay in India? Yes. No. Maybe.

In any case, you also have to rely on body language and non-verbal cues to assist your comprehension.

Please and Thank You

"Give me water," I heard a gentleman say to the air stewardess, and I thought he deserved with his water a piece of my mind. "She is not your servant," I muttered silently, judging him on what I perceived as a haughty attitude and a lack of manners. This and other pervasive instances of such "demands" came as quite a shock to me until I realised I was the one in need of educating, specifically in language.

It was not until I learnt Hindi that I understood why such requests appear like demands. In Hindi the notion of "please" is inherent in the way the verb is conjugated. When the Hindi word for "give" is translated into English, Hindi speakers may assume that "give me" is in a polite form. Therefore in the gentlemen's mind, his request could have been "(could you please) give me water". Similarly, asking a waiter to pack your leftover food in Hindi is "pack *karo*" or the more polite "pack *kijie*", both of which when translated into English would make anyone sound bossy: "Pack!"

There are formal words for please (*kripiya*) and thank you (*dhanyavaad*) in Hindi, but I tend to hear them only in airport announcements and not in common speech. At all other times, "please" and "thanks" are used. Occasionally, you may hear thanks in Urdu (*shukriya*). This and *dhanyavaad* are considered formal usage and are appropriate for written correspondences and in business and social settings where a degree of formality is required. Some consider *dhanyavaad* rather than *shukriya* to be the more "Indian" term.

You may find that a word of thanks may be heard less often than you are accustomed to. In India, people view doing things for others (especially others to whom they are close) as their *dharma* (duty or responsibility), thereby requiring no explicit need for thanks. Profusely thanking someone may be interpreted as trying to create distance in a close relationship. Some may actually find it insulting. So instead of thanking your host again and again for the wonderful meal, say instead "I really enjoyed the delicious food and the opportunity to spend time with you." An Indian host would be happy to know that her efforts have been noticed and appreciated.

Whilst profuse thanks are not often heard, profuse "no, thanks" are always ignored, especially when it comes to touts. You will soon find that "No, thank you" is rarely enough to deter them, along with urchins and street vendors who see your politeness as a sign of weakness. A stern forceful reply is required, as much as it makes you cringe inside and feel like a bad person. I usually say "*Nahi* (no)!" forcefully but when the pestering continues (and some will follow you for a long time or tug at your clothes and bags), I channel my inner *maharani* with a commanding "*Jao* (go)!" A close friend of mine developed an anti-harassment face (she calls it her "resting bitch face") for such times. She is a warm, smiley person by nature, but when she has that face on, even I would think twice about approaching her.

DRESS AND MODESTY

One of the easiest and fastest ways to fit in is to dress like a local. Not only does a whole new sartorial world open up to you but you also blend in better with the crowd. Clothing broadly falls into two categories: unstitched and stitched. Unstitched cloth would be the *sari*, *dhoti* (men) and turban. Their most striking feature is that they are worn draped, tucked or wrapped, requiring neither tailoring nor stitching

and can be adjusted to fit any growing girth, as in the case of pregnancy or the middle-age spread. Stitched clothes include the *kurta*, *lehenga*, and pyjama for ladies and the *sherwani* (men) for men, in addition to trousers and shirts.

Women

Mrs Dayal told me a story about a relative who was up to her knees in seawater because of a tide that had come in sooner than unexpected. The captain hurried her to climb the ladder onto the boat but she refused because it would mean having to lift her *sari* and expose her legs to the other passengers. She eventually did board the boat but only because her husband, water rising up his trousers, pushed her forcibly up the ladder. This illustrates the traditional view on female modesty: legs and thighs are always covered come hell or high water, and will invite looks when not.

This practice is not as deeply entrenched in cosmopolitan cities like Mumbai, where short skirts go fairly unnoticed, but

The Whole Nine Yards

Ranging between five to nine yards the *sari* has been traditional attire for Indian women for centuries, endowing them with elegance and sensuality.

The *sari* consists of three parts: the *pallu* (end-piece), *jamin* (the field) and *kinara* (border). Many people select a *sari* based on the intricacy of the *pallu*. A *choli* is a short tight-fitting blouse worn with the *sari*. When I got my first *choli* tailored, the tailor told me that the blouse should allow me to breath but just enough to stay alive. The petticoat worn underneath has to be similarly tightened until it securely cuts into your skin since it holds the *sari* up at the waist. The draping of a *sari* is where the art begins and I was fortunate to have Mrs Dayal and Madhu teach me. I can tie my own *sari* now but it takes me at least 30 minutes and several exasperating attempts. Mrs Dayal does it in under five, and therein lies the difference between an expert and a novice. She can also tend to the garden, go marketing and nap in a *sari* with perfect ease whereas all I can do is stand up straight and breathe lightly. Draping a *sari* requires practice and patience, and its reward is the moment when you bring the *pallu* across your midriff and flip it over your shoulder. In an instant you transform from a tangle of cloth into an Indian Cinderella. It is like magic with the aid of an unlikely fairy godmother: safety pins. One or two if you are experienced; five for me.

Saris range in fabric from heavy silks to cooling cotton and light chiffons and georgettes. The lighter it is, the easier it is to drape but in terms of refinement, silks are incomparable. The *sari* is also a cultural indicator. Indian women take great pride in their *saris* and having a good story to tell about where you obtained your *sari* or showing knowledge of unique regional fabrics will therefore be appreciated. A *sari*'s distinctive weave, motif, colour and draping style vary by region. Therefore it is worth picking up a few on your travels within India as meaningful souvenirs. Favourites include Chanderi (Madhya Pradesh), Kantha (West Bengal), Ikat (Odisha), Bandhani (Gujarat), Kanchipuram (Tamil Nadu) and the highly valued Banarasi (Uttar Pradesh). Some women have them tailored into Western dresses if they cannot manage a *sari*, but I love them as they are.

in places like Delhi, where conservatism runs as high as that rising tide, it is best to keep one's legs concealed. Dressing modestly is even more important when travelling to rural areas not just for your safety, but I think also out of respect for the cultural norm.

Traditional Indian clothes for women cover from the waist-down but not necessarily from the waist up. In the case of the *sari*, the navel is left exposed as it is believed to be a source of energy and creativity. Personally, the sari is the most beautiful garment I have ever worn. It is *the* definition of feminine; it hugs the curves and gives a beautiful silhouette, but it takes practice to wear one because there are many considerations to think about, the biggest being it unravelling in public. But once mastered, it will be your go-to outfit for elegance and grace. Wear appropriate ones to fit the occasion and season. Silks and handloom *saris* are good for formal events; georgettes are suitable for parties and in the summer.

The Big Cover Up

In addition to the scarf, shawl and wrap, add the *dupatta* and stole to your vocabulary and wardrobe (it does fill up fast). A *dupatta* is essentially a long scarf and a stole is a short one. A shawl on the other hand is much larger in size for wrapping around the body, making its use confined to winter. The best ones are the pashmina shawls from Kashmir, and you should invest in a good one during your stay in India. Quality differs and many shops claim they sell 100% pashmina but the cheaper ones are usually silk or cotton blends.

It was Mrs Dayal who introduced me to the real deal (it takes a local to let you in on where to get the good stuff). I first met her *shawlwala* Ahmed at her home. He came with nothing but a big scruffy black duffel bag out of which he produced the most exquisite pashminas I had ever seen. They were all handmade in the traditional *kalamkari* technique, a skill that had been in his family for generations. He told me that it takes three months to complete one shawl and, judging by the intricacy of the pattern and intensity of his squint, it came as no surprise. Hours of needlework by day and night went into each piece. Ahmed was invited because Mrs Dayal's cousin was looking for a warm legacy to hand to her granddaughter. Pashmina shawls are regarded as heirlooms. Mrs Dayal herself owns one that is over 100 years old. A specific type of Kashmiri shawl is the *jamawar*, which historically took decades to make and were commissioned by and gifted to royalty. The original *jamawars* are highly prized, if not priceless. Today *jamawar* designs and motifs are replicated by skilled hand weavers such as Ahmed.

My favourite accessory has to be the stole because of its multiple uses in India. Firstly, it is anti-stare, which means that when your chest becomes the focus of stolen glances, the stole covers it up. In summer I use it to protect my head when the heat gets too intense or across my face when there are too many flies around (they will land on your lips!). Rain? Dirt storm? Too cold? In a temple? Food stain? The solution lies in one small piece of cloth.

Quintessentially Indian, the *sari* varies across India, from colour and draping style to fabric and pattern.

The other traditional wardrobe staples for women are the *lehenga-choli*, *anarkali*, *salwar kameez*, and *kurta*. The *lehenga* (also called *ghaghara*) is a large ankle-length flouncy skirt traditionally from Rajasthan and Gujarat. It is worn together with the *choli* (blouse) and a large veil called an *odhni*. *Lehenga-choli* is commonly worn for formal events such as weddings. The closest garment to a Western dress is the *anarkali*, which has an empire cut and a flared bodice worn over *churidar* (leggings) or palazzos and can be dressy or casual depending on the material. The *salwar kameez* was traditionally worn by women in the north, particularly in the Punjab (hence it is also called the Punjabi suit) but it is now common across India. It consists of the *salwar* (baggy trousers) and the *kameez* (a long shirt or tunic). A long scarf called a *dupatta* is draped over the chest and flipped back over the shoulders. Nowadays the *dupatta* is widely used as a stand-alone fashion accessory that can be worn scarf-like over shirts.

A *kurta* (or sometimes called *kurti*) is a loose-fitting long shirt or tunic that falls below the waist and sometimes below the knees. This is the most common outfit for casual daily use. It can be dressed up with a *dupatta* or worn alone. For a more traditional look, it is worn over *salwar* pants, a *churidar* or a *lehenga*. For a more modern look, pair it with jeans or breezy palazzos. This is by far the main staple for expatriate wardrobes as they are easy to find, comfortable, affordable and can be easily modernised depending on the fabric and design chosen. In the north, you can get beautiful hand block prints in light Indian cotton, the best material for summer. In addition to the traditional looks, there are also a host of Indian designers who use traditional Indian textiles cut in contemporary or Western silhouettes. This alone can add scores more to shopping trips and wardrobe space.

Men

The *dhoti-kurta* is the traditional outfit for men. The *dhoti* (also called *lungi*) is a piece of cloth tied around the waist and tucked between the legs. It is considered daily wear for men, especially in rural India. For formal occasions, the *sherwani*, a long coat, is worn over *churidar-pyjama* pants. For casual daily wear, men usually wear a *kurta* over trousers or jeans.

In general, I have seen less men donning traditional wear in cities, preferring instead the Western long-sleeved shirt worn loose over trousers.

Jewellery

India is the place where jewellery is especially loved, appreciated and acquired. As a global centre for lapidary (gem-cutting), precious stones are plentiful and likely to be more affordable than in your home country. This includes diamonds. Stones can be purchased alone and then set to any design of your choosing.

The main risk, however, is whether you are getting the value you are paying for. Unless you are an expert, there are unscrupulous people out there who could be selling you a piece of glass or inflating the price far beyond the real value of the stone. It is best to get a recommendation from a local, especially if you plan to buy large quantities or bigger rocks. The safe bets are the chain stores.

But for a taste of tradition, there are also the secret dens known to the select. I was taken to the bowels of Old Delhi on a hot afternoon, a small price to pay for the chance to see one such place more commonly referred to as a traditional jewellery shop. We stopped at a nondescript door. Behind it sat an old man at an even older wooden counter. At my friend's instruction, he reached for a drawer full of plain envelopes and poured out their contents. Precious stones tumbled onto the counter in rapid succession, a rhythm he and the generations before him undoubtedly perfected. Proprietors of these types of family businesses span generations and their customers do too. Word of mouth and trust are the reason why people return.

If you are looking to start with mid-range precious stones

(generally of a lower quality), they are commonly found everywhere, even online. Friends are also likely to give recommendations. Because such stones are inexpensive, I just buy them if I like them and thus have significantly multiplied my one-gold-necklace collection. Be forewarned that it is hard to ignore the sparkle of India, even more so when all that glitters really is gold.

> My fashion sense has always had minimalist leanings so when I was invited to my first wedding in India, I donned a simple black dress paired with a small gold necklace. Elegant anywhere else but India. I stood out or rather faded out into the inky night sky (it was an outdoor reception). Around me, ladies glittered and sparkled in colourful sequined *saris* and gems and jewels, rivalling the stars above and creating their own universe. No earlobe, neck, wrist, finger and ankle went unadorned (save for mine). I learnt two things that night: never wear black to a wedding and for jewellery, more is more.

Gold

Indians are the world's largest consumers of gold. India's love affair with gold spans centuries and is rooted in the Hindu religion. Gold symbolises life and beauty. Seen as auspicious, it is widely bought and used for happy occasions, such as festivals and weddings. Indian brides are usually given enough gold jewellery to render them immobile from the weight. Gold is also used in temples across India where the grateful or penitent absolves themselves through gold donations. Ancient temples have collected billions of dollars in jewellery, bars and coins over the centuries. Temple gold is estimated at about 3,000 tonnes, more than two-thirds of the

Follow the Yellow-Brick Road to Jaipur

On the golden trail of jewellery, nothing beats a trip to Jaipur. It is known as the "pink city" because of the colour of its buildings but in actual fact, it is iridescent with its colourful jewel-encrusted history and its famous gem industry, particularly emeralds. As a centre of lapidary, it specialised specifically in the cutting of emeralds and diamonds, and jewellery shops can be found every few paces as a reminder that you're not in Kansas anymore. Many precious stones sold in Delhi and other parts of the country come from Jaipur, so a trip to the source is indeed a pilgrimage to the heart of bejewelled India.

Two traditional techniques originating from this region are *kundankari* (inlay work with gems) and *meenakari* (enamel work), both techniques often seen on the same piece. This ensures that the front (with *kundankari*) and the back (with *meenakari*) are equally beautiful. We had a Jaipur jeweller invited to a party in Delhi to showcase his antique collection of traditional Kundan jewellery—jewellery that employs the *kundankari* and *meenakari* techniques, traditionally with uncut diamonds and other gemstones. As I adorned myself with earrings, rings and bangles made of uncut diamonds, rubies and emeralds, I had a glimpse of what I would look like as a Rajput princess of the past. Forget about ruby-red slippers, real rubies are far more magical.

gold held in the US bullion depository at Fort Knox, Kentucky.

For average Indians, gold is also financial security. Rural housewives store their meagre savings in trinkets, whilst those in cities do so in family vaults, amounting to an estimated 17,000 tonnes of gold in jewellery and other heirlooms. I asked Santosh where he keeps his money. He said, on his wife's hands. For many Indians there is little faith in financial institutions, making gold the best accessory to savings.

SOCIAL ETIQUETTE

India is still a traditional society and therefore knowing basic social etiquette will ensure that you do not offend unintentionally, even though Indians will generally be forgiving if you do. They are also unlikely to point the mistake out to you, so you may be unknowingly committing the same mistake repeatedly. The best way to learn is to ask a friend or observe those around you.

Practices may differ between regions, cities and social strata, but the following are generally the common values across India and have to do with the Hindu concept of cleanliness. The most important thing is to be mindful of social and cultural norms, and be considerate and respectful in your attitude towards them.

Take Off Your Shoes

When entering an Indian home, offer to take off your shoes. The host will likely let you know if it is necessary but it is good to make the gesture first. In Brahmin homes, shoes are often taken off before entering. Taking your shoes off is a must in temples and mosques, and there are often places to deposit your shoes for safekeeping, sometimes for a small fee. Use these services. I had a friend who wanted to save

10 rupees and decided to leave her shoes outside. She went home in her socks.

Do Not Point Your Feet at People
It is a sign of respect to bend down and touch an elder's feet in India. But other than this, feet are considered unclean and therefore you should not point the soles of your feet or shoes at people, especially at gods when visiting places of worship. Similarly, touching people or objects (particularly books) with your feet or shoes is also unacceptable. If you accidentally do so, apologise immediately. If you have to sit on the floor, tuck your feet in as tightly as possible.

Do Not Use Your Left Hand
The left hand is considered unclean as it is used to wash oneself after defecating. Therefore you must avoid using your left hand to eat with as well as to pass food or objects to people. Similarly you should not touch people with your left hand or receive or give items with it. Some shopkeepers consider it an insult if you were to pass them money with your left hand. Remember that the right is always right. Giving and receiving a gift or business card with *both* hands, however, is considered respectful.

Be Careful When Sharing Food and Drink
Although sharing food is part of Indian culture, do not let your lips touch other people's food, for example, biting into a *roti* and passing it on, or double dipping. Do not share utensils such as spoons. This is because of the belief that coming into contact with another's spit (called *jootha*) is polluting. This could be why coffee is drunk without the lips touching the rim of the cup in the south, where traditional rules are

followed more strictly. Similarly, when drinking out of a shared cup or bottle, Indians will pour the liquid directly into their mouths without their lips touching the rim of the receptacle.

Be Respectful Towards Elders
Respect for elders is deeply engrained in Indian society; therefore, treat older people with exceptional courtesy.

Don't Wear Tight or Revealing Clothes
Indians adopt a conservative standard of dress, particularly in rural areas. Women are expected to dress modestly, with legs and shoulders covered. Pants are acceptable but shorts and short skirts can be considered offensive. Men should wear shirts and trousers in public; shorts and sleeveless T-shirts are reserved for the beach or "for hippies", the latter being an invitation to be treated as one too. Western dress, such as jeans and knee-length dresses, are prevalent in cities and will not offend, but avoid shoulder-barring blouses and slinky mini-skirts unless you are travelling by car all the way to a party.

Stay well groomed and dress respectably. Looking grungy may be cool to some of us but many Indians find it hard to understand why allegedly wealthy foreigners would want to dress in the same way as those in the lowest ranks of Indian society. Dressing respectably improves the impression you make and gets you more respect (especially if you're a woman).

Don't Show Affection in Public
Kissing and hugging are associated with sex in India and are considered obscene if done in public. Even in Indian movies, the hero and heroine rarely kiss. Affection is implied instead

through suggestive glances and playful frolicking around flora. In more conservative areas, holding hands is also not acceptable. However, it is okay for two men to hold hands as this is a social gesture of brotherliness and not at all an indication of sexual orientation.

Give Appropriate Gifts

Indians are very hospitable, so although it is not expected, it is good to reciprocate with a gift when invited to parties or celebrations. Indians traditionally give gifts of cash at weddings or celebrations. You need not do the same, but giving something, such as a hamper or ornament for the home, is appreciated. Yellow, green and red are considered lucky colours, so try to incorporate them in the wrapping.

When invited to a home, you are not expected to bring a gift but if you do, flowers or a box of sweets are appropriate. Avoid white flowers (used at funerals), leather items (if you are visiting Hindus), or items made of pigskin or alcoholic products (if you are visiting Muslims). When receiving gifts, Indians do not open them right away, preferring instead to do so in private when all the guests have gone.

Respect the Rules at Places of Worship

Religion is an important part of everyday life both in rural and cosmopolitan India. Temples, mosques, churches and Sikh *gurudwaras* are places of worship, so if you are allowed entry, dress modestly and respect the rules. Women and men are expected to cover legs and shoulders (and sometimes the head). This is where a *dupatta* or stole comes in handy.

When entering a temple, mosque or *gurudwara*, you must remove your footwear (socks are allowed in some instances).

Some temples restrict non-Hindus all together from entering, especially those in Kerala and Odisha. Menstruating women are also prohibited in temples and mosques. Jain temples do not allow any leather products, such as watchstraps, wallets, belts and handbags, to be brought in.

A temple or mosque's inner sanctum is usually off-limits to non-believers but you can walk around the grounds. Taking photographs of deities may be prohibited in some places so if you are stopped, apologise and keep your camera. It is best to ask permission first before taking any photographs.

In temples and *gurudwaras*, you may be offered *prasada* (sacred food). Receive it politely with your right hand.

Offer Water to Anyone Visiting Your Home

Offer a glass of water or a cup of tea to anyone who steps into your home or office. This also applies to delivery boys and repairmen who do normally expect that little bit of hospitality. I was told this custom came from rural India where people walked long distances to get to another's home. Whatever the origin, it is a thoughtful gesture and that is why I have included it here.

Even if you do not offer water, people will directly ask you for it with a short and sharp *"pani?"* (water). I usually buy small bottles of water for such instances. Interestingly, many prefer the water at room temperature even on the hottest days, which does save you the trouble of having to chill it.

PERSONAL SPACE

The concept of personal space seems to be alien in India or at least in the way it is understood in the West, where we generally acknowledge that there is a physical and emotional "buffer zone" around individuals that can be accessed only

by very close friends and relatives.

In India, that empty spatial zone does not exist. For instance, you may find a nice empty bench to sit on in the park. Before you can settle into quiet solitude, someone will come and sit next to you even if there are other empty benches in plain sight. In another scenario, you and your partner have settled into great seats at the cinema with plenty of elbow room and an unobstructed view of the screen. Ten minutes later, an Indian family comes in and sits right next to your elbow, leaving you staring at the completely empty row in front wondering if they are seeing something there you are not. Not long later, a couple makes their way in and shuffles through that empty row. You mentally tell them to keep moving but they stop right in front of you and sit down. Your buffer in India is people, not that abstract concept of space.

Nothing illustrates this more than a queue in India. It is

rarely an orderly line; it is a mass of people pushing, struggling and jostling in front of a counter, standing close enough to each other to form one clump of bodies. If someone is standing too close behind you, it could be that he is just keeping the normal Indian distance (no distance). If you feel uncomfortable with the lack of distance, turn around and tell him (or her) to give you some space.

For women, note that there could be instances where someone may be taking advantage of the situation so if you are travelling with male friends, they should be behind you in a queue. In Indian culture, men keep their distance from women, so if they sit too close to you or touch you, this is not normal behaviour.

Buffering is not limited to bodies. Be prepared that whatever you do, people will surround you with their stares. It can be as mundane as going to buy fruit and somehow the act of walking around with fruit in your hand is worthy of attention. The staring can be intense and discomforting, but it is something that you have to learn to deal with. Take comfort that all eyes are not directed at just you. Staring is a

The Queue-Cutter

You are standing there patiently waiting your turn when all of a sudden, with great precision, someone steps right in front of you just as you are about to approach the counter. This is the queue-cutter, a common feature in many Indian queues. He uses the pause from your jubilation that you're next in line to slip himself in before you. He banks on the fact that you are so elated with being next, you won't mind waiting for one more person to clear. He employs this together with the strategy of confusion. He may linger by your side as if part of your group or the group before you so no one knows for sure if he has the legitimate right to be there. He uses ambiguity to literally get ahead. Whatever the tactic employed, there will be neither sense of shame nor reproach from the counter staff. On the contrary, queue-cutters cut with an air of entitlement, as if his sense of (self) importance is evident to all those behind him.

national sport. Anything both ordinary and out of the ordinary can attract a crowd of people who will gather and look. You can say it is because Indians are generally curious people, which extends to engaging you in conversation about your personal life very quickly. This is normal.

Not all violations of personal space are negative ones. I once wore a *sari* to a dinner and it was unravelling because I had not tied it tightly enough. I went to the bathroom to retie it and the lady attendant (there are usually bathroom attendants in higher-end hotels) saw me struggling and offered to tie it for me. Everything was going perfectly until it was time to tuck the pleats into the petticoat, whereby her entire hand went inside my petticoat, grazing against my lower half. She didn't flinch (I did) and looked pleased with herself for being so helpful. I realised that the gesture, rather than seeing it as a violation of personal space and underpants, embodied the Indian concept of family that can extend to the space outside it. A female is also a sister, mother, aunt. Here, her lack of the concept of my personal space reminded me that we are all part of a giant sorority of sisters that permeates cultural and social borders.

MAKING FRIENDS

Friends may be found at work or at school, regardless of whether you have children or not. The American Embassy School (AES) in New Delhi conducts many after-school adult-learning classes, and I found these to be a great way to meet new people from India and other countries in an environment that is familiar and safe to form new friendships. It is incredibly easy to bond because almost everyone at AES has faced the similar challenges of starting a new life in India. Fellow parents and classmates soon become fast friends, and meals are often shared beyond the campus café.

You can also expand your social circle by joining other group activities, such as yoga classes, Bollywood dance classes, an ashram (if you're deeply into yoga), a volunteer group—all of which will give you ample opportunity to meet new people.

Meeting for the First Time

As a foreigner, you will constantly come across people who want to strike up a conversation even if they are not articulate in English. Whether meeting for the first time on a train ride or in a formal professional event, the flow of conversation is essentially the same.

Conversations usually start innocuously by asking where you are from, which is then followed by a usually shocking stream of intrusive questions like your marriage status, who your father is, your occupation, how much you earn (yes!) and other details your best friend may not even know. Do not be offended. It is partly Indian curiosity, partly hospitality that they take an interest in you, and partly the Indian need to determine social position (see Social Identity on page 76).

When caught with uncomfortable questions, it is acceptable to give vague answers or even white lies. It is also perfectly fine to reciprocate with a few intrusive questions of your own. You can leverage this opportunity to broaden your understanding of India and its culture. English-speaking Indians and members of the large middle class are also usually well informed and generally enjoy a good conversation.

Conversations

Indians love opinionated discussion and the more educated individuals readily dive into debates. As long as you know what you are talking about, you can air your opinion without fear and may be more appreciated for it than sticking with safe platitudes. Cricket and politics are subjects of great interest to men so it helps to have some basic knowledge of the two for small talk. If not, asking about each other's family is universally engaging for both men and women.

Once a relationship has been built, any topic is acceptable, but it is advisable to exercise discretion over sensitive topics such as the caste system and India's social problems. Indians can be quite passionate about their country and may take offence if you cross the line (only another Indian can freely criticise India). Also, do not make comments about skin colour, as Indians are very conscious of skin tone. Avoid using strong swear words in all instances.

Dating

Remember that many marriages in India are arranged and that the concept of dating is not as common as it is in the West. Indians may face family disapproval for going out with a foreigner, so be sensitive to the context. On a date, men are generally expected to pay.

LGBT

India is still largely a conservative country and homosexuality is criminalised and punishable with a 10-year jail term. Being gay is seen as shameful and many homosexuals remain closeted. At home many face intense pressure from their families to marry by arranged marriage.

In the major cities such as Mumbai, Delhi, Kolkata, Chennai and Bengaluru, things have started to turn, with increasing social acceptance and a growing gay nightlife scene, although this remains largely underground. Information on gay events and getting to know others in the LGBT community rely on word-of-mouth and through social network apps such as Grindr. In November 2015, Delhi hosted a Queer Pride March, which reflected the community's rising prominence and gains in social acceptance. However, discrimination remains widespread.

Interestingly, while being gay can get you charged in India, being transgender gets you rights in contrast. A revolutionary ruling in 2014 by India's Supreme Court created a protected third gender category for *hijra*, the collective term for transgender people, eunuchs and the intersex (people with male and female anatomies). This enables them to identify themselves as *hijra* (not male or female) on government documents and allows them access to welfare programmes, education and employment opportunities.

Hijra

There are an estimated two million *hijra* in India. The *hijra* were recognised in India long before their legal rights were codified. In the royal courts gender-neutral eunuchs occupied privileged position as guards to the royal harem. However, in later times, they were labelled as pariahs and driven to live in city fringes. There they formed their own *hijra* communities, which developed its own religion, social hierarchy and customs. Some Indians consider them sacred and their blessings auspicious. For this reason, *hijra* earn their livelihood by exchanging blessings for cash at traffic stops or by performing at festivals and celebrations, such as weddings and births. Santosh spent twice as much on his first son's birth celebration than on his second because his family believed that hiring a *hijra* to bless the firstborn would ensure further blessings upon the family.

Once, Ben and I were on a train when a group of loud, laughing *hijra* boarded, clapping in their signature style and asking for money. I observed that almost everyone gave them some spare change (and those who were reluctant were playfully groped until they did), whereas a malnourished boy who had come in to beg before them was duly ignored. It was only later that I found out that *hijra* are said to also have the power to curse. They also seem to go exclusively after men because whenever Ben and I encounter *hijra*, they do not even look my way. One reason is that many *hijra* think of themselves as women, referring to each other as "she" and dressing in women's clothes.

PRACTICALITIES

WHAT TO BRING

Unless you are settling in rural India, many comforts from home may already be available in India. You might not get the variety you get at home, but you can certainly find some of the basic equivalents. Here are some items to note before you pack.

Food

If cheeses and olive oil are a main part of your diet, you may want to bring a starting quantity as the variety available in India is limited and expensive. The same goes for Asian sauces such as oyster sauce, fish sauce and soya sauce. Whilst you can still purchase them with relative ease, they can cost up to twice as much. If you are moving to Delhi, some embassies have their own commissary for their citizens and diplomats, which you should research before you make your large purchases for shipment. Commissaries typically sell common food items you get back home.

Toiletries

Toiletries are affordable in India. I learnt this too late and ended up shipping a few dozen bottles of shampoo and enough toothpaste to sustain a village. Major brands are produced in India and you can purchase them at a fraction of the price, but if you are using specialised products, then you should bring them. An item that is significantly more expensive is tampons. Commissaries may sell them but in regular stores, they are hard to find. Sanitary napkins are more commonplace and affordable (as they are produced in India).

Clothes

Bring seasonal wear if you are moving to Delhi since the climate is temperate. Leave the skimpy summer dresses behind.

Medicines

Bring your prescription medicines but you can leave behind any generics such as diarrhoea pills. You can easily purchase your generics in India.

Electronic Items

Gadgets such as cameras and computers can be shipped as these tend to be more expensive. Household appliances, on the other hand, can be bought in India.

Check with your moving company what is allowed in your shipment. Some may prohibit foodstuff as the shipping containers are heavily fumigated before the journey. They should also advise you on taxes that need to be paid for customs clearance, especially on electronic items. Get a reputable company that would know how to get your cargo cleared. My friend's shipment was stuck at customs for three months because she was missing the "necessary paperwork", which could mean anything from really having missing papers or a lack of an "incentive". An experienced company would be able to handle such situations or avoid them altogether. Check with your embassy or company for recommendations.

VISAS AND RESIDENTIAL PERMITS
Visas

You will need a visa to enter India. Indian visa rules are not always clear so those who plan on visiting or moving to India must begin by identifying the correct visa. Visa regulations are subject to change at short notice so you should first start by contacting your respective embassy or consulate for the latest details and visit India's Ministry of Home Affairs (www.mha.nic.in) for updated visa information and application requirements.

You can apply for an Indian visa at your local Indian Embassy, or approach a VFS Global private processing agency (www.vfsglobal.com). Visas can take a long time to be processed, so it is best to start the application as far ahead of time as possible. If you have secured a job in India, your company will be able to advise you on what type of visa you should apply for and how much time it will take.

The most common types of visas are:

- **Tourist Visa:** An Indian tourist visa allows you multiple-entry visits and is valid for six months from the date of issue. As of 2014, e-tourists visas are available for citizens of 40 countries. The visa is valid for a single entry with a maximum stay of 30 days from the date of arrival, and can be obtained twice in a calendar year. Citizens of some countries are eligible for Visa-on-Arrival at selected airports in India. It entitles the holder to stay up to 30 days.
- **Student Visa:** A student visa is valid for the period of study in India. It has to be renewed every year, up to a maximum of five years. You will have to provide proof such as a letter of admission from the educational institution.

- **Journalist Visa:** Journalists and professional photographers can apply for a three-month, single-entry journalist visa. You will need to provide proof of your professional status.

- **Employment Visa:** You will need this visa if you want to work for an organisation registered in India or to do volunteer work. You will have to provide proof of a job offer as well as academic/professional qualifications to apply for this visa. Employment visas for India are usually valid for between two and five years, depending on the applicant's profession.

- **Business Visa:** This is for entrepreneurs or investors who want to conduct business in India. It is a multiple entry visa and allows a stay of up to 180 days. Business visas are valid for six months, though you can also obtain longer-term business visas. A business visa cannot be converted into an employment visa. Unless you are employed by an embassy or work in international organisations like the UN, you will need to apply for either an employment visa or business visa to legally work in India. No separate work permit will be needed thereafter.

Residential Permits

If you have a visa that is valid for more than 180 days, you will need to register with the Foreigners' Regional Registration Office (FRRO) or the Superintendent of Police (SP) of the district within 14 days of arriving to obtain a Residential Permit. (Diplomats and officials and their spouse and children are exempt from this on a reciprocal basis.)

The experience, as one friend put it, was akin to slitting your wrists and watching yourself bleed slowly. Bring all your documents, more than what is required or stated, and make sure you have an irrational number of copies of them. Documents include:

- application forms,
- your passport,
- passport-size photographs,
- a copy of your visa,
- a letter of guarantee from an Indian host or sponsor,
- lease agreements.

This same friend had brought all the necessary documents as stipulated on the website but he had the unfortunate luck of encountering a *babu* (Indian government official) seemingly bent on making it difficult for him. He required multiple trips, each with a waiting time of as-and-when-the-*babu*-felt-like-working. Making multiple copies of documents is pre-emptive because you might get pushed from one counter to the next, across floors, halls and levels so if you are out of copies,

you are out of luck and have to return to fulfil yet another surprising requirement.

For those who would rather not test the limits of their patience, there are agencies that can help you renew your permits. Service fees are generally high because of how infamously frustrating the process is if you were to do it yourself. The high fees also go into making sure that your application lands at the top of the correct *babu*'s in-tray.

Your permit documents not only verify your resident status in India but allow you to enjoy domestic rates at hotels or entry to monuments, a small consolation for the hoops through which you had to jump.

ACCOMMODATION

Finding a place to stay is the decision with the greatest impact on your everyday life so it is worth weighing the pros and cons carefully before you tie yourself down to a lease. Seek the help of a Destination Service Consultant or an experienced real estate agent who has served expatriate clients as they may

Babus and the Great Indian Bureaucracy

The *babu* is a particular creature the public loves to hate but must deal with for any kind of administrative transaction. He is a bureaucratic genie and knows he has the power to grant you your wishes.

He wasn't always known to be a necessary evil. The term *babu* was originally a term of respect, attached to a proper name in the same way as "mister" is. In colonial times, it referred to a native Indian clerk or Indian civil servant. Gradually the term became frequently used pejoratively to refer to bureaucrats of the Indian Administrative Service (IAS) and other government officials. While many sit at the highest echelons of government, the one that all of us are likely to encounter are the ones that sit behind the counters.

The *babu's* task is to uphold the tangle that is Indian bureaucracy and red tape. In this system, you are required to run around as inefficiently as possible to gather the necessary requirements, forms and proofs for submission. Forms are to be filled in duplicate or triplicate and are required to be accompanied by more forms, documents, proof, proof of proofs, certified copies, stamped copies, all of which are laid at the shrine of officialdom. Your time and patience are but small sacrifices for the blessing the gods of bureaucracy bestow: the rubber-stamp approval. Getting to the dull thud of one is where the art truly lies.

Your success in getting things settled in India such as visas, permits and mobile phone applications hinges on how well you can deal with the *babu* handling your matters. Be polite and calm. Make sure you fill out all documents correctly. Do not leave blank spaces, use the same signature throughout, follow your name exactly as it is written in your passport. Some experiences go smoothly without incident; others have to be "helped" along. Rest assured that no one escapes having to go through the process of dancing on hot stones and running around in circles. The slow turning wheels of India's infamous bureaucracy will never stop. Work with it, ride it; just don't let it crush your spirit.

be familiar with the needs that you might take for granted, such as running water.

Rents vary according to cities. Rents in Mumbai are the highest. The price for a tiny apartment in Mumbai may get you a small house in Delhi or a huge bungalow in Chennai.

Types of Housing

Accommodation in Mumbai is usually limited to apartments with a range of price points in this category. However, for

BHK is a common term that means "Bedroom, Hall and Kitchen" so a 2BHK apartment is 2 bedrooms, 1 hall (living room), 1 kitchen.

spacious Delhi, other types of housing are available:

- Contrary to the name, **farm houses** are mansions spread over a few acres of land usually located in exclusive gated communities on the outskirts of town.

- To stay closer to the city centre and still enjoy the luxury of space and amenities, you can consider **bungalows**, which are large independent homes usually set within a garden or compound.

- **Apartments and duplexes** are the most popular among expatriates as they are spacious enough without being too big to handle. Apartments are also the main type of housing found in middle- to upper-class neighbourhoods. Families who have children or pets often opt for ground floor units to have the benefit of the garden. Upper floor units, usually with balconies, prioritise views and privacy.

- *Barsati* are small one- or two-bedroom units located at the top floor or roof of a building and often opens out into a roof terrace. Rents are lower because the top floor is unpopular as it heats up in summer. You can get some really nice ones but a visit to check out the premises is a must as some can be run-down.

Where to Live

If not already taken care of by your company, your accommodation budget dictates largely where you end up living. Neighbourhoods popular with foreigners tend to also have higher rents, but also more reliable infrastructure. You also have the advantage of having help nearby if needed. For example, if your driver did not turn up for the day, you can ask a neighbour to swing by and pick up your children for school since she would also likely have children going to the same school.

For those who prefer a more immersive experience or need to be closer to your workplace or school, you can opt for local neighbourhoods. Before you do, ask about the water supply since many of such neighbourhoods do not get a constant piped water supply throughout the day. Some rely entirely on water trucks that come at dawn, which means that there could be days with no water if the truck does not show up or if you fail to wake up in time. Electricity may also be erratic.

Top Floor Not the Top Choice

A top floor unit is a tempting proposition because of the views and breezes, and you have an entire terrace at your disposal for BBQs and sun bathing. However, the top floor unit is the one that gets the full brunt of the summer sun, especially in Delhi where roofs are flat. Indian homes are built with minimal or no insulation, which means that in winter, the house is chillier than the outside and in summer, you must tolerate insane temperatures in the discomfort of your own home. At 50°C heat, you might want to think hard if the views are worth baking for.

What to Check For

Never be fooled by what you see. Looks are deceiving and you have to know what to check for in order to get hassle-free accommodation. I use this term "hassle-free" because it is important to get a place with the *least* likelihood of things breaking down or going wrong *after* you move in. This is more common than you think. Here are the tips I've compiled after hearing stories of problems and regrets:

Don't Assume New Is Better

Ben lived in Mumbai for several years in an old apartment in Bandra. The elevator always frightened me because it seemed like a contraption far older than its intended lifespan. There was no sliding elevator door, just a wooden swing door you open to mark where the elevator begins. Once in, you pull a metal gate across the opening for it to start with a jerk and move up to whatever floor you had pressed on its big tactile knobs.

Ben's friend, in contrast, had scoffed at Ben's pre-Independence residences and moved into a tall new modern apartment with great views of the Arabian Sea. During the monsoon season, rainwater would flood its fancy lobby but that was a small price to pay for Mumbai breezes and high storied hopes. However, when his shiny metal elevator plummeted down a few floors, he learnt that one cannot assume new is better. His hopes fell with the fall and he moved into a unit on the second floor of an apartment building as near-decrepit as Ben's.

As for Ben, he never had any problems with his old apartment because sometimes in India, old is gold. They were built to last, not to shine.

In another case, this time in Delhi, my friend was smitten by an apartment that had just been built with fancy fixtures, marble floors, large glass windows, new air conditioners, new everything. He hastily signed on the dotted line without adequate checks, confident in the assumption that new is hassle-free. Several months later at the onset of summer, he turned on the new air conditioners and went about his errands. He returned to find his living room floor flooded and waterfalls cascading from the air conditioner blower units. Shoddy supervision and inexperienced workmen had mounted the air conditioners without installing piping, and nobody, including himself, cared to check. Suffice to say, significant hassle ensued to get the situation rectified.

Check the Water

When you enter any unit, turn on the taps and check for two things—the colour of the water (if it's brown, it means your pipes are rusty or contaminated) and the water pressure. My friend's new Grohe showerhead could only muster a trickle of

water, enough to keep a small fern alive and nothing else. Yes, it was a new apartment and yes, there was hassle involved in repairing it. Also test the flushes and double check if there is a geyser (a hot water heater) in each bathroom because winter is a poor time for a cold shower.

Smell the Air

For homes that have been closed up for a while, it is normal to get a musty smell. What you should be looking out for are bad smells like mould and sewage when you enter. Our friend in Chennai was often sick with diarrhoea and she did not know why until we visited her apartment. It smelled like sewage. This is irreparable.

Ask If There's a Back-up Generator

Don't assume there is one or that you will always have power. Delhi is notorious for its power cuts, especially during the summer. Sometimes the landlord will only provide an inverter, which has limited capability to power up the whole house. If a generator is critical to you, ask for one in the negotiation. (see Electricity on page 161).

Survey the Neighbourhood

Although coming home to peace and quiet is good, you should pick a neighbourhood or house that is not too quiet and secluded because more people on the street means less likelihood of someone breaking in unnoticed. Also ask around if the neighbourhood is prone to flooding (especially important in Mumbai and Delhi) and what the traffic situation is like during peak hours. If access is limited to one or two roads, you may then spend too much time waiting to get in and out of your enclave. You should also note the time needed to get to school, your office and the nearest amenities during rush hours, preferably by revisiting your shortlisted properties during peak hours to verify if this is something you can tolerate daily. The agent will always underestimate the time if you ask. Also check if there are issues in the neighbourhood related to piped water supply and power outages.

Meet Your Landlord If Possible

There is no hard and fast rule here, but Ben and I considered the landlord as a factor in our decision-making in that they must be easily reachable. A friend's landlord was residing overseas and so he was literally too far removed to share my friend's urgency about a broken generator in the height of summer. Even if the landlord lives in the same city, you will still be dependent on him responding to your distress in a timely manner. Ben and I were very fortunate to have a great landlord and it vastly improved our stay. We were nearly hassle-free for the duration of our lease partly because the landlord lived in the same building and therefore problems affected us both. Mrs Dayal ensured that preventive maintenance of the house was done routinely, water was always kept in ready supply and things that needed attention were repaired immediately.

Leases and Security Deposits

It is important to sign a proper lease, as you will need it as proof of residence to apply for other services such as Internet and mobile phone lines. Some landlords prefer to sign informal agreements to evade tax. Do not agree to this. The minimum lease term covered by rent control laws is 12 months. A shorter-term lease is called a lease-and-license agreement, which allows up to 11 months. Landlords tend to prefer them, as they are not covered under rent control laws. Seek the advice of your real estate agent pertaining to this kind of agreement. Security deposits are generally two or three months' rent. For many, getting the security deposit back can be challenging and therefore knowing the landlord well helps.

Real estate agent commission fees are usually about half a month's rent. They may offer additional services like maintenance and furniture rental.

Short-Term and Shared Accommodation
If you are staying for less than a year, short-term stays are available but harder to find. Yuni-Net (Delhi), an online Yahoo group, is a good place to start. There are also serviced apartments you can consider. If you are looking to share with other single expatriates, a good place to find postings on shared accommodation is again on Yuni-Net (Delhi).

SETTING UP HOME
Electricity
India's electrical current is 220–240 volts, 50 Hz when it is running. Power cuts are a feature of life, especially in the summer months when the power grid gives up and calls it a day. The heat is magnified manifold by the temporary death of the ceiling fan or air conditioner. It truly is a test of endurance to sit there and accept the situation that can last any time between 20 minutes and a few hours to an entire day. Add to this the knowledge that it could have been done on purpose in what is called "load shedding", which means that power is turned off in some areas to better share the limited resource. Where you stay also makes a difference as to the frequency and duration of load shedding exercises. I was told that the posh areas rarely see their air conditioners cut and it takes a calm mind to not get upset that your comfort is being compromised so that someone important can have an uninterrupted supply of air-conditioning for his household 24/7.

We did not have a back-up generator (called *genset*), only

an inverter, which, because of its limited capacity, could only power the essentials like ceiling fans and some lights. It did not have enough power to keep the refrigerator running so when this happens, I kept the fridge shut to prevent the cold air from leaking out. In a particularly bad it-felt-like-forever stretch (I was too delirious from the heat to note the exact number of hours) when the fans eventually stopped working, I fled the house to seek refuge at a *genset*-powered friend's house nearby. This underscores the importance of the neighbourhood (it is hard to escape power cuts completely but you can minimise its occurrence), having a back-up *genset* and having friends nearby whose house where you can seek refuge. I have never experienced a power cut after 6pm but in other neighbourhoods, this can happen. Always keep flashlights and candles handy.

Because of cuts, you also get power surges when the power turns back on. Make sure you get a voltage stabiliser for each of your expensive electrical appliances and devices, such as the refrigerator, TV and computer, to prevent power surges from severely damaging them. They are inexpensive and easy to find. We also protect our mobile phone and laptop chargers with surge protectors. Once you learn the preventive techniques and coping mechanisms, the next time a blackout happens, it will be no sweat (figuratively, of course).

Electricity Bills

We paid our bills by cash and that requires going down to the BSES (Delhi) office. You can send your driver down to pay the bills for you. Try to give the exact amount, as oftentimes the cashier will claim he does not have change. You can also pay online but that will require an Indian credit card or an established arrangement with the bank.

It is important to check your bill every month and look out for irregularities. My monthly bill averages Rs6,000, which is on the slightly lower side for expatriate families. My friend, on the other hand, had a monthly bill of Rs25,000, which was unusually high, given that her house was average-sized and her usage conservative. All of us naively assumed it was an administrative mistake, and she went to great lengths and hassle to get it resolved (key word: hassle!). After a few months of consistently high bills, an Indian friend told her that someone could be tapping into her electricity, or the meter had been tampered with and was moving faster than it should. She engaged an independent electrician to weed out the problem: Her landlord's nephew was living in the unit below and his air conditioners were linked to her meter, quite intentionally. She immediately turned off the affected switches so that the nephew could feel the heat of her wrath. If you suspect something like this is happening to you, turn off all appliances in your home and check if the electric meter is still running.

Gas

Some homes come with a piped-in gas supply for the kitchen. Many do not and rely on gas cylinders to power the stove. You can apply for a cylinder when you move in. When the gas runs out, a gas man will come and replace the empty cylinder with a full one. It is advisable to weigh the cylinders at the point of purchase. A friend, who was using cylinder gas, had been replacing her cylinders every few weeks when one typically could last for months. When she asked the gas man why the cylinder was so light, he said authoritatively, "Madam, gas is light," which she accepted until she realised that he was

Double-check that you have separate water, gas and electricity meters. Although the assumption is that you would have separate meters for your unit, it is best to confirm this.

selling her near-empty cylinders. She switched to another gas man and bought a scale.

Internet

You can apply for an Internet connection from Internet service providers (ISP) or mobile phone service providers, such as Airtel and Reliance. Internet speeds may vary. Our house could get the maximum Internet speed but a friend's house not more than six doors away could only get half that speed even though we were paying the same monthly subscription rate. It did not make sense, but that's the way it is. It took him six months to get a resolution on the issue; mainly he eventually accepted his half-speed Internet, the bandwidth completely taken out of him to pursue it any further.

It took about three weeks to fully set up our broadband connection but after that, it was relatively stable except when it got too hot outside (I'm not sure if there is any scientific reason for this). One day it stopped working and I called the service provider to come fix the problem. A technician came about two days later and checked the connection indoors and outside. "Squirrels," he said nonchalantly when he saw me, "that is the problem."

Apparently when workmen came to install the wiring for the Internet, they ran the cables through the mango tree instead of looking for proper structural support. The squirrels, irritated by the intrusion to their home, started nibbling at the cables until they broke through it. "Can you fix it?" I asked. No. His job was to diagnose. Another man will come to fix the wiring. Then yet another man will come to check that it is working. That is how one job requires three people and one to two weeks to complete. The wiring guy eventually came and I asked him if he had rerouted my cable since the root cause of the problem was cute tree-dwelling rodents. "No, madam. But I give you thicker cable." My mango tree broadband support has been doing just fine.

Cable and Satellite TV

India's national network is called Doordarshan, but if you want a wider range of international channels, you will need to subscribe to cable or satellite TV. Paperwork is inevitable but less tedious than setting up other services. It took two months to finally get our cable TV to work but it was one of those services where I had heard very few complaints. Satellites may be already installed at the roof so check with your landlord prior. Direct to Home (DTH) satellite TV connections are also reliable. Interruptions tend to occur on cloudy and rainy days, or in the case of my friend, when the neighbourhood peacocks perch on his satellite and affect the transmission.

The curious thing about the English channels in India is that they also come with English subtitles, meaning you could be watching an American comedy in English, and reading what they say…in English. I actually found this useful because you can have the volume down low and still be able to follow what's going on.

Telephones and Mobile Phones

Mobile lines are overtaking landlines so unless you have one already installed, think about saving yourself the hassle and opt for a mobile connection instead.

Many people have two lines, one from each phone company as backup. There are always arguments as to which company offers a more stable connection. I say it depends on the city and area. Airtel seems to be more reliable in Mumbai but not so in Delhi. Some say it depends on where the tower is. We have a Vodaphone tower just opposite our house but its signals rarely reach within the house. It's not uncommon to see Mrs Dayal running out into the garden to answer a call. I have one communicative window where I literally need to stand in order to get a stable signal for my "im-mobile" phone.

Plans can be prepaid or postpaid. Prepaid lines means you pay upfront for a certain stored value that will be deducted each time you make or receive a call. The downside is that a call can get cut off midway when the value runs out. The benefit of using a prepaid scheme, however, is that when you leave India, you can just let the line lapse. In comparison, it took 12 months to cancel my postpaid mobile line, during which they were billing me every month despite my best efforts to inform them of the cancellation. Therefore it is not just setting up a service that is challenging. Cancelling water, electricity, Internet and phone lines may be equally so, and the reason often cited by landlords to retain some, if not all, of your security deposit after you have moved out.

Furniture and Appliances

Check with your company if you are entitled to furnished or unfurnished residences. From my experience, the furnished ones are aesthetically challenged in many ways. It may be worth your while to negotiate for an unfurnished apartment with an added monthly furniture retainer that allows you to choose your own furniture on a rental basis. Some real estate agents provide this service. This arrangement suits the needs of people who do not wish to bring back furniture from India or do not have the time to get the basics in place, such as the bed, refrigerator, sofa, dining table and chairs.

India makes beautiful furniture, textiles and decorative items. If your taste is for clean modern designs, then it will be harder to find. But if you are into handcrafted furniture rich in heritage, you are in the best place to buy them. A hand-painted Rajasthani cabinet, an intricately carved Lucknowi table, a Kashmiri side table etched with brass, a mother-of pearl bureau, a gilded mirror — all these make beautiful pieces in your Indian home as well as talking points in your home country if you bring them home. Ask your real estate agent or friends where to find these shops.

These days you can also buy furniture online wherever you are. Pepperfry.com and urbanladder.com carry a trendy and affordable range and on websites such as Yuni-net, you can buy second-hand furniture from expatriates leaving India. Look out for private garage sales in your expatriate networks as these are fire sales where you can get necessities like heaters and air coolers at a steal.

Another way is to attend an auction, which is a public garage sale that is handled by an auction company rather than the owners themselves. The concept works in the same way as a garage sale except that the auction company gets a cut of the total sales in return for handling advertising, registering of guests and sales transactions.

Do not bring your household appliances unless you cannot part with them. They can be taxed (check with your moving company). Expensive ones may also die if you do not protect them with voltage stabilisers and surge protectors. Household appliances are easily available in India, from Indian brands to global ones such as Philips and Panasonic, which have their made-in-India ranges. The first home appliance you should prioritise is a water dispenser that holds 20-litre bottles of purified drinking water, as tap water is not fit for drinking.

DOMESTIC HELP

Even the most independent homemaker will eventually hang up her gloves and call it a day or rather reclaim her day in

India. Homes in India require daily cleaning and maintenance to an extent unimaginable and when you can easily and affordably find someone to cook, clean, take care of the children, do laundry and wash dishes, the idea of getting domestic help becomes irresistible. Dreams of free time and hobbies suddenly become a tenable reality at the drop of a mop.

To assuage any guilt you might be having, having domestic help (servants, to use the popular term) in India is common and not exclusive to the upper crust of society. No, you will not become a pampered princess overnight and will probably be mindful that this fairytale will come to an end when you return to your home country. Culturally, having help is also expected of you as Indians see doing menial tasks for yourself as a lowering of your status.

Whether you agree with this or not, I offer another compelling reason: hiring servants allows someone, especially low-skilled women, to earn a much-needed honest day's wage in a safe, stable environment. In addition, you have a wonderful chance to positively influence the lives of your staff and their families.

The average Indian household may have more than one person in their employ. Generally it is common to have servants specialising in only one function: a maid to clean, a *dhobi* (laundry person) to wash and iron, a cook to prepare meals, a driver, a *chowkidar* (watchman/guard), a *mali* (gardener) and an *ayah* (nanny) to take care of the children. So should you decide to go down this path of assisted domesticity, your new job becomes that of management. You, as the *sahib* (boss) or *memsahib* (mam boss), will now have to deal with HR issues, such as employment terms, expectations, how to keep them loyal to you, employee squabbles and disciplinary issues when they arise. Your ability to manage all this effectively will determine the kind of relationship you have with your staff; the aim of course is to have a strong, long-lasting one.

Finding Staff

You can tap on the international community for references either online through digital forums such as Yuni-net or more reliably, by word of mouth. Many repatriating families would usually like to help their staff find a new family to work for before they leave, so it is worth seeking out these opportunities. Organisations such as the American Women's Association keep a registry of servants who have previously worked for its members.

The important thing is to get the word out and it will spread quickly. Often, a friend's maid or driver, upon hearing that you plan to hire, will recommend their cousin, sister, husband, etc. That was how we got to know Madhu and Santosh. So effective is word of mouth that sometimes random strangers with no affiliation to anyone may show up at your door, nervously clutching crumpled testimonials and reference letters (which may or may not be genuine). Hear them out but do so with due caution.

The problem is not finding someone, but finding the *right* someone. In all the above cases, you should ask candidates to submit their resumes, shortlist suitable ones and arrange for an interview about a week later.

If all this is too much, there are agencies who can do the legwork for you. Domesteq is one such Delhi-based agency specifically designed for the expatriate community. They will ensure that references are checked and documents verified before making recommendations.

Selecting Staff

You should meet potential candidates face-to-face before making any decisions no matter how strong the recommendation. Firstly because you want to see if there is any chemistry between you and the candidates since they may be living in your home and interacting with your family. The second reason is to verify information. Ask them questions about their last job, why they left, etc. In the process, you glean information about their work ethic and what they value, which helps you to manage them easier.

When calling them for an interview, you should be prepared with the following:

- **Scope:** Define your needs and, if you prefer an all-rounder, make that very clear upfront that they are required to perform several tasks. List them if needed.
- **Salary and Overtime Rates:** Benchmark and offer what is fair (see page 172). Overtime rates apply to drivers because the norm is an eight-hour shift.
- **Working Hours:** Decide on the working hours.
- **Servants Quarters:** If you have quarters to offer, servants usually are willing to take lower base salaries for a place to stay in order to save on rent, water and electricity bills. Note that this means you are expected to cover the cost of utilities in addition to their full salary.
- **Holidays and Days-off:** Some servants are used to having every holiday off (or none at all). There are many public holidays in India so you might want to select certain holidays as days off. Diwali and Dussehra are usually a must.

At the end of the interview, tell them clearly that you have not yet decided (unless you have). Since English is not the first language, they may mistake enthusiasm as a job offer. One maid we know quit her job soon after an interview because she misread her interviewer. When she learnt she was not hired, and could not get her old job back either, she was devastated. Be clear in your communication so you do not leave anyone in a worse-off position. The same goes for a new hire. Tell them that you will give them a trial period of a week or two before you confirm them. This gives them some room to manoeuvre and also allows you time to see if they are suitable.

Before making a decision, call their referees to ask why they left their old job because what they tell you may be different from what really happened. An added precaution is to get your driver (if you have one already) to go to the stated address to make sure they live there. Once you have all the information in place, my final advice is to go with your gut and cross your fingers. Hiring the right people is as much rigour and fact corroboration as it is luck. Keeping them loyal to your household, however, is effective management.

Managing Staff

Despite your best efforts, it is not unusual to have a few tries with maids and drivers. They could run off for a number of reasons unrelated to you or the way you treat them. I believe it has much to do with their character and that is why I place emphasis on character over salary at the point of hire. Generally good people want to stay and if you give them further reason to stay by the way you treat them, you will nurture loyalty, trust and a win-win relationship. Perhaps Ben and I were lucky that we had good people to start with. Nonetheless I am sharing my management strategies, which I believed helped in creating a job they valued and wouldn't have wanted to jeopardise. It's simple: manage, motivate and reward. But above all, be kind.

Pay Them Fairly

Undeniably, wages form the minimal incentive to stay. If their wages are too low, they will jump ship at the next offer. You will know when this happens because they will not turn up for work and will not be contactable. If you are not ready to start with a high base, then offer salary milestones they can look forward to like annual increments.

The table below shows the duties and indicative monthly salaries in rupees paid by local Indian families and expatriate families in Delhi and Mumbai, depending on experience and

Job	Scope of Work	Local rate	Expat rate
Driver	Driving, maintain car, run small errands	12,500	12,500-20,000
Maid	Cleaning, mopping, laundry, ironing	6,000	8,000-12,000
All-rounder maid	As above + grocery shopping, basic cooking	7,000	10,000-20,000
Cook	Grocery shopping, cooking, washing up	8,500	12,000-15,000
Ayah (nanny)	Child care, night duties (if required)	8,500	12,000-15,000
Guard/ Night watchman	Guard premises, manage water pump, control access to visitors	9,500	Employed usually through a security company that screens and trains them. Rates vary.

Source: babajob.com.

English fluency. Wages in other cities are typically 10 to 30 per cent lower. Those with past relevant experience generally command more, and like many things, you do get what you pay for.

Be Kind But Don't Overdo It

Be kind because it is good for your soul and good for their lives, but do so gradually as they may not be used to it. However, do not "spoil" them as this will affect the way they interact with their next family, who may have a different management style. I knew of someone who gave his maid carte blanche to do anything in the house: bring friends over, drink his beer and help herself to the food. When the boss left, it was hard for the maid to keep another job because she could not accept treatment any less than what she was used to. So keep in mind that spoiling them can also spoil their employability chances after you. Training them well is a much better contribution to their lives.

Demonstrate That You Care About Their Development

This can be built up gradually over time. One such way is to teach them new skills such as how to cook special dishes from your home country. This makes them more marketable after their employment with you. Aim to be the one that leaves them better off as a result of knowing you. When they realise there is value in staying with you, they are less likely to be tempted by higher monetary offers.

Be Nice But Maintain Professional Distance

You can be nice but make it clear that there is a line they should not cross and that you expect everyone to take their job seriously. We went about this by making it clear the behaviour we expected and the grounds for immediate termination, such as theft (lack of integrity).

We fired our first driver because he did not show up for work on New Year's Day when we had repeatedly told him that New Year's Day was not a day off. He chose to intentionally ignore our instruction. Therefore, it was not his act of skipping work but his defiant attitude that got him fired. He crossed the line.

Be Forgiving

People make mistakes, so if the mistake is genuine, let it go. It is, however, important to explain why you are upset so that it is not repeated. If needed, issue a warning. If the mistake is due to lack of training, put in the effort to instruct as many times as your patience can bear. Look at their attitude towards correction as a gauge as to how trainable they are.

Reward Them For Performance

You can factor in performance bonuses to encourage and reward good work. The usual expectation is a one-month Diwali bonus but nothing stops you from giving more for doing their job well.

Other Things to Note
Cultural Differences

Be mindful of the gender divide and what is socially acceptable for Indians. Touching or friendly hugs are usually not advised. In the case of male help, it can also send the wrong signals. My friend complained that her driver was more open to her husband than to her, and she mistook this for chauvinism. It could well have been, but also recognise that Indian men are brought up to keep their distance from women.

Unspoken Hierarchy

The servants will establish a hierarchy among themselves according to gender, caste, age and job. Generally, drivers are seen at the top of the ladder, followed by older male maids (butlers). In Mrs Dayal's home, her butler took it upon himself to order everyone else around in her absence, and a bossy know-it-all can create unhappiness for other staff if left unchecked. You can choose to let the hierarchy take its natural course or not. I did not allow that to happen and stressed mutual respect regardless. It fostered more teamwork between Madhu and Santosh with the traditional divides unsupported, and thankfully it went well. It might not be so in all cases.

Colourful Excuses

When a servant says he has to go back to his village urgently because his father or uncle or brother died, it can mean he plans to find another job. If he returns after a few days, it means he did not get the other job. Of course, he could be telling the truth and his family unfortunate enough to encounter numerous deaths. Even more unfortunate is how one particular family member seems to have died multiple times (some will lose track of how many times they use the same person as an excuse). Only you can tell fact from fiction and a strong relationship will ensure you never get such *bahaane* (excuses) told to your face.

Concepts of Hygiene

You may assume that your maid or *ayah* knows the basic standards of hygiene but it pays to just check in once in a while to correct anything that falls short in this no-compromise area. A trained maid will wash her hands before touching food and after cleaning the toilets. Another issue you could encounter is body odour. My friend, in gasping desperation, finally bought her driver deodorant and taught him how to use it. Trained maids and drivers are usually quite conscious of keeping themselves clean and odour-free, but this is a conversation you might need to have.

My friend made the unfortunate mistake of hiring someone quite young and inexperienced to clean his home and left her unsupervised whilst he went to work. He had given her a set of coloured towels and instructions: blue towel for dishes, red one for the toilet, green one for the floor. For months thereafter he suffered continued bouts of diarrhoea. One day when he was at home, he had the opportunity to see how the girl went about her work. Red towel for the toilet, red towel for the floor, same red towel to dry the dishes. Flabbergasted and already sick to his stomach, he asked her why she had only used one towel instead of the set as he had instructed. She replied that it was a waste to use three towels at the same time. There was no concept of hygiene, only that of frugality.

Privacy

You *will* lose a certain amount of privacy when you hire a maid or *ayah*. Those who are not trained may not understand the Western concept of privacy and personal space, especially when they themselves live in a one-bedroom apartment together with five other family members. Address this by training them to knock when entering and setting rules as to when and where they can engage you. For example, a study or bedroom can be deemed off-limits and that becomes your inviolable private zone.

If your privacy cannot be compromised for whatever reason (one chap I know insisted that walking around in his underwear unimpeded was non-negotiable), then consider getting a part-time maid instead. This arrangement also works well for single professionals.

Well-trained help, especially drivers, are taught to be discreet about their presence and silent in their conversations with others when it comes to your family matters.

Expectations and Compromises

The benefit of an experienced maid, *ayah* or driver is that the training has been done by someone else, or at least in the basics, leaving you to fine-tune things according to your style and temperament. However, you will often find the standard of work still below expectation. If it is not due to laziness or stubbornness but to the lack of education and exposure, then accept that it will never be according to what you expect. At best, you can train and hope for small improvements within their capability and understanding of the world you came from. At some point, all expatriates will reach the conclusion that they should live and let live, and pick the correct battles.

> If there is a little more dust on the cabinet than expected, here's the truth: dust is inescapable in India. Manage your expectations.

However, compromise should not come at the expense of you or your family. Dishonesty, shoddy work, continued carelessness, poor work ethics and bad habits should never be tolerated.

Domestic help will also hold unspoken expectations of you. These came from the old feudal system where the *sahib* was expected to take care of his servants for life (and they stayed for that duration).

One typical expectation is loans and you might find a servant coming to ask you for a loan soon after starting work. You may choose to make clear from the onset that such requests will not be entertained. Or give it careful consideration with stipulations, for example, working for it: do more overtime, clean the windows, etc. This minimises the risk of them securing the loan from you and then disappearing forever (too many stories about this). On your part, create opportunities for additional tasks (even if you do not need them) so that they learn that money should be honestly earned. If it is an urgent request such as a funeral, or their mother/wife/child is sick (the most popular one), then let your conscience guide you.

The key is to treat each loan like a loan and not a hand-out (unless it is intentional). Be serious about the repayment schedule such as doing monthly deductions from salaries no matter how small the sum may be to you. If you are too casual about repayment then they will be too, and this can set an unhealthy precedent.

Since the domestic staff industry is completely unregulated, you are also expected to take on full responsibility when you hire domestic help. You are required to pay for medical expenses if they fall sick. If they are staying in your quarters, you are expected to cover the cost of utilities (and sometimes food) for them and their family.

Termination

If a servant has committed an act on your "immediate termination" list, you should confront them and determine if giving a warning or firing them is more appropriate. If they are indeed guilty of it, many will quit in order to save face from getting fired. If you want to terminate them because of a more subjective reason, such as you can no longer tolerate their incompetence, then you should compensate them with a severance of at least one month's salary so that they have something to tide them over while they look for another job.

Also provide them with a reference letter.

If you have to terminate them because you are leaving the country, then a bonus of at least one month's salary is expected. It is always a good gesture to try to find your staff a new family to work for, especially if they have been loyal to you. Sometimes it is the only decent thing to do.

I know of a person who left her maid high and dry after she left India. The maid showed up at my gate crying and looking for help. She was not paid a severance and as she was staying in the quarters, she also lost her home when her boss moved out. The boss had often praised her for her work so it came as a surprise that the maid would be abandoned so easily. I think we all owe a duty of care to our staff to see that they move on well. If not, what you get are random strangers knocking at your door looking for work. These people could be those who were fired for legitimate reasons (and hence you should be cautious) or more pitifully, those who were quickly forgotten once their bosses moved on.

WORKMEN

This is a mixed breed of the knows-what-he's doing to the pretends-to-know. If you chance upon the former, hold on to his calling card and pass the word on to your friends because a reliable person you can call is much harder to come by than you think. The latter category can leave you with a bigger problem than what you started off with.

We once called an electrician to do some simple rewiring. He arrived empty-handed and asked us for tools (this should have been a clear indicator of what lay ahead). He then used our screwdriver to forcibly pry open the switch covers, rewired whatever was needed and shoved the covers back on, leaving holes and gaps around the rim where the plaster had fallen off because of his indelicate hands. I pointed to the mess he made—my badly scratched switch covers, gaps in the wall and plaster dust all over the floor. There was nothing but surprise. To him, the task was to rewire. Nobody said anything about doing it nicely or with common sense in mind.

And then there are other times where you are just the unlucky victim of shoddy workmanship. My friend's neighbour was having some renovations done. It must have involved hacking and hackneyed workers because my friend came home to a giant hole in his bedroom wall, an obvious and tragic mistake. The workers and supervisor (if any) had conveniently disappeared for the day, leaving him gaping, like the hole. The lesson here is never assume that common sense is common.

So at the risk of sounding like a control freak, always supervise the work when you can because even paid supervisors don't show up or don't care. If you cannot do it, get your driver or maid to supervise because when others are watching, there is less likelihood of careless workmanship. Your maid or driver can also point out to the worker when he is damaging something in the process of him fixing it (it happens!).

If you pass by a construction site and look at the people working on it, it does explain why air conditioners are mounted without piping, windows do not line up and sewage can leak in a new building. There are rarely people with hard hats, work boots, safety gear and other such signs to instil confidence. Instead you will find bare-footed labourers, women laying bricks, mothers carrying sand on their heads while they hold their babies, and their young children nearby tethered to a pole. This is hardly the profile of experienced workmen but sadly it is a commonplace sight and oversight.

GETTING AROUND

The Indian Road

If you are familiar with computer games where you try to move forward whilst dodging gunfire, bombs and enemy craft, then the Indian road might feel familiar. The goal is similar: to move forward safely without touching or getting touched by fellow-road users whilst keeping an eye out for pedestrians, beggars, traffic cops, bullock carts, cyclists and cows that invade the same space as speeding cars. The rules of the road vary according to how visible the traffic cop is.

The biggest unspoken rule is that might is right so the kings of the road are the trucks that bully smaller vehicles into submission—and the elephant, which needs no description. Driving on Indian roads requires the development of a keen sixth sense to know how to anticipate the unexpected in the nick of time, which results in a very surprisingly small number of accidents despite the very large number of harrowing traffic violations.

Here are what I think are some unwritten rules of the Indian road:

- Lane markings are road decoration. If there is a space, get into it.
- Road rules are guidelines, except when a traffic cop is nearby.
- Signalling a turn is a waste of finger activity. Just turn.
- It is okay to make a right turn from the second lane even if someone is heading straight in the rightmost lane because you are invincible.
- The cow is the mightiest of road users. Do not ever knock one down unless you want an angry mob surrounding you. If they want to graze in the middle of the road and create a traffic jam, this is their prerogative. Traffic only *moooves* when they do. There are also special cow ambulances you can call for hurt cows.
- Do not let the road be silent, for how else can you call it an Indian road. Honk as often as you can because

A cow enjoys some *chapati* as traffic builds up to a halt around it.

the road chorus is always in need of fresh voices to raise its irritating volume. Furthermore, the kings of the road have given their royal endorsement with their large "Horn OK please" signs. Honks are a language and experienced drivers know how to interpret its series of Morse codes. Two short light-handed beep-beeps says "I'm here", because side mirrors are more often used to check in on hair rather than looking out for adjacent vehicles.

- Speed into a traffic circle as if the momentum of the circle is pulling you in like a black hole.

Indian drivers are both bad and good drivers in that they have the ability to avoid each other whilst flouting every law in the Highway Code. Because awareness of international driving norms is not widespread, the bar is set very low: don't die. This makes Indian drivers surprisingly courteous in giving way to others and very forgiving to even the most brazen examples of dangerous driving.

So You (Still) Want to Drive

If you plan on driving in India, you will need an international or local driver's licence. An international driver's licence must be accompanied by your country-issued driver's licence and is only valid within a year of arrival, after which you will have to apply for a local licence. Seek the assistance of a driving school or an agent to help you with that. Depending on the requirements, you may be asked to go for a driving test. Passing may be easier than you anticipate.

Ben's experience illustrates the wide range of test standards. His test centre was a small building manned by a few humans and policed by goats. At his turn, he climbed into the old test vehicle with the tester. "Start engine, move forward," the tester said gruffly. A few metres later came another curt instruction, "Okay, reverse". Ben reversed back to the original starting position. "Okay, pass," declared the tester. Ben learnt of a new factor to passing in India: whether there is enough budget to fill up the test car's fuel tank.

The roads and its flanking pavements are not just arteries; they are a community in themselves. A stop at a red light is a two-minute glimpse into the lives of the road's inhabitants: women cooking under bridges, a child defecating on the sidewalk, drunks sprawled out on the sand, a cigarette seller, a girl selling flowers car to car. It can be emotionally painful until frequency makes it numb. At other times, the road is a solution. In rural India, farmers sometimes scatter freshly harvested crops on the road so that you dehusk them as you drive over them.

Buying a Vehicle

There are no restrictions on foreign ownership of vehicles, and Indian and international brands can be purchased easily. For diplomatic plates, consult your embassy on the procedures for vehicular purchase and registration. If you are buying second-hand, it is best to purchase one from another expatriate who is leaving. Note that if you buy a vehicle that had a diplomatic licence plate, you are required to pay the taxes to convert it into a normal plate (unless you are entitled to a diplomatic plate as well). You will be required to get the necessary paperwork done such as transfer of ownership, vehicular insurance and pollution checks. If your driver is experienced, he will remind you when the insurance and pollution certificates are up for renewal and will get it done on your behalf.

Taxis

Metered taxis are ready available in cities like Mumbai and Kolkata, plying the streets in search of passengers like invading black beetles (the Ambassador cab looks like one to me). In Delhi, you can either call for a taxi or hail one at a taxi booth. Taxis can also be hired for fixed periods of time.

Before you begin any journey, check that the meter is reset and working to avoid surprises at the end of the ride. If you are travelling alone (especially for females), take note of the driver's name and other details as an added precaution, especially if you are not familiar with the city. In recent times, booking taxis using apps like Ola and Uber are increasingly popular in all the major cities.

If you are completely new to a city, use the prepaid taxis at the airport so that you do not have to haggle with a driver who will know when you're fresh off the boat (or plane). Prepaid taxis will have their own counter and you pay a fixed fare according to the distance. You will only need to tip the driver and nothing more.

For sightseeing trips, there are (better-maintained) tourist taxis. You are expected to give the driver some money for

The Ambassador car, whose design has hardly changed since 1958, was the first car to be made in India and still plies the roads today mostly as government vehicles and taxis.

meals and tea when you stop for a break and a tip at the end of the day as he receives only a small fraction of what you have paid the taxi company. If you are staying overnight, you are expected to cover his room and board. Check with your hotel as some may have arrangements with nearby hostels.

Hired Cars

If you do not have a vehicle, renting a car can be a more stable option than relying on taxis. Hire one with a driver (specify English-speaking) as renting just the car alone may cost about the same. Furthermore, it is not advisable to drive yourself on Indian roads no matter how skilled a driver you think you are. Reputable car companies like AVIS and Hertz operate in India through local partners. You can also check with your hotel or company for other reliable local car rental companies.

Auto-rickshaws

If taxis are the beetles of the road, auto-rickshaws (or autos as they are called) are the locusts, finding strength in numbers. Every day thousands of these small, noisy, smoke-spewing death traps clog up intersections and fill up any remaining spaces between traffic. Yet they are indispensible to keep the city moving when other forms of public transport fall short. In cities that see epic traffic jams like Delhi, the small auto has the ability to squeeze, weave, mount and take narrow pot-holed shortcuts. The fare for the ride includes the dose of adrenaline that comes with it.

Hailing an auto is a matter of sticking your hand out when one buzzes nearby. In cities like Mumbai and Chennai, the *autowala* automatically starts the meter when you climb in. In Delhi, some *autowalas* did not get *that* memo, so it comes

The ubiquitous auto-rickshaw differs in colour by state.

down to you to "remind" them to start the meter (which will mysteriously not be working for a great number), or negotiate the price before you head off. Your bargaining power is dependent on your nationality, the weather, your destination, demand and whether you require them to wait. Knowing the roads will minimise any sightseeing tours or scenic routes they may intentionally take you on. At the end of the journey, they may present you with a fare card if there have been recent changes to the base fare or additional surcharges that are not reflected on the meter. This is legitimate.

A tip is normally not expected for the driver and his driving skill of invincibility. In Mumbai and Chennai, change is actually returned. In Delhi, it can be sometimes conveniently overlooked so try to have small notes on you. Overall, an auto-ride is a quick, efficient way to get around the city if you do not mind the choking pollution and risk to life and limb.

A ride on a cycle-rickshaw is always a timely reminder to go on a diet or hit the gym.

Cycle-rickshaws

A cycle-rickshaw is one that is powered by a human on a bicycle, usually a shrivelled old man with strength beyond your young strapping capability. This eco-friendly mode of transport is good for short-distance travel where streets are narrow and congested. Some areas in Delhi, like Old Delhi and Lajpat Nagar, are predominantly accessed by cycle-rickshaws, which can easily be found outside train stations and key bus stops. Fares have to be negotiated before pedalling off.

Buses and Metros

There would be little reason to ride a bus unless you want to witness first-hand the Indian courtesy of "there's always room for one more", never mind the people already hanging off the door. Ben was once forced to take a public bus in Mumbai, considered to be the best modern bus system in India. He left his vehicle with the flat tyre in the care of his driver whilst he bordered a public bus with a box of cheesecake in hand on his way to a dinner engagement. At his destination, he leapt off the vehicle clutching a cheese pancake. Not only did the ride alter the box and its content drastically, it also required athletic finesse to jump off a moving vehicle too overly burdened to come to a proper halt.

Metros differ between cities in term of the extent and state of the network. The best so far seems to be the Delhimetro, a modern rail system with a wide network of stations and clean, comfortable carriages. Women-only carriages are available, which is respite during peak hours where the courtesy of "there's always room for one more" may find discourteous hands too close for your comfort. With its modern reliable trains, Delhimetro is a good and inexpensive way to move around the city and beat the traffic. Autos and cycle-rickshaws waiting outside the metro stations allow you to continue your onward journey home.

SHOPPING

The awe and temptation felt by the early colonisers at seeing India's incredible range of goods continue to grip the shoppers of today. India's traditional bazaars such as Chandni Chawk (Delhi) and Chor Bazaar (Mumbai) are as old as they are legendary, teeming with vendors, goods and bargain hunters jostling for space in its small narrow lanes. At the opposite end of the retail spectrum are the posh high-end malls that are gaining popularity across India, though few in number. In between are the mainstays of Indian retail — the neighbourhood markets, bazaars and shopping complexes —

Getting Directions

The key to getting correct directions is to ask at least three people so you can triangulate the response. It is likely you will get three differing answers because Indians generally do not like to turn you down so a wrong direction is better than none at all. For example: "Turn left at the Haldiram's then turn right at the green gate. Go straight and at the wall with the telephone, make a left." At Haldiram's you should stop and ask again. If the next stop is the green gate, then you're off to a good start. Directions tend to be in terms of landmarks instead of road names. Look out for sweetshops or unique markers at intersections. *Autowalas* are the best people to ask, as they may be more familiar with the small streets than pedestrians. If lost in a residential neighbourhood, a watchman is a better person to ask for directions.

that cater to the vast majority and that make Indian retail varied and colourful.

The way to shop in India is inefficiently. Retail is designed for you to travel from store to store and in the process uncover other spending possibilities. If getting all your groceries and household needs under one roof in under an hour is what you are used to, be prepared to have your perfect world shattered. In the course of a grocery/errand run, you will need to visit at least two stores. Meat is sold at the butchery, eggs at the grocery store, milk at the Mother Dairy outlet, fruits at the roadside *vegetablewala*, Western products at the "supermarket", seafood at a specialised market, medicine from the chemist (drug store), bread at the bakery, alcohol at wine shops. An errand run in India is closer to an errand marathon, so here are the most common types of stops you will encounter:

- **Supermarket:** These usually air-conditioned all-in-one stores can be found in the major cities, but tend to be small with limited variety. They are better known for stocking Western products that may not be available in regular grocery stores. You can buy meat and vegetables, but you are not likely to get the freshest available and may be paying higher prices. If you are short of time, the supermarket is a good compromise.

- **Neighbourhood Markets:** These ubiquitous neighbourhood markets comprise separate stores for meat, general groceries, medicines and toiletries (chemist/drug-store), appliances, housewares, flowers, fruits, books, as well as service-related ones like tailors and doctors. They are buzzing centres where people, services, goods and animals congregate. The small one opposite my house, blandly called 'A'-block Market, has a Bengal Sweet Palace, a doctor's office adjacent to a butcher, a currency exchange, a chemist and a resident pack of aggressive stray dogs. Within this category of neighbourhood markets are broad variations that take their cue from the neighbourhood in which they are situated. Upscale Khan Market in Delhi is a popular high-end shopping arcade with grocery stores, bookstores and branded apparel stores amidst hipster restaurants and cafes. An increasing number

A friendly neighbourhood store.

of neighbourhood markets located within middle-class
neighbourhoods have gentrified, whether intentionally
or not, to become hip-*esque* shopping destinations.
Not by design though, but by leaving things as they
are—tangled mess of wires, narrow unpaved lanes,
unpainted walls: the stuff cool shops and funky cafes
love to set up business in.

- **Specialised stores and markets:** Because Delhi has a
  large international community, there are also specialised
  stores stocking Korean and Japanese food. A particular
  favourite food market for expatriates in Delhi is INA
  market. It takes 20-30 minutes (no traffic) to get to from
  South Delhi where many expatriates live and yet people
  still come because INA sells some of the freshest
  meat and seafood around. Some of its vendors also

speak Japanese and Korean. Here, you can get fresh Asian vegetables such as bokchoy, sauces and other groceries that are not available in the usual grocery stores and roadside vegetable carts. I cannot comment on the experience (hint: fly-infested in summer), but INA might be the closest thing to a one-stop shop sans air conditioning. Prices reflect their expat clientele so if you plan on buying regular vegetables and fruit, support your neighbourhood *vegetablewala* instead.

- **Street carts and temporary street markets:** At almost every corner in residential neighbourhoods, you will find a *vegetablewala* or *fruitwala* selling fruits or vegetables. They may be "permanent" in that they are always there at that particular spot, or roving, when they move around with their cart door-to-door. I once bought a palm tree from one of these roving street vendors. Generally, I try to buy from such people if their prices are

My *vegetablewala* displays his stock of fresh vegetables neatly on the ground under the shade of a large neem tree.

reasonable in order to support the small-scale vendor. I have a favourite *vegetablewala* down the road that I choose to buy from even though I know he is a bit more expensive than the bigger one further down the street. In return, I get a friendly pair of eyes who watches over me when I'm out alone taking my evening walks around the neighbourhood. Sometimes the street vendors come together to form an informal street market, which is held regularly on certain days. At the height of mango season, their carts brim with golden goodness. Street markets allow me to go window-shopping, India-style. This involves Santosh driving slowly past the carts as I yell out my order from the car window:"1 kg onions", "1 kg mango".

- **Malls:** High-end malls catering to the upper middle class is a fairly recent phenomenon. These malls tend to be located near expatriate or upper-middle-class neighbourhoods. Malls such as High Street Phoenix (Mumbai), DLF malls (Delhi and Gurgaon) and Phoenix Marketcity (Bengaluru) carry luxury and high street brands, and increasingly have tenants catering to a young upwardly mobile professional demographic. Despite their growing presence, Indians still love the buzz and variety associated with shopping complexes (such as Connaught Place in Delhi), bazaars and shopping enclaves.

- **Bazaars:** Bazaars are part of the traditional Indian retail landscape and are known to carry everything imaginable. In Delhi, what differentiates the other bazaars from Chandi Chawk are scale and level of chaos. Smaller but just as lively are the infamous two bazaars of Sarojini Nagar and Lajpat Nagar. Sarojini is good for housewares and clothes (you can get factory overruns of some international brands whose apparel are made in India) and Lajpat Nagar is good for clothes and textiles. A trip to Sarojini, like any other bazaar, must be prepared for in advance. It is cash only—leave the credit cards and expensive stuff at home. This is especially true for Chandni Chawk where pickpockets abound. Dress modestly and don't drink anything (there are no restrooms that you want to use). If you can do this, shopper heaven awaits.

- **Shopping enclaves and shopping belts:** Delhi's middle-class shopping scene tends to be concentrated in small residential enclaves such as Hauz Khas, Greater Kailash (GK) and Shahpur Jat. In Mumbai, whole streets are dedicated to retail. Whether in Colaba, Hill Road or upmarket Pali Hill, the numerous shopping belts in Mumbai make the city one of India's best for shopping.

When I first told Madhu I was going to Chandni Chawk, she turned pale. "No jewellery, keep your cash in your pocket, dress like a local, look poor, look ugly, carry your cheap bag in front of you at all times, pay attention," was her rapidly fired advice. Santosh had the same reaction as he dropped us off near the bazaar. He looked worried. "Call me anytime, mam. Anytime," were his parting words. "I stay by car because people steal cars," he added. Good to know. The first thing that greets you at Chandni Chawk is the human crush and chaos. It is truly the best mind-training exercise for anyone: to be able to focus on all the trinkets, the smells, the sounds, the pickpockets, the experience, the charm, the filth, the gropers, the bargains, the traffic, the food, the puddles, the live wires, the jewellery, the incense, the yells, the hum, the honks all at once while navigating cramped lanes fighting for air and personal space as people push you from behind and brush you from the front (heed Madhu's advice to carry your bag in front of you). What an adrenaline rush it was. Five hours, 5,000 rupees and a sigh of relief later, I reached home. Madhu called me to ask if I was okay. The car was also okay. Achievement level unlocked.

Bargaining

No one does this better than the Indian aunty-ji. It comes from having (or loving) to bargain all her life. The first thing she will tell you is to never pay the price quoted to you. Bargaining is a game and the shopkeeper is expecting you to play it, so don't disappoint him. The rules are simple: you start by asking about the price, then feign horror at his reply. This paves the way to either ask for a discount or state your price, which should be lower than what you are willing to pay. What happens after this comes down to stamina. Who wins is a matter of who gets worn down first. Getting him to show you the item in every single size and colour and every possible other permutation is one way to accelerate the process. The look of bored indifference must be maintained consciously at all times. When you zero in on the item you want, the next stage is to find fault with it. The aunty-ji employs this to film award standards. The scene goes something like this: "I don't like the handle", "the colour is stupid", after which she returns the item in disgust and indignantly walks away. I have yet to perfect the mock look of loathing so I bank on the easier tactic: time. Be the first shopper. Many shopkeepers believe that the first sale determines the luck for the rest of the day so they will be motivated to agree on your price.

If timing is not convenient, then try confidence. When you go to the markets, there are two main prices: one for the foreigner and one for the Indian. The price you get is determined by how confident you are in bargaining and how well you know the prices of goods. That means you should visit several shops to compare deals before narrowing in on that one particular shop. To enhance my bargaining power and prowess, I took up Hindi (it helps!). If you can get the Indian price, you know you've become *desi* (local). Note that you should not renege once the seller accepts your price, as it is considered rude. So only start the bargain game if you are truly interested in the item.

Bargaining is part and parcel of the shopping experience at India's bazaars.

The aunty-ji also knows not to be deterred by a price tag or sign that says "Fixed Price"; it's fixed for those who don't ask, she will say. She can usually get a few rupees knocked off but there are some places where bargaining is simply not done: supermarkets, bigger stores and government emporia, for example. Know where to bargain, when to bargain, and when to stop. Again, once you are fairly familiar with prices, you know when you're getting the foreigner price (about twice as much) and I generally do not want to support such shopkeepers as a matter of principle. On the other hand, if the *coconutwala* charges you an extra 10 rupees for a coconut, let him have that little extra (US$0.15, to put it in perspective). Know when to pick your fights.

SCHOOLS

For parents with kids, there are public schools, private schools and international schools to choose from in India apart from the School of Hard Knocks you have chosen to enrol in. Differences relate to fees, curricula, learning environments and pedagogy. Most parents send their children to private or international schools if they can afford it, with international schools being the most expensive. Popular private and international schools face very high demand so it is best to look into this as early as possible before you leave for India. Long wait lists are the norm. If your children's education is covered under your employment terms, do make sure enough allowance is allocated for school fees.

International Schools

International schools are ideal for expatriates who want their children to continue with their home country's curriculum and language to minimise disruption to their children's learning.

This continuity also makes it easier for children to reintegrate into their country's education system upon return. American and British international schools can be found in the major cities and offer familiar teaching methods in a good learning environment. In Delhi, the first preference would be the embassy schools—the American Embassy School (AES) and The British School, followed by the French school, German school and Japanese school, which all maintain their respective country's teaching language. Alongside these are Indian international schools.

Private Schools

Indian private schools combine the best of both worlds by providing ample opportunity for international students to integrate and learn about the Indian culture while receiving quality education. Indian private schools are held in high regard. However, they have high-pressure competitive learning environments that emphasise results and rote learning. This may not suit some international students who are accustomed to other learning styles. A small number of places and a tedious admission process are some of the challenges. Some schools allocate a quota for international students and this may improve your children's chances of getting in.

Public Schools

Public schools are not advisable as facilities, quality of teaching and teachers as well as curriculum are unlikely to meet your expectations. The instruction medium may also not be in English.

Other Schools

For younger children, there is a wide range of private nurseries and kindergartens to choose from, such as Montessori schools. For older children, boarding schools are another option to consider. Many of these schools are prestigious premier schools, which have produced some of India's best. They can be co-ed, all-girls or all-boys schools. Boarding schools typically emphasise an all-rounded education focussed on academia and personal development.

MONEY
Currency

The official currency in India is the rupee, abbreviated as INR or Rs, which comes in denominations of 2,000, 500, 100, 50, 20, 10 and 5. The rupee is further divided into 100 paise, but these are hardly in circulation, people preferring to round prices up to a rupee. The most useful notes to have in your wallet are Rs500 and Rs100 as many vendors do not have enough change to break a Rs2,000 note unless your bill comes close to that amount. Small change may be returned to you in coins and in sweets such as mints. This unofficial other currency only flows one way; you cannot pay in mints. Otherwise, coins are in denominations of Rs1, 2, 5 and 10. Indians may also refer to the cost of something as "bucks" in informal speech. "This scarf cost me 200 bucks!" "Is it Gucci?" you ask. "No, it's Sarojini." (200 rupees).

Indians prefer to transact in cash rather than credit card or cheque. This applies even to large amounts so it is not usual to see Indian women whip out an envelope stuffed with notes. In one extreme case of preferring cash to card, an Indian student paid her entire private school fees in cash. Since the largest denomination then was Rs1,000, the money came packed in a large truck accompanied by armed guards.

Banking

There are numerous Indian and international banks which offer services including Internet banking. Bank branches and ATMs can be found in major cities and towns. You may be charged a small fee if your card is not issued by an Indian bank. Credit cards are also widely accepted but as a precaution, I pay by credit card only in established businesses.

Opening a Bank Account

Most banks offer a non-resident (NRO) savings or current account for expatriates who earn an income in India. Ask the bank for a specific checklist of documents needed to open an account. As banks in India have a reputation for tedious bureaucracy, many expatriates will enlist the help of their company to open a bank account. A word of advice is to settle your bank account early before you leave India. I have a friend who is still resolving issues related to closing his bank account long after leaving India.

Taxes

Taxes in India can be confusing. Generally expatriates who live in India for more than 182 days in a year are considered tax residents and will therefore have to pay tax on their local income. It is recommended to consult your company or a tax specialist to determine what tax category you fall in and what portion of your income is subject to tax. Note that India has double taxation agreements with its major trading partners, which means that you cannot be taxed in both countries at the same time. Consult a tax specialist to determine if your country falls under the agreement and to determine which country you should be filing your taxes in.

Cost of Living

India is often seen as a cheap place to live in, which is why new expatriates are surprised to find that living costs in major cities can be high. According to Mercer's 2016 Cost of Living Survey, Mumbai and Delhi are the most expensive Indian cities to live in, followed by Chennai, Bengaluru and Kolkata out of a survey of 209 cities around the world.

Accommodation will be the biggest expense, especially in Mumbai. Local groceries are affordable but expect to pay a premium for imported foods. In Delhi, the prices of vegetables go up three times in the summer because allegedly a third spoils in transit. Eating out can also be pricey in Delhi and Mumbai compared to other Indian cities.

HEALTH AND HEALTHCARE

A medical check-up and vaccinations were the pre-posting requirements for us before moving to India. When I arrived at the hospital for the shots, an attending nurse had a clipboard with a list of all the vaccinations that were available for me to choose from. When I told her I was going to India, she shot me a sympathetic look, then flipped to a different checklist with a list of all the vaccinations NEEDED for India: 13 in all over a course of two months. For someone who hates needles, 13 is a giant pain in the...arm, but it highlights the extra care you need to take to protect your health in India.

Mosquito-borne illnesses like malaria, dengue and chikungunya are fairly common, especially during the monsoon season. Always slather on mosquito repellent. The brand that seems to be the most effective is an Indian brand called Odomos, formulated for India's commando-like mosquitos. There are also devices such as plug-in citronella dispensers and electric coils.

Rabies also poses a risk and can be contracted by stray dogs, monkeys and rats. In Delhi, it is illegal to kill strays and so the risk increases as their number goes up. Some can turn aggressive for no reason. Monkeys in popular tourists areas can be bold enough to snatch food from your hand and inadvertently scratch you. See your doctor immediately if you or your family member has been bitten or scratched, even if you have had the rabies vaccination.

Healthcare Services

India offers a range of healthcare options from mainstream medical treatments (allopathic) to homeopathic and Ayurvedic treatments. India's private hospitals are well known for medical tourism and see patients from other countries seeking a variety of treatments. Indian doctors and specialists have a good reputation partly owing to the volume of cases they encounter in their professional career. Falling short is usually the result of poor sanitary practices by other staff or the lack of facilities, particularly in public hospitals. For general ailments, doctors (called General Practitioners or GPs) have clinics located in hospitals or in neighbourhoods, sometimes in a residential unit. You should go by references from the expatriate community in your city. The same applies to dentists. A good private clinic would be clean and professional with well-trained staff. The cost of healthcare may be borne by your company; if not, general procedures are largely affordable.

After a prescription is written up, medicines can be bought at a chemist. The chemist stocks a range of prescription and over-the-counter Western medicines, some homeopathic ones and general toiletries. Medicines are extremely inexpensive as India is one of the world's top pharmaceutical producers of high-quality generics. The price difference can be large enough for friends and relatives to make you their drug mule each time you return from India. My mother had a thing about Vicks inhalers, which were significantly cheaper in India.

Personally, Indian generics seem to work better on me and I also benefitted from the guidance of a fantastic pharmacist at my neighbourhood chemist. However if you are currently taking specialised medication, it is best to consult your doctor or specialist on the appropriate continuation of your prescription.

FOOD POISONING AND DIARROHEA

The most common attack to your health is food poisoning and the humourous term "Delhi Belly" does little to alleviate the discomfort and distress it produces each time, every time. It is almost considered a rite of passage that befalls all who step into India and only then can one be considered initiated.

Food poisoning arises due to contamination of water and food, and despite your best preventive efforts, it can strike without warning. On my first trip to India, I ate *idli* from a train station vendor but only suffered food poisoning from a breakfast buffet in a five-star hotel. Pace your despair; your senses and gut do get stronger with every bout as you learn how to avoid, navigate and cope. Diarrhoea eventually becomes part and parcel of life in India and you soon wear your experience like a badge. In no time at all, you know how to advise your guests running to the loo at a drop of a *chapati*. You console them, tell them what to look out for like a guru imparting wisdom as you hand out hand sanitisers, wet wipes and anti-diarrhoea pills from your overstuffed handbag.

This is what I imagine you would say with the air of someone who has seen far too many stomach emergencies:

- Always eat fully cooked food, never half-cooked and never ever raw. Skip the salads, cut fruit and fruit juices unless you are confident about the sources.
- Don't take ice. Apart from the possibly dirty water used for the ice, ice blocks can also be transported in dirty

The way ice blocks are transported is one of many reasons behind the advice to stick to chilled bottled water.

containers. Ask for chilled drinks instead and use a straw as the cap may have rusted.

- Wipe the top end of cans before drinking from them.
- Be selective with the street food; it is a risk even for the experienced.
- Wipe your utensils down before use.
- If it's not too severe, go easy on the medicines. The best way is to get all the bad stuff out of your system as quickly as possible. Hydrate well. No milk.
- We can only hope that the cook washed his hands after coming out from the toilet or after scratching himself.
- We can only hope they used a clean towel to wipe the dishes.
- We can only hope someone did not sneeze or cough into your food.
- Don't think of it as diarrhoea but as an uninitiated detox.
- Welcome to India.

WATER

Contaminated water is often the cause of diarrhoea. The traceable culprit is usually contaminated ground water or old leaky pipes that have let through contaminants such as sewage. When new to India, it is best not to take any chances until you get used to the water, even in hotels. Take the known precautions seriously: drink only bottled water, brush your teeth (and rinse your toothbrush) in bottled water. When you shower, make sure water does not enter your mouth. I used to spit after showering (and the habit has stuck). Gradually, you will get used to the water quality in your home and may find brushing with tap water uneventful.

When setting up home, the economical solution is to buy a water dispenser. When buying your 20-litre refill bottles,

check that the seal is unbroken as some dishonest vendors may fill them up with tap water. Tap water is never safe to drink, but usually good enough to wash dishes and vegetables. I usually use bottled water for the final rinse. If

Hairfall

If the lack of clean water frustrates you enough to make you want to pull your hair out, don't bother—the water will do it for you. Many expatriates, both women and men, complain that they returned to their home countries thicker around the middle and thinner on top. Fortunately, many Indian women are living, walking shampoo models and can offer you advice on how they keep from clogging up their showers. Indian women love their locks and religiously follow hair regiments, many of these passed down from mother to daughter. My friend swears by onion juice to stimulate hair growth, her dark-haired 80-year-old grandmother as living proof. Another uses a family recipe of yogurt, honey and coffee to keep her hair naturally dark and silky. If having onion-head makes you cry, there are many other traditional hair tonics and oils you can buy. Since salon (pronounced saloon, no cowboys) services such as hair spas are affordable, you can safely embark on your anti-balding efforts without guilt. While you are saving your crowning glory, throw in the affordable manicure and pedicure too (done simultaneously by two different people). This wild wild west of hair spas, scalp massages, mani-pedis and leg rubs are exactly what us hair-fallin' gals need, so I say yee-haw ladies, go for them *saloon* sessions.

you love salads, my Italian friend recommends soaking the vegetables in a vinegar solution. Another salad-loving friend soaks her vegetables in a mild bleach solution. Be it sour vegetables or chemically tainted ones, it goes to show the care needed to stay safe.

AIR POLLUTION

Whatever does not affect your gut affects your lungs. India has four of the top 10 most polluted cities in the world, with Delhi coming in 11th in a global survey conducted by the World Health Organisation (WHO) in May 2016, a slight improvement from its unenviable top position in 2014. This issue has become a serious concern for expatriates considering a posting to Delhi, where daily pollution levels are often in the "unhealthy", "very unhealthy" and "hazardous" ranges especially during the winter months. For families with asthma-sufferers, India's air pollution is a problem. Air purifiers can help alleviate the effects and you should buy top-of-the-line ones if you can afford it. The US Embassy and Consulate Generals in Delhi, Chennai, Hyderabad, Kolkata and Mumbai monitor air quality levels and daily readings are easily accessible from the US Embassy website (www.newdelhi.usembassy.gov/airqualitydata). If it crosses a certain threshold, embassy schools would usually stop their outdoor activities.

EYE POLLUTION

You can try to hear no evil, speak no evil, but seeing no evil requires much practice, particularly when it comes in the form of two pervasive male habits: peeing and crotch-touching in plain sight. You can attribute the first to the shortage of clean public toilets. Therefore, men relieve themselves at the side of the road (because they can) in full public view, lined up like a stiff procession of golden fountains. Under trees, against walls, on pavements, below signboards: everything not in the public toilet IS the public toilet.

This outward display of manhood waters Indian cities differently. In Delhi, wet spells are frequent. Only the gods are able put a stop to this behaviour. This is why some walls are pasted with various pictures of gods. To ensure that all bases are covered, Christian icons share the same cement as Hindu deities, Sikh gurus and Buddhist monks with one unifying message: you pee here at your own peril.

While I understand why "it is easier to piss in public than to kiss in public" (a common saying), I cannot fathom why men fondle or touch their parts in public. I do not know if it's because of the heat or to check that all is as it should be down there (it's hard to verify), but it seems to be done unconsciously or rather in conscious disregard. I have shaken one too many hands or accepted change from the same hands that seconds before were visibly touch and go. It appears to be like an unnerving nervous twitch or like a period at the end of a sentence where it marks the completion of one activity before another begins, such as waiting at a light to cross the road. Its pervasiveness may be due to its high entertainment and relaxation value going by the many crotch potatoes around reaching for their remotes. After a while, you learn to turn a blind eye.

TOILETS

Women seem to be at a disadvantage when it comes to this particular area of need. Toilets, if any, are few and far between and even if you can find one, it might be so unwelcoming that you are forced to choose between the imprint of the nauseous experience on your brain forever and privacy. You will soon learn to master various degrees of bladder control and self-inflicted dehydration. Or if nature calls, learn to call back directly on nature behind a large bush.

One of the toughest times I had was on our first train trip, which was an uneasy 13 hours. I grew increasingly incensed as my parched lips and dehydrated self saw men and Ben mindlessly drinking water. The audacity! I picked a few fights with the love of my life just to release that frustration and when I was about to burst, I set off to the greater adventure of a train toilet. I thought you could smell it a mile away, but there was no odour in the air. I realised why when I entered the confines of the aptly named water closet. In the place of a bowl or squat toilet was a giant gaping hole in the floor with a view of the tracks below. The deed required circus-worthy skills: strong thighs, good balance to keep steady on a rumbling moving train while securing keys, spectacles,

and loose change that may otherwise be lost forever. All this whilst fighting the updraft as you downdraft. Whatever you leave behind adds to the cumulative track record on India's long rail system.

You may find relief in knowing that malls and restaurants have facilities that match their patrons' wallets, usually manned at all times by an attendant (who may use the same cloth to wipe the taps and the toilet bowls). There is always an audience listening as there is someone cleaning. What is common to almost all restrooms is a small hose called a bidet spray that for many Indians takes the place of toilet paper. It is easy to use, just point and shoot in a snap, and when used together with toilet paper yields a remarkable feeling of clean. My Belgian friend said that the thing she missed most about India, above lifestyle, food and culture, were these bidet sprays. In some Indian restrooms with no sprays, you may find a low tap with a small bucket or pot under it. That is also the way to flush the toilet. Always being prepared,

I keep rolls of toilet paper in the car for emergencies and a roll of toilet paper (de-cored) in my handbag.

I have to warn you that not all tourist attractions have tourist-standard restrooms so you have to plan ahead. The same goes with hitting the road because getting caught in a traffic jam is a particularly awful form of torture, especially for women. Watching men pee by the side of the road almost seems like a taunt. Even if you wanted to let it rip, it may not be safe for you to do so, which leaves you little room but to cope with your rising tide of frustration and anxiety welling within.

POVERTY

Poverty in India has an especially visceral quality to it. India is home to the largest number of impoverished people in the world. Therefore learning to deal with its widespread and confronting nature is part of adapting to India. It can spur you to volunteer or donate, but it can also desensitise you over time. A poor woman begging in the street soon becomes just another beggar in the street until she eventually becomes invisible. Therefore guard your eyes and heart from both extremes. Learn when to give, what to give and who to give to for the impact you want. I knew of a couple in Delhi who bought new blankets for a homeless family since people do die of cold in the winter months. When they next checked in with the family, they found that the blankets had been sold for extra money. Whether the money was used wisely to buy food or used foolishly by the husband to buy booze or cigarettes remains unknown (although they suspect the latter). If giving money to a family, it is better to give to the women. Even better is to do so through an organisation.

The cityscape of many Indian cities is punctuated by slums.

Beggars

Pity them or loathe them, beggars test your conscience as much as they can test your patience. Some are so persistent that pity can turn quickly into irritation, especially when they use their own hungry children for heightened effect to pester you for *baksheesh*. And then there are also the obviously downtrodden: the starving widow, the man with missing limbs, the blind child, so that the only salve to your conscience is to relieve yourself of some spare change.

In the case of child beggars, take note that the money you give may go to their handlers instead. I always carry pre-packed bags of biscuits to ensure the children directly benefit. Food is always a good choice. My friend Tammy, a person with the biggest heart I know, takes the trouble to go around to give out leftovers and gifts (on special occasions) to the homeless family that lives under the bridge near her home in Delhi.

If you would like to start small, look no further than within your walls; charity begins at home. Though your staff may not be in dire need, they will have needs you can meet.

WOMEN'S SAFETY

It is an unfortunate truth that women, both local and foreign, have to contend with unwanted male attention, often on a daily basis. Sexual harassment ranges in severity from staring to "eve-teasing" to rape. The world was made more aware of the issue of women's safety in India after the brutal rape of a Delhi woman in December 2012. Even prior to the horrific incident, Delhi already had an unsavoury reputation.

While it is never the woman's fault for the abuse or rape, conservative mindsets remain entrenched in society that allow men to blame and harass women with impunity. Some blame ultra-conservative upbringing where Indian boys have little to no interaction with girls outside the family, making them more susceptible to traditional stereotyping of women.

These are steps foreign women can take to be safe:
- Dress modestly. Wear local clothes like a *salwar kameez*, as this will help you blend in.
- Move around in groups.
- Avoid going out alone after dark. Taking a taxi alone at night is not recommended.
- Be constantly aware of your surroundings.
- Do not be overly friendly with male strangers.
- Take the "women-only" carriages in trains and metros.

Eve-teasing

Eve teasing is a euphemism used in India to refer to verbal or physical sexual harassment in the public sphere including molestation and "flashing" but falls short of rape. The aggression can range in severity from sexually suggestive remarks to catcalls to surreptitiously brushing against a woman to groping. The euphemism comes from "Eve" of the Old Testament and "teasing" which makes light of the disagreeable act of harassment. It is often described in India as innocent play and is common in public spaces and on streets and public transport. Although eve-teasing is illegal, it still remains widespread and unchecked.

A common stereotype of foreign women is "being easy", so whilst Indian men may keep a respectful distance from Indian women, they may not do so with foreigners.

Even conservatively dressed foreign women who go by all the rules still face harassment because a man with indecent intentions will not let your

modesty stop him. So unless attitudes towards women change, a woman will continue to be routinely subject to "eve-teasing" by the Adams who are willing to shatter her paradise for their own amusement.

How to Respond

The first step is to ignore rather than engage, because any engagement may be mistaken for interest or even encouragement. If things get uncomfortable and your hints to back off are not being heeded, then a forceful and rude reply is needed and deserved. Make a scene if you need to. If the situation escalates, seek help from policemen or authority figures near you.

Go Away

If beggars are surrounding you and you are beginning to feel unsafe and uncomfortable despite your polite "no" and "no thank you", it is time to up your volume. *Jaa-iyeh* is a (still fairly polite) way of saying "go away" in Hindi. If it's getting too much, a rough *jao* (pronounced *ja-oh*, a ruder "go away") should put an end to the pestering. I used to think that it is discourteous to be so brusque with anyone but I learnt that it is the only tone taken seriously when under harassment.

CHAPTER 6

FOOD

> ❝I know that one lifetime, one memory,
> is not enough to eat, know and absorb India.❞

—Chitrita Banerji

If there is any food to wake, shake and numb the taste buds, it has to be Indian food. With the combination of aromatic spices, each dish is a pleasurable punch to the tongue, and occasionally to the gut. For many people, Indian food is curry, which is further simplified to anything that resembles a brown spicy gravy. But being in India, you soon realise that this is just the tip of the culinary iceberg. Just below the curry line are the depths and breadth of its regional cuisines. Beyond just delicious, they also provide a tangible look into India itself.

Indian food is simplistically divided into North Indian and South Indian, reflecting the similarly simplistic geographical divide. North Indian food tends to be Mughlai food accompanied by a variety of *rotis* (breads). South Indian food is more rice-based with the heavy use of coconut.

Regional cuisines reflect the diversity of India's geography, climate, religion and history, which together determine the distinctive flavours and cooking styles of regions. For example, West Bengal's love affair with fish is due to its location in the Gangetic delta where seafood is abundant while Gujarati food reflects its predominant Jain population.

Mughlai cuisine refers to the recipes and cooking style developed during the Mughal Empire. It generally refers to the cuisine of North India (particularly in Delhi) and in Hyderabad.

For my taste buds, no factor stands more distinct than the influences from afar in India's storied past with traders and colonisers, who brought with them their styles of cooking and new ingredients. The Portuguese introduced bread and baking to the Malabar Coast as well as new crops such as chilli and potato. The defining *biryanis* and *pulaos* of northern India are recipes from the imperial Mughals, who also introduced the pineapple to India. The British too made their mark, particularly in Kolkata, resulting in a fusion style called Anglo-Indian. Thus, the resulting culinary labels of Goan, Anglo-Indian, Mughlai, Hyderabadi, Awadhi, Parsi, and Chindian all bear testimony to the centuries of cultural interaction with Persia, Central Asia, Europe and China. Together with the regional labels of Bengali, Kashmiri, Tamilian, Andhra, Northeastern, "Indian" food is dramatically and emphatically more than just curry alone. Now that's food for thought.

Curry

The word "curry" derives from *kari*, a spicy dish from Kerala and Tamil Nadu. It became synonymous with Indian food in the Western world partly due to restaurants called "curry houses" that were set up by Punjabi immigrants in Britain. The Punjabis have a culture of eating out and in India, they developed roadside restaurants called *dhabas*, which sold simple food cooked in a *tandoor* oven for people on the move. The proliferation of *dhabas* helped spread the taste of *tandoori* food to the rest of India and popularised the idea of eating out. Similarly, these "curry houses" in Britain catered to the local Indian population as well as British officers who had once stayed in India and who had acquired a taste for Indian flavours. Punjabi food soon became the taste of "Indian" food in the West.

Just like it did for centuries, Indian food today continues to absorb the influences and tastes of its time. Changing demographics and a greater exposure to fast food has yielded a McAloo Tikki burger at McDonalds, a *tandoori* chicken burger from Burger King or a chicken *tikka* pizza from Pizza Hut. Putting any disdain for fast food aside, this alone is worthy of a food stop. The McAloo Tikki is not merely a spiced potato patty between buns; it represents India's remarkable ability to evolve, adapt and imprint itself on anything. Indian food therefore is much too broad and too complex to be confined to the singularity of curry, and yet it owes its identity to one all-important component: spices.

I love Indian food so I sought to master the Indian kitchen by learning how to cook. Lofty ambition aside, it makes good sense to learn how to make your own Indian food because you can modify recipes to suit your tolerance to spices as well as to cut down on the incredible amount of ghee that normally flavours Indian restaurant food. Ghee, if you didn't already know, is clarified butter. I had attended an Indian cooking course and discovered that ghee is not only a cooking medium but also the answer to just about any question. What do I fry this in? Ghee. What makes this taste so good? Ghee. Why does it smell so nice? Ghee. You've put on a couple of pounds since I last saw you? Ghee. (It's true!)

Intimidating as it may seem, the first start and half the battle is to buy the spices required for Indian cooking. And there are indeed a lot of spices. My first venture saw me at the centre of my own spice trade in the aromatic corner of the market, haggling with my inner voice of reason, asking what this and that was for, trying to figure out the spice names and their English equivalent. Like traders of yore, I brought back sufficient quantities to satisfy a homeland. It wasn't smooth sailing cooking up a storm in a teacup but one gigantic mess later, my first dish of *aloo gobhi* (potatoes with cauliflower) made landfall. After a few more tries, I discovered that like Chinese cooking, India also has its basic building blocks that gives the cuisine its characteristic taste. To me the flavour of North India lies in *garam masala*, ginger-garlic paste, cumin (*zeera*) and yogurt/curd (*dahi*). To this I add a trio of additional spices to improve the taste: coriander powder (*dhania*), turmeric powder (*haldi*) and chilli powder (*lal mirch*). As time progressed, I developed my own style of Indian cooking I call "restrained alchemy", which sees me sparingly combining a repertoire of about 10 spices to create Indian-tasting food.

A tip for storing spices: Common to every Indian kitchen is the Indian spice box known as *masala dabba*. It is a pie-shaped metal receptacle containing inner compartments for the various spices. Given the range of spices used for even the simplest of meals, it makes sense to have the spices on hand in one receptacle instead of in separate bottles.

REGIONAL FOOD

Food is as characteristic of a region's identity as its language. Although they share many commonalities in terms of spices used and cooking style, knowing the differences will enrich your appreciation of the range of flavours within Indian cuisine. I have included a summary here of the most distinctive regional labels in their broadest form: northern, southern, coastal and northeastern, as well as the most common state-specific flavours that can be found within and beyond their state boundaries.

North India

When one talks about Indian dishes in other parts of the world, it almost always refers to North Indian signatures like *tandoori* chicken, butter chicken, kebabs and *biryanis*, which are essentially Punjabi and imperial cuisines. North Indian food tends to incorporate milk-based products such as *paneer* and *dahi* (yogurt/curd). *Dahi* is a key ingredient for marinating and thickening, resulting in creamy curries and sauces, which are usually eaten with various types of *rotis* (breads).

Kashmir

Kashmiri food is heavily influenced by the cooking style of Central Asia and Tibet. The preferred meat is lamb. Dishes are cooked with a generous use of yogurt giving it a creamy consistency and coloured with locally grown saffron. The Kashmiri banquet called *wazwan* is a 36-course meal that is served on a large ornate plate piled high with rice and the first few courses. Each successive course is then served separately. Meals always end with *kahwa* (green tea), which is sweetened and flavoured with cardamom and almond.

Punjab

Punjabi food is Indian food to the West. The familiarity of its signatures dishes like *tandoori* chicken and *dal makhani* (lentils slow-cooked in butter) is comforting especially when everything else on the menu is unpronounceable. The other internationally well-known Punjabi favourite is butter chicken. Its origin, however, is not in the Punjab but a small kitchen in the Moti Mahal restaurant in New Delhi. The Punjab's dairy and agrarian economy means that milk products such as *paneer* (cottage cheese), yogurt and *lassi* (yogurt drink) are very much part of the Punjabi table as well as seasonal favourites such as *sarson ka saag* (slow-cooked mustard greens) and *baigan ka bharta* (smoked and pureed eggplant). The holy city of Amritsar boasts of its batter-fried fish.

Rajasthan and Gujarat

Rajasthani cuisine is a mingling of the culinary traditions of the princely Rajputs, Mawaris, Jains and Muslims of the region. Rajasthani food is primarily vegetarian. Because of the scarcity of fresh vegetables in the state's arid climate, most dishes are lentil-based, such as *dal-baati*. The food is simple, robust and almost always cooked with a heavy hand of chilli and ghee. In Jaipur, dishes are a blend of Rajput and Muslim tastes. Gujarati food is strictly vegetarian, owing to its large Jain population, and is considered one the most sophisticated in India. It is sweetened with *jaggery* (a type of sugar) and meals are served on a platter called a *thali*. Gujarat's steamed lentil cakes called *dhokla* are popular breakfast and snack foods across North India.

Delhi: Mughlai

Mughlai cuisine allows you to eat like a king (*did*). Rich, refined, flavourful and multi-coursed, it is imperial cuisine from the kitchens of Mughal India. The imperial chefs brought with them the culinary traditions and flavours of Central Asia and Persia and over time these became the rich curries, fragrant *biryanis* and creamy *kormas* that we know today. Meals typically begin with kebabs and progress to the main course, which comprise various meat and vegetable curries accompanied by rice (plain basmati, *biryani* or *pulao*) and an assortment of *rotis*, such as *naan*, *rumali roti* (a handkerchief-like *roti*), *paratha* and *poori*. For a taste of authenticity, Karim's restaurant in Old Delhi is run by descendants of chefs of the Mughal court.

Uttar Pradesh: Awadhi (Modern-day Lucknow)

Awadhi cuisine reflects the elegant lifestyle of the royal Nawabs. It is subtle, refined and considered unmatched in culinary India. The essence of Awadhi cuisine comes from the traditional method of cooking called *dum pukht* where food is cooked over a slow fire in a sealed clay pot, allowing the ingredients to cook in their own juices. Lucknow's *biryani* and delicately flavoured *pulaos* are famed across India as much as its lamb (*seekh*) kebabs and minced-lamb (*galouti*) kebabs. The latter came about because it was considered uncouth for nobility to be seen biting into pieces of meat.

West Bengal: Bengali, Anglo-Indian, Chindian

Freshness is important to the Bengali palate. A typical Bengali meal can be summed up as fish and rice accompanied by fresh seasonal vegetables. Bengalis prefer freshwater fish, and favourites include the *bhetki* and *hilsa*. Bengali food derives its distinctive flavour from a five-spice mix called *panchphoron* as well as the bitter-sharp taste of mustard

Roti (bread)

Roti is flat bread made of wheat flour (*atta*) and cooked on a *tava* (flat skillet) or in a *tandoor* oven. It is popular in North India whose arid climate supports wheat cultivation. There are a variety of *rotis* that are region-specific but the most common across North India are *naan*, *paratha*, *poori* and *chapati*. *Poori* is a deep-fried bread that when freshly made puffs up with air and resembles a beach ball. *Paratha* is layered dough fried in butter or ghee. They can be stuffed with potato or lentil for a substantial breakfast or snack. *Chapati* is much thinner and considered by many to be a healthier option since it is made with only *atta*, water and a pinch of salt. I learnt how to make *chapati* from Madhu, and by her standards, I would have failed the Indian wife test. Whether custom or hearsay, she told me that back in the day Indian mothers would ask a potential daughter-in-law to make *chapati* as a test of marriageability. Perfectly round ones is a mark of a potentially good wife. Going by my results, I would have been eating my amoeboid *chapati* alone for the rest of my life.

oil, in which the food is cooked.

Bengali cuisine is sensitive to a balance of tastes so sugar is added to counter the bitter taste of mustard. In the state's capital of Kolkata, the Anglo-Indian bent from the days of the British Raj still reign. Typical Anglo-Indian dishes are roast lamb, prawn cocktail and *mulligatawny* soup, which is a soup modified from Tamil Nadu's *rasam* (a type of soup) and served on its own to fit the Western sequential serving style of soup-entrée-dessert. *Kedgeree* (from an Indian porridge called *kichdi*) is served at breakfast with boiled eggs and smoked fish in Kolkata homes, as are toast with omelette.

Kolkata is also home to India's first and only Chinatown. Known as Tangra, it was set up by the early Hakka immigrants who came to British-run Calcutta to work in the leather tanning industry. Chinese restaurants have become a common sight in the city, although most dishes have adapted to the Indian palate in a mixed style termed as Chindian. Favourites include chilli chicken and originally clear soups spiced up and thickened with cornstarch. Noodles have crossed significant territorial and cultural boundaries to become well accepted across India, served up even at Punjabi *dhabas*.

South India

The coconut grows in abundance along costal and southern India, making it the defining ingredient in the cuisine of the south. Rice and rice preparations (rather than wheat- or millet-based products) also characterise South Indian food.

abundance

Tamil Nadu: South Indian, Chettinad

Tiffin food is traditionally a "light meal between meals" taken at mid-day. Now it is common for tiffin foods to be eaten at breakfast time or as an afternoon snack.

South Indian food often refers to the food of Tamil Nadu, which is vegetarian and rice-based. A typical meal consists of rice, vegetables and curd served on a banana leaf and accompanied by *sambhar* (*dal* broth), yogurt-fried chilli, pickles and *rasam* (thin pepper soup). Its claim to fame however is found in its *tiffin* food.

The best known are *dosa* (rice pancakes), *idli* (steamed rice dumplings), *vada* (deep-fried lentil doughnuts) and *uttapam* (spicy pancake). All are eaten with *sambhar* and three types of chutney in the colours of the Indian flag; green coriander, white coconut and orange chilli-tomato.

By contrast, the Chettiars from the Chettinad region are meat eaters. Pepper chicken and other Chettinad dishes are characteristically very spicy.

Andhra Pradesh and Telangana: Andhra, Hyderabadi

Andhra cuisine is a blend of ingredients from North and South India; cumin and chilli from the north are mixed with the mustard and curry leaf of the south. Dishes tend to be spicy and sour, flavoured with a liberal use of chilli, tamarind and lemon to wake the appetite from the sluggishness of the perennial heat of the region. Hyderabad, Telangana's capital, developed its own distinct cuisine because of strong Muslim influence. Arab, Turkish and Persian tastes have found profound expression in its signature dish, the Hyderabadi

Biryani

Biryani is a mixed rice dish cooked with meat, herbs and spices. Lucknow (Awadhi) and Hyderabadi *biryanis* are the most famous and always a subject of debate as to which is better. But there are many regional variants and thus reason enough to start a *biryani* bucket-list. These include Dindigul *biryani* (Tamil Nadu), Bhatkali *biryani* (Karnataka), Thalaserry *biryani* (Malabar Coast), Kolkata *biryani* (it has potatoes) and Bombay *biryani*. The Lucknow and Hyderabadi *biryanis* are similar in that they come from the royal kitchens whose masters, the Nawabs and Nizams respectively, were the epitome of refinement and sophistication and who demanded their food be just as so. The difference between the two *biryanis* lies in whether the meat is cooked separately from the rice (Hyderabad) or together in the *dum phukt* method (Lucknow). Both yield exquisite tastes. I lean towards Lucknow *biryani* but only because I derive pleasure from breaking the dough seal on the clay pot to release the strong whiff of spices, ghee and meat. You just can't beat this on a hungry winter's day.

biryani. The ruling Nizams were notorious for their lifestyle excesses, and the rich sophisticated food of Hyderabad reflects their decadent leanings.

Coastal India

Coastal cuisine refers to the cuisine of the states bordering the Konkan and Malabar coasts (southwestern India) stretching from Maharashtra to Goa, Karnataka and Kerala. Coastal food is characterised by a wide range of fresh seafood dishes and the liberal use of coconut and cashews. Rice is the dominant staple.

Maharashtra: Parsi

Mumbai is a cosmopolitan metropolis and a melting pot of cultures and food. Hindus, Muslims, Christians, Jews and migrants from all over India enrich Mumbai's culinary offerings in addition to the ready availability of high-quality Western food. Particular to Mumbai is the cuisine of the Parsis, who are of Persian ancestry. They are well known for their legendary baking skills (Shrewsbury biscuits from Pune are a must) and a dish called *dhan sak* (meat and lentil casserole). The other food synonymous with Mumbai is the *pao bhaji*, a small square loaf of bread served with minced vegetables cooked in a hearty tomato sauce.

Goa

Goan food is unmistakably Portuguese in influence with names such as pork *vindaloo* and *sorpotel*, which are signature dishes. Fresh seafood and vegetables feature heavily in a typical menu and they are eaten with rice or bread (*pao*). Dessert is almost always *bebinca* cake.

Kerala

The many coconut groves of Kerala hint at its cuisine's most important ingredient. Coconut features in all of Kerala's dishes from mains to dessert. Keralan fish curry, a lightly spiced coconut curry, is a signature dish. Food is eaten with *appam*, a delicate steamed rice pancake made with coconut milk. *Puttu*, another staple eaten with curry, is made of ground rice and grated coconut steamed in bamboo cylinders.

Northeastern

Heavily influenced by neighbouring China and Tibet, the most famous product of the northeastern states is the *momo*, steamed dumplings filled with meat and vegetables accompanied by a side of broth. There was a *momo* seller who sited his little stall opposite my house on the street corner. He saw roaring business well into the night, especially

The *momo* seller opposite my house sites his stall adjacent to a refuse collection point but still manages to attract a steady stream of hungry customers daily.

on winter days when steamy hot *momos* were perfect to combat the chill. I learnt how to make this simple dumpling and the closest equivalent to my mind is the Chinese *sui kow* or Japanese *gyoza*. The hardest part is doing the skin just right (it has to be thin) and pinching it at the top into a leaf-like pattern, both of which failed spectacularly in my novice hands, rendering the *momo* a no-go.

STREET FOOD

Note that sometimes the water used to cook street food may not be clean. I stick to *chaats* that are fully cooked, such as those fried in a vat of hot oil.

Residents of Delhi are notorious in their love for street food, and the proliferation of little food carts makes snacking throughout the day too easy. These savoury snacks are called *chaats*, essentially variants of fried dough eaten with yogurt and chutney and topped with spicy sprinkles. By far the most common is

Roadside *pakora* stalls are a common way to grab a quick snack.

It's easy to spot the Golgappa seller with his stall stacked up with fried empty shells.

the *samosa* (potato-filled turnover) and *pakora* (vegetable tempura), both eaten with chutney and sometimes ketchup. Another favourite is *pani puri* (also called *golgappa*) in which deep-fried hollow dough balls are filled with potato, *dal* and onion, and then dipped into tamarind water to flood its crispy chamber. The correct etiquette is to pop the dripping ball whole into your mouth and bite it to release the slush of ingredients.

Chaat specialties vary from city to city. In Mumbai, *sev puri* and *bhel puri* are a must. Other common street foods in Delhi are *bhutta* (corn-on-the-cob roasted on makeshift grills), cold fruit juices and *kulfi* (ice cream). The street food that cuts across all social strata has to be the *jalebi* (deep-fried dough spirals smothered in syrup). Savoured at streetcarts in the

I *aam* Mango

The intensifying rays of summer indicate the coming of one of India's best fruits: mango (*aam*). As the leading cultivator of mango, accounting for about half of the world's production, there are over 1,500 varieties of mango in India to occupy your summer days and diet. Each state will claim that their mango is the best in taste and flavour, but the undisputed king is the Alphonso mango from Maharashtra. In Mumbai, they come as fresh as they get, sweet and deeply satisfying. But in Delhi, perhaps owing to the long road journey, I find the freshest (and to my palette, the best) are the Dussehri and Langra varieties from nearby Uttar Pradesh. In India they can be found in every corner heaped on wooden carts by the road ripening under the sun, garbed in juicy red and yellow with their sweet perfume and taut roundness.

India's love affair with mango goes back thousands of years where it captured the imagination and taste buds of both laymen and clergy, conquerors and kings through the ages. It was used by the early Buddhist leaders and came to represent faith and prosperity in Buddhist legend. The enamoured Portuguese took the fruit back and introduced it to the Western world as "mango" (from the Malayalee word *maanga*). Its greatest admirers were the Mughal emperors whose fondness for mango pervaded each successive generation. The *aam panna*, a traditional drink to cool the body, is said to have come from the Mughal court.

The mango today retains its plump significance in Indian life. Mango leaves are strung up with marigold as door garlands (called *toran*) and hung at entrances during festivals and events. The leaves are used in religious worship (*puja*) and during ceremonies such as weddings where they are symbols of life, luck and prosperity. The mango is also an iconic motif in Indian art and design, its curvaceous shape inspiring the paisley pattern. In my household, the mango tree was the centre of the garden. Not only was the tree a decades-old reminder of the Dayals' family history, it provided shade and fruit for squirrel, bird and human. Tree-ripened mango, mango *lassi* and Mrs Dayal's homemade mango *achar* were the best of summer's gifts. Persian poet Amir Khusrau called the mango "the fairest fruit of Hindustan". I think its greatness lies in its Hindi name—*aam*, because it certainly is what it is.

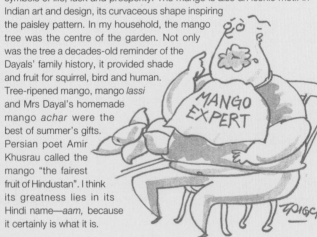

alleys of Old Delhi to wedding banquets in upscale hotels, *jalebi* seems to be a universal favourite for both young and old in the north. Taken just-fried with a scoop of cold vanilla ice cream, it is a wonderful way to round up the calorie count.

TYPICAL INDIAN MEALS
A Typical Indian Meal

A typical Indian meal comprises various dishes eaten with *rotis* and/or rice. The number of dishes indicates how elaborate the meal is but the format is largely the same, with an unspoken four-dish minimum. Dishes are accompanied by crispy wafers (called *papad* in the north, *poppadom* in the south), pickles (*achar*), chutney and chopped fresh onions and chilli sprinkled with lime juice. Mr Dayal eats his meals with mint and coriander chutney, which he said is excellent for health and digestion.

Dishes are served all at once. There will usually be a *dal* dish, which is a thick and nutritious stew made with various lentils. Ben's favourite is *dal tadka* (*tadka* means tempering with garlic, chilli and cumin). There would also be at least two vegetable dishes: a dry vegetable dish like *bhindi fry* (fried okra) and a vegetable curry. Non-vegetarian meals could include additional meat dishes, usually lamb, chicken or fish. The food is scooped onto a dinner plate and eaten with rice or with hot fresh *rotis*, which are placed on a side plate.

Meals usually end with something sweet. In the north, dessert takes the form of *kulfi* (a

Indian food makes an indelible mark not only on the taste buds but also the tummy. Because dinner is usually a late affair, it is not uncommon to finish dinner then go straight to bed. On the bright side, you could say Indians never go to bed hungry and it is only a few hours that separate the last meal from the next.

traditional Indian ice cream), *phirni* (rice pudding) and *gajar halwa* (dry carrot pudding only available in winter). In the south, rice continues in the form of *payasam* and *pongal*,

Sweets

Indians love their sweets and the country itself shows it—the entire Indian subcontinent is shaped like a giant sweet tooth. Completely different from Western candy, Indian sweets (*mithai*) are milk-based confectionaries taking its name to an extreme. They are formidably sweet and take some getting used to for the uninitiated and sugar-averse. The first time I tried *gulab jamun* (fried spongy balls soaked in a rose-flavoured syrup), I made the mistake of popping an entire ball into my mouth. As I bit down, my brain froze from the amount of syrup released in that one bite.

Nibbling is the only way to eat *mithai* and after a few dozen nibbles, my hands-down favourite is the *rasgulla* (*paneer* balls soaked in light syrup). Ben's *mithai* of choice is almond *barfi* and like many Indians, he has a preferred sweetshop to buy it from. Mine was all too conveniently located opposite our house. Bengal Sweet Palace was its name and it was always the busiest shop on that stretch with people milling outside chomping on large *laddoos* or savoury *dhoklas* as stray dogs and crows lay waiting for crumbs. Sweetshops are prolific across Indian cities big and small for sugar highs and navigational help. They have become the hallmarks and landmarks of the Indian street. Nobody knows where "Vasant Vihar 'A' block" is but if I say "Bengal Sweet Palace", an *autowala* will get me there.

Although *mithai* are made all over India, Bengalis have the sweetest reputation for it, evidenced in the many sweetshops that are Bengali-run or named. For this reason, no one leaves Kolkata without a box of *sandesh* or *rasgulla* in hand for gifting. Bengali sweets differ from non-Bengali ones by its use of *chhana* (similar to *paneer*) instead of evaporated or whole milk. In the south, sweets are usually made of rice. *Borrelu* (Andhra Pradesh) are deep-fried balls made from a batter of *dal* and rice and filled with sweet coconut. *Unni appam* (Kerala) is similar to *gulab jamun* but uses rice, banana and coconut. Made with generous amounts of ghee, sugar and cardamom, *Mysore pak* is considered the "royal sweet" of the south because of its beginnings in the kitchens of the Mysore Palace. It is traditionally served at weddings and other festivals in South India. *Khir* (a North Indian variation of South India's *payasam*) is my favourite rice-based dessert. It is traditionally prepared during special occasions and festivals. Madhu taught me her recipe for *khir*, which requires boiling rice, milk (coconut milk in the south), sugar, cardamom, saffron and raisins together to form a pudding, which is eaten warm. I modified the recipe by halving the amount of sugar, replacing raisins with dried cranberries and almonds, and chilling it before serving because when you make it for yourself, who *khirs* what you add and how you eat it.

both sweet rice puddings. Common to both and forming the mainstays of desserts are Indian sweets, which are consumed at the end of meals (and also very much between them).

Breakfast

An Indian breakfast can seem heavy and almost lunch-like. Common breakfast foods vary according to region but generally in the north, *parathas*, poha (flattened rice) and *dhokla* are common breakfast foods. Mumbaikars and Goans tuck into *pao bhaji* and *vada pao* (*vada* sandwich) in the morning while Bengali households have *luchi* (*poori*) with curry. In the south, *tiffin* dishes like *idli* and *dosa* are popular. Keralans would start their day with *puttu*. Northeasterners may have *momos* for breakfast or *thukpa*, a Tibetan noodle soup. In the Dayal household, breakfast is a tomato-onion-chilli omelette on buttered toast served along with *masala chai* and a small bowl of *channa dal* for the man of the house and the squirrels in the garden.

Lunch

With almost a complete meal for breakfast, lunch tends to be a light midday meal commonly referred to as *tiffin*. The concept dates back to the British Raj although some argue it existed long before. Typical *tiffin* food would be *idli* and *dosa*, South Indian favourites that have become popular in the north. Lunch could also be another complete meal. In the major cities, the lunch hour is used to catch up with colleagues and friends over food. Restaurants, fast food joints and roadside food carts cater to the office crowds but it is also fairly common for Indians to bring their own packed lunch from home.

In the case of Mumbai, homemade lunches have become

an entire industry. Every day thousands of specialised delivery men called *dabbawalas* deliver packed lunches from home to loved ones (or lazy ones) throughout Mumbai.

Dabbawalas

Like mailmen, the *dabbawalas* of Mumbai are indispensible fixtures of the city's daily life but instead of mail, they bring parcels of home-cooked goodness from 100,000 suburban kitchens to offices all around the city. Their routine involves picking up the food from home kitchens, coding them, delivering them to the office address, then returning the empty lunch boxes (called tiffin carriers or more commonly *tiffins* or *dabbas*) to the original kitchen from which they came. Come midday, Mumbai's 4,000 plus *dabbawalas* ("the ones who bring *dabbas*") fan out into the city on train, bicycle or foot to deliver hot fresh lunches to hungry working folk. It is not simply a door-to-door service. The *dabba* can reach the exact floor, department and desk of each of the estimated 150,000 recipients, all without the use of technology. Instead, the century-old industry relies on its own unique coding system of markings. And they rarely make mistakes. A typical dabba *meal* comprises *roti*, rice, *dal* and a vegetable dish packed in a three- or four-tiered stainless steel *tiffin*. Wives use *dabbawalas* to deliver lunch to their husbands, but some also take orders from outsiders. Ben used to order a *dabba* from a Jain housewife. It always came on the dot neatly placed on his desk. Once finished the *tiffin* is left at the same place for the *dabbawala* to pick up. Ben has never returned a *dabba* unhappy or with food left over. This, I imagine, must have been the greatest compliment to the cook as well as a nod to the humble *dabbawala*, who consistently delivers on his famed efficiency.

Teatime and Chai

Afternoon tea could have been a British import or born out of necessity if lunch was indeed light as intended. Whatever the reason may be, late afternoon means a break that involves *tiffin* foods, street snacks and sweets accompanied by a hot drink—*masala chai* in the north, filtered coffee in the south.

Masala chai is black tea brewed together with milk, sugar, cardamom, cinnamon and other spices. It is served piping hot in small glasses. There is no particular way of drinking *chai* except to do it quickly before a milk skin forms over the

Art installation using *khurri* cups.

surface and, of course, to enjoy it completely. Apart from its comforting aroma, the spices used in making the drink are known to have many health benefits, especially related to digestion. Many Indian women have their own passed-down recipe of spice blends. On the go, *masala chai* is sold in trains (by boys who jump up onto the train at station stops), planes,

TEA IS VERY BIG HERE

and along the roads. The drink will be poured into flimsy plastic cups that you have to handle delicately but, on occasion, you get the traditional environmentally friendly clay cups called *khuris*. After finishing your tea, you smash the *khuri* onto the ground for it to be remade into new ones.

India's tea-drinking culture is pervasive. India began producing tea in the 19th century when the British set up tea gardens in the northeast, particularly in Assam, Sikkim and West Bengal (Darjeeling). Today India is the world's largest producer of tea and employs over a million people, two of whom I know personally. Madhu's parents live in one of the many tea gardens in Darjeeling where they have been employed all their lives. When she returns from a visit, she brings me a bag of tea home-smoked in her parent's yard. There are various tea varieties grown in India. Darjeeling tea is called the "champagne of teas" because of its golden colour and light muscatel flavour. The tea required for *masala chai* requires a darker variety such as Assam tea, which has a stronger, punchier taste.

As India is a tea-growing country, tea is plentiful and inexpensive to purchase with a vast range of qualities available. Specialty tea shops in tea-growing regions and in major cities package and sell estate-grown teas. These make great gifts for overseas friends or for yourself in the form of a couple's retreat or family vacation in one of India's tea gardens, where you get to sit and sip some of the best of the world's teas at its source.

HOW TO BEAT THE HEAT AND A COLD

If the food is too hot (spicy), there are several discreet ways to cool off without reaching for the water and soda. Reach instead for yogurt-based food such as *raita*, which is curd mixed with cucumber, tomatoes or *bhoodi* (tiny fried gram flour balls). A *lassi* (yogurt drink) will also help sooth the stomach almost instantly.

In the case of heat from the weather, I find that nothing refreshes more than *nimbu pani*, fresh lime squeezed into water. It is common to be served *nimbu pani* in summer when visiting homes. A variant, fresh lime soda, is made the same way but with soda water. At restaurants, you can have the drink sweet or salty (if you don't specify your choice, salty is the default). The salty variant is sprinkled with a pungent black salt (*kala namak*), which is an acquired taste. You can also go for "sweet-salty".

When the weather turns gloomy, rainy and cold, Indians reach for *masala chai* or filtered coffee (depending on the part of the subcontinent). In Kashmir when temperatures

Kashmiris are said to keep a hot flask of *kahwa* handy in their coat pockets for drinking and for warming themselves.

Ayurveda

India has a long history of using foods to heal the body. This is the science of Ayurveda, an ancient Indian system of natural and holistic medicine that is based on the idea of balance in bodily systems. According to Ayurveda, each person has a natural constitution or inherent trait called *dosha*. Our *dosha* defines our appearance, personality and how we are affected by different foods. There are three *doshas*: fiery (*pitta*), cool (*vata*) and earthy (*kapha*). A person is usually dominant in one *dosha* and will have imbalances in the other two. Ayurveda seeks to restore this balance through what we eat in order to return our bodies to optimum health.

To determine your *dosha*, you can visit an Ayurvedic doctor or try online tests, which are convenient but not necessarily accurate. From one such test, I am a *kapha*, and *kaphas* are prone to bloating and weight gain (right, it's not my love for cake). To restore my balance, I must avoid sweet food (not going to happen) and choose more astringent food like bittergourd. I quickly concluded that Ayurvedic eating is not for me, not for the lack of faith in Ayurveda but that of willpower. However, I believe in the potency of natural ingredients, which form the basis of traditional remedies to effectively address minor problems and for general long-term health. There is ample proof that natural remedies work and yet there are other concoctions where I remain somewhat sceptical such as the old wives' cure for sagging breasts—boil neem oil with powdered pomegranate rind, then make into a paste and apply. I'm happy with my fruit as they are.

drop below freezing, *kahwa* (green tea) is consumed throughout the day. There are also "heating" foods to warm the body, such as ghee, *urad dal* and herbs like *methi* (fenugreek), which are found in many dishes.

When the chill is inside your body, an Ayurvedic recipe called *haldi doodh* (turmeric milk) is the traditional go-to remedy for the common cold. This drink is also fast gaining popularity in the West. Turmeric offers many health benefits since it has both anti-inflammatory and anti-oxidant properties. Taken at night, it promotes sleep and relieves an array of ailments including colds, sore throat, indigestion and diarrhoea. Some basic knowledge about Ayurvedic foods will help you benefit from the wealth of traditional natural remedies that have been known to Indians for centuries.

EATING IN AN INDIAN HOME

We were often invited to dine with the Dayals, sometimes for special occasions and sometimes for no reason other than spending a nice evening together. If you have been invited to an Indian home for dinner or a party, it will help to know the typical order of events to best prepare yourself for the night ahead.

Before You Leave the House

The first thing to note is that Indians eat late. If you are used to taking dinner at 7pm, it is advisable to have a snack before you leave the house because dinner is usually served around 9pm (or later). You are not expected to bring a gift but more people are doing so. Appropriate gifts are flowers (avoid white flowers, as these are associated with funerals). a bottle of hard liquor (a Hindu host will appreciate it) or a box of Indian sweets.

Arriving

If not already stated, ask the host what time you should arrive, and then arrive a little later than that—20 to 30 minutes late is usually expected. Being punctual is usually too early for the host, who may still be in the midst of setting up. Indian guests often arrive for dinner between 7.30pm and 8.30pm.

The period before dinner is usually the main time to socialise unlike in Western or Asian homes, where the socialising is done after dinner with a hot beverage or stiff drink. In an Indian home, guests have an hour or two to chat before the meal is served. During this time, drinks like beer (Kingfisher, of course), hard liquor, juices and soda will be offered, along with an assortment of *namkeen* (salty-savoury snacks) or a variety of appetisers (called starters). Dinner is typically between 9pm and 11pm.

At the Dayal house, pre-dinner snacks consisted of the royally good chips from Bengal Sweet Palace and fresh homemade *vada* to which Mr Dayal would gleefully take out his stash of whiskey. Then he, Ben and Johnny would settle on the sofa for quality time. Starters, if served, tend to be favourites like chicken *tikka*, *paneer tikka* and an assortment of kebabs, all of which are like meals in themselves. You have to learn to pace yourself. The first time I was invited to an Indian dinner party, I thought the starters were the main course. By the time dinner was served, I was full and ready to call it a night.

And Finally Dinner

You usually sit where the host indicates at the dinner table, which may be set Western-style with tablecloth, napkins and cutlery. The table setting usually comprises a dinner plate, small side plate for *roti* and a small bowl called *katori* for *raita* or soup. Soup may be served separately to start off the meal after which the main courses are served all at once. They may be completely vegetarian or a combination of "veg" and "non-veg" (vegetarian and non-vegetarian) accompanied by *roti* and rice.

Guests are often served in a particular order: the guest of honour is served first, followed by the men. *Rotis* are brought hot and fresh off the pan by attentive servants, whose job is to monitor the *roti*-eating progress of those at the dinner table. *Rotis* are torn off, then used to scoop curries and vegetable dishes.

It is acceptable to use a spoon to assist in the scooping of food. A fork or knife are not often used unless in very formal settings or as dictated by the host. The degree of informality is indicated by whether the host themselves use their hands (and it generally signals that they are comfortable with you if they do). The most used utensils are the tablespoon followed by the fork; knives tend to be taken out only at breakfast for spreading butter.

Indian meals are usually eaten with the hand, which is said to add tactile pleasure and increases enjoyment. The correct etiquette is to only use the right hand for food, with the left placed on the lap.

In the course of the meal it is okay to ask for more food. In fact, a hosts sees it as a compliment if you ask for more. "You barely ate," was Mrs Dayal's frequent admonition despite us polishing off numerous *chapatis*, rice, and several helpings of vegetables and chicken. This is typical Indian hospitality: warm, generous and gracious. Guests are typically honoured (and over-fed) at all expense, and this trait cuts across India and all social strata. I have visited many households, and all will serve you the best of what there is in the kitchen, feed you till you are bursting and then complain you did not eat enough.

If your waistband is fully stretched and now cutting into your skin, a polite rejection to another serving of food would be to touch your stomach and say that you are really full and can no longer take in anymore. With this, you would have honoured your host's hospitality and she can rest assured that she has fed you well. Do leave a small amount of food on your plate as this indicates that you are satisfied. Finishing all your food means that you are still hungry and will concern the host that she has not given you enough to eat.

In the south, you may be served a meal on a banana leaf or a *thali*, a metal plate on which a variety of food is placed. A *thali* is not meant for sharing. Our first South Indian meal was at Shridar's home in Vijayawada. We proceeded to the rooftop where mats were laid on the ground. After washing our hands, we sat down with our hosts. The servants placed banana leaves before us and then scooped food from metal buckets onto our leaf-plate. I watched Shridar as he mixed the curry with the rice deftly with his fingers into a rice ball before plopping it neatly into his mouth. I was told this is characteristically a South Indian way of eating. After the meal, the far end of the banana leaf should be folded inwards towards you as this is a sign of gratitude and an indication that you liked the meal. Take careful note of the direction because folding the leaf outwards away from you is a sign of condolence during funeral wakes.

Dessert usually marks the end of the meal. Guests rarely linger and leave soon after dessert. By then, this could be well past midnight. With a full meal, good company and warm hospitality, an Indian dinner experience is the stuff of sweet dreams and even sweeter memories.

Kitchen Boundaries

In your culture, it might be considered polite to peep into the kitchen and ask if the host needs your help. Unless you are very close to your hosts, avoid doing so in India, especially if you are a man. In very conservative Hindu households, a person who has consumed beef is thought to have a "polluting" effect in the kitchen. Modern households may not adhere to this, but it is still best to ask before entering the kitchen.

EATING OUT

Unless you live in a very remote area, you can usually find a range of restaurants for every price point, from roadside *dhabas* to five-star hotels in the major cities. Cosmopolitan cities offer both Indian and global cuisine. I find that Delhi, perhaps owing to its large international population of diplomats, has a slightly wider range of global cuisine than Mumbai. It is easy to find Japanese, Chinese, Korean, Italian and French restaurants that serve authentic fare without travelling vast distances or crossing oceans. Mumbai, on the other hand, wins on its superb Western food and gritty-chic eating-out atmosphere, especially in hipster places like Bandra and Lower Parel.

Dotting the culinary landscape in all cities are the major fast food chains, especially in areas that see a lot of tourists. It is worth giving them a try, not just out of desperation because you are tired of spicy food, but to see how fast food adapts to the Indian taste. KFC does not have "original flavour" chicken but two versions of spicy (it's hard to escape from spicy in India). Burger King's mutton burger and McDonald's chicken *tikka* wraps (also spicy) more than make up for the fact that beef burgers will never be available in Hindu India, except at some hotel restaurants.

Reservations and Restaurants

You need not make reservations if you plan to have dinner before 8pm. Restaurants in India are typically empty at 7pm. Diners start streaming

If you see "beef" on the menu, do not bother to ask the waiter if it is really so. He will say yes but it will typically be buffalo meat (commonly called beef). Buffalo meat is chewy and many say leaves a slight aftertaste. Instead stick to chicken or lamb, which the Indians do to perfection.

in from 8pm onwards and the restaurant only reaches full swing at around 10pm. For early diners, Indian meal times work well so that you're ready to settle the cheque when Indians have only started to browse the menu. Similarly, the average lunchtime is 2pm so early diners get the choice seats. Kitchens don't fire up till about noon so the best time to go for an early lunch is about 12.30pm.

Indian restaurants can usually adjust the spiciness of the food when requested. However, it is up to the cook to interpret what mild means so prepare for anything between

Ending On a Sweet Note

The bill may come together with some traditional bead-like candy (called *mukhwas*) if you are dining at an Indian restaurant. Made with fennel (*saunf*), coriander seeds and cumin, these are breath fresheners and help with digestion. They are so effective that I have replaced my mints with *mukhwas*.

Kitty Parties

At some restaurants, you may find a large group of women coming in to have lunch together. This is called a "kitty party" and refers to a traditional monthly get-together of ladies, usually housewives (who may or may not be cat-lovers, as I first mistakenly thought). Traditionally at such a party, members contribute money to a central pool (called a kitty) and lots are drawn to decide which member will get the entire sum for that month. Today, luncheons and get-togethers are also called kitty parties. The common aim is to bond. Siting next to a kitty party in progress is hearing about everyone's opinion on something and someone (often simultaneously). Can the claws come out any more?

bland and still spicy. Leftover food can be packed or "parcelled" as they say in Delhi. A simple "parcel *karo*" (please pack) to the waiter is the appropriate instruction.

Tipping

Tipping is practised in mid- to high-end restaurants even though service and other mandatory taxes have already inflated the bill by about 30 per cent. There are no particular guidelines on how much to tip (some say 10 per cent), but generally it is Rp100–500, depending on the size of the bill. Service can range from shoddy to astonishingly pampering, the latter being a consistent norm in India's five-star hotels and restaurants.

HOSTING A PARTY

As the chill descends upon Delhi the party spirit rekindles. Parties can take the form of a potluck, where everyone chips in with a dish. Potlucks are generally informal where the food is served buffet style. If you have guests from different backgrounds, a potluck is a good way to try food from various countries and in turn trade recipes and make friends.

Formal parties require invites to be sent out ahead of time with RSVPs expected. A call a few days ahead to your guests is usually needed to confirm the attendance even if this does not guarantee that the guest will show up. Be prepared for this scenario as well as for guests who show up with an extra friend in tow. Do not be taken aback or offended; see this as a compliment. Indians are very hospitable and when they behave this informally around you, it usually means that they feel closer to you. Furthermore, all guests, whether invited or not, are highly honoured in Indian culture. Nevertheless, those familiar with Western etiquette will first ask if it is okay to bring a friend. A good host is expected to be warm and gracious in both situations.

Food

As a host, it is advisable to ask ahead of time if there are any dietary constraints, especially in the case of a formal sit-down dinner. Hindus and Sikhs do not eat beef and many Hindus are vegetarians. Muslims do not eat pork or drink alcohol. To avoid the many permutations for a large party, a meal served buffet-style is the most sensible option. It allows for a range of food that caters to various religious restrictions and dietary preferences. It can also accommodate unexpected guests and guests who are late (which is not unusual).

I find that it is always good to include a dish from your own country as a way to introduce guests to your culture. If that dish is non-vegetarian, you should announce this fact along with a description of the dish. But stay within the comfort zone of Western and Asian foods that Indians are generally familiar with, such as pasta and noodles. Also, choose something that is savoury. The Indian palette is accustomed to food with strong tastes, given the richness of Indian cuisine. There is also a preference for sauced-based dishes and sweet desserts.

Have Your Cake and Feed It Too

If you attend an Indian birthday party, you will find the usual familiar birthday wishes sung before the cake is cut by the birthday boy or girl. But when it comes to serving the cake, this is where many foreigners are stunned into reacting badly. It is customary for the birthday boy or girl to feed cake to family members and friends with their hands. It is considered an intimate gesture, so do not freeze awkwardly or worse, reject the cake from the celebrant. Receive that hand-fed morsel of cake gracefully; it's all part of the fun anyway.

Remember that vegetarian food generally excludes anything with eggs. Do check that your desserts, especially cakes and baked goods, do not contain eggs if you are catering for vegetarians. Cake shops do sell eggless versions of their cakes so do your homework ahead of time. As for what kind of cake to buy or bake—I find that Indians love anything chocolate. Who doesn't really?

CHAPTER 7

ENJOYING INDIA

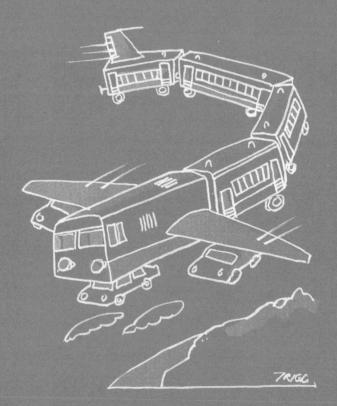

> ❝It was as if all my life I had been seeing
> the world in black and white and,
> when brought face-to-face with India,
> experienced everything re-rendered
> in brilliant technicolour.❞

—Keith Bellows

Enjoying India is enjoying the glass half full whilst dealing with the daily challenges that empty you of enthusiasm. Many newcomers only start to live again after the initial struggle of settling down is over after which comes acceptance (or numbness) and finally, enjoyment. There are infinite ways to channel stress, broaden your outlook and even change your person if you know where to look and how to get there. Therefore choose your poison and imbibe India. Cheers!

TRAVEL

Travel not only opens your mind to the infinite facets of India, it also lets you escape from your maddening crowd to join other such crowds in new places with familiar quirks. Journeying through India is really about going deep whilst spanning wide, rediscovering humanity and insanity in all possible places and particularly at the final destination—ourselves.

Planes

In recent years, domestic air travel has become common and affordable, making it the quickest and sometimes safest way to get from point to point in one piece. Different domestic carriers have varying standards of punctuality and professionalism, but the "experience" of air travel will usually come from your fellow travellers.

The pomp starts at the airport with the Wheelchair Parade, an inordinate number of elderly people who breeze through security upon their human-fuelled chariots. At the plane door, they leap out of their prior infirmed condition and walk normally to their awaiting seats. You can only marvel at these miracles of modern air travel before your attention is redirected to the Seat Warmer, that one particular character you find sitting firmly in your seat because she likes yours better. She might feign ignorance as she pretends to fumble for her boarding pass from a deep pocket of her deep handbag, in the hopes that during her search, you too might search your heart and acquiesce to her ruse. Stand your ground, air comrade. Take back that (aisle) seat. As the cabin fills up, so will the Water Boys who illustrate that the act of boarding a plane is terribly dehydrating. These are the people who will keep the flight attendants so busy fetching little pails of water that other passengers are left to tumble unassisted down the aisles themselves. After the parched are watered and Jack, Jill, Raj and Priya have settled down into their rightful seats, a member of the cabin crew will mark the start of the flight by jadedly asking everyone to turn off their cell phones because she knows they won't. Then she sits down, buckles up and stows away her frustration until she reaches cruising attitude.

Trains

For a more grounded experience, take a train journey on board the third largest rail network in the world. It could certainly look like a third of the world is travelling with you, judging by photos of Indian trains where people hang out, off, or on top of, stuffed carriages. But in reality train travel is quite comfortable depending on the type of train and class of seats.

The Rajadhani and Shatabdi Express trains are premium express trains that can save you time and discomfort, but you forego the authentic experience of having wind (and sand, dirt, smoke and other crap in the air) in your hair, the cool wet dew of morning or someone's spittle landing on your face (it happened to me), and the kindness of strangers as they "adjust" to make room for just one more person in a berth already full five persons ago.

If you are a woman (or group of women) travelling alone, note that there are women-only compartments in trains.

Before considering a cross-country train journey, check out the Indian Railways website (www.indianrail.gov.in) and other websites listed in Resource Guide (page 336) to get tips on which ticket is right for you and how to book them. The three pieces of advice I have are to book the tickets yourselves (or through a proper travel agent), not expect anything you are used to and watch your bags like a hawk. Bring rope or a lock and chain and tether your belongings to you like a ball and chain if you are not in the AC (air conditioned) classes.

TRIGG

Recounting our first experience in what not to do, we had arrived at our small hotel in Chennai and approached the concierge desk to book train tickets for the next day. On hindsight, the man standing *near* the desk dressed in normal clothes was not the hotel concierge but a convincing opportunist who had perfected his spiel about the grave difficulty of foreigners obtaining train tickets. We were much too young then to recognise cheats, much less their tactics of scaremongering. So we naively handed this alleged ticket miracle worker the sum he asked for with nary a bargain. Little did we know this marked our first life lesson on trust in India.

The next day he showed up punctually at dawn's break to pick us up and drive us to the train station. He asked us to wait outside presumably because it was crowded inside and then vanished into the dark urine-filled innards of the Chennai Central Railway Station. About 15 minutes later, he emerged with tickets in hand (he had gone in to buy tickets from the ticket counter, no miracle there). We followed him through a maze of sprawled homeless people amidst a garble of signs, overhead announcements, flies, beggars and touts to the right platform to wait for the train. When the train pulled in, he "helped" us on board by shoving all others aside so that we could clamour in peace up the steep stairs. Then with a toothy smile, he handed us our tickets before slinking away into the safety of anonymity.

We looked at the tickets once the train began to pull away. Sleeper Class Ordinary it said, the cost of each printed clearly and precipitously lower than what we had paid for and expected. A few hours later, they proved more valuable in other ways. Long story short, we lost our seats and I nearly lost my mind on that 13-hour ride through open land, open windows and open defecation. But we also experienced the open hearts of South Indians who shared their seats and their food. This was perhaps the real life lesson on trust in India: that it can surprise you, whether in the way that it's taken from you or by the way it turns out. Still, lock your bags! And don't look out your window at dawn.

About 10 years later, older and wiser, we took an express train (AC First Class) from Delhi to Jhansi. It was fully air-conditioned with assigned cushioned seats, meal service and glass windows. No *hijras* came on board dancing and clapping, no beggars, no *chai* boys walking through the aisle stuttering "*garam chai chai chai chai*" before leaping off the moving train as it pulls out of the station. The journey, whilst *relatively* safe and comfortable, ironically lacked the colour of the first "Ordinary" one, proving that Indian ordinary is really quite extraordinary. The glass on the sealed window also does something to you, making you feel more like a spectator watching the movie outside your window rather than being a part of the hurtling drama that is the Great Indian Rail journey.

Cracks of Dawn

An overnight train journey allows you to wake up to the sun rising gently over the Indian countryside, making slowly visible the tender fields of crops and crotches. Railway tracks seem to be the choicest spots for shanty folk to be caught with their pants down (or *dhotis* up) in the act of the morning ritual of greeting the sun with their cracks of dawn. And nothing gives you a better view than your train window.

For a reason yet unknown to me, people face the tracks and will smile at you as they openly defecate. There are even patterns suggesting that this is a communal activity. There are the perchers, those that squat in a line by the tracks with a respectable spacing between each person, the chatting pair in the fields facing each other because good gossip knows no boundaries, the tribe that forms a crotch circle, and lastly the introverts, whose solitary heads dot the fields in the far distance. The United Nations has recently estimated that up to 595 million people in India do not have access to toilets, and they generate about 65,000 tonnes of faeces every day, polluting water bodies and spreading the risk of disease.

Despite the government's efforts in constructing 8 million toilets (2016) under the Swachh Bharat (Clean India) mission, India still has the highest number of people defecating in the open because old habits die hard for the many who choose to continue to do so even after having newly-made toilets. The reason has partly to do with religion because many Hindu households believe that excreta should be kept away from the house and that cleaning toilets is the job of lower caste members. Abject poverty and ignorance about hygiene are other reasons why open defecation remains widespread, although numbers are declining.

As India tries to eradicate the practice of open defecation by 2019, the biggest stumbling block is not the lack of toilets, but rather the difficulty in convincing people to start using them. But progress is being made to educate and inculcate its practice. The sun will come up tomorrow on rural India, but today still very much belongs to the dawn.

Automobiles

A car is a scenic way to travel IF the roads are decent. For longer trips, you must have a liking for the open road, *dhaba* food, boat rides (because some roads are that bumpy) and the flagrant disregard of road rules. You must also have the ability to relieve yourself anywhere since there are very few proper bathroom stops (because along an Indian road, everywhere is a bathroom stop).

For short weekend getaways or day trips out of your city,

a chauffeur-driven car is the most relaxing way to travel. Just remember that you are expected to pay for the room and board of your driver if you are staying overnight. To get the best of both worlds if you are tight on time, pre-hire a car with a driver in your destination city. He can pick you up at the airport or train station and will serve as a reliable guide for the remainder of your trip within or around that city. Unless you are on a tight budget, I find this to be the most hassle-free solution than to have to constantly negotiate with taxi drivers in a new city.

The Delhi Exodus

Every year in May, Delhi empties itself out, leaving behind the have-nots and the could-nots and, in the very few cases like me, the will-nots. I loved Delhi too much to escape because there is no need to escape from my version of paradise, even if it comes with flies and heat. But May to September is a lonely time for the city, abandoned by Delhiites and expatriates for better climes and better times. It's the season when the travel bug bites the hardest and airfares are the highest. Book early if you must flee.

FESTIVALS

There are hundreds of festivals in India. It is said that if each festival day was declared a public holiday, the entire country would be in celebration for most of the year. Instead, 17 have been chosen as public holidays. These are good opportunities to soak in the culture and celebrate it with a happier India. Festival days fall into one of three main categories—national, religious or seasonal/harvest.

National Festivals

Patriotism runs high on the three national holidays. **Republic Day** (26 January) marks the birth of the Indian republic

Ordinary citizens find their own unique way of showing their patriotism.

when its constitution came into force. **Independence Day** (15 August) commemorates India's freedom from British rule in 1947. **Gandhi Jayanti** (2 October) celebrates Mahatma Gandhi's birthday.

Religious Festivals

India is a spiritual land and its religious festivals not only mark religious affiliations but also play a central part in ordering the lives and rhythms of time for Indians. Many regions have their own unique festivals and those celebrations common to all would have regional variations in the way and intensity in which they are celebrated. Because the country is predominantly Hindu, the festivals celebrated with great fanfare tend to be Hindu ones.

Dates vary year to year for Hindu and Muslim festivals because both follow the lunar calendar.

The most prominent are:

- **Holi** (March): Holi is a spring festival celebrated with particular exuberance and abandon in North India. It unofficially marks the end of winter. During Holi people throw *gulal* (coloured powder) and water at each other, men and women mingle freely, and *bhang* (marijuana) is traditionally consumed to heighten the euphoria. For your own safety, it is best to go to Holi parties hosted by your friends rather than to join a street celebration where men may use it as an excuse to grope women openly. Even if you do not consciously participate, anyone out on the street is considered fair game for children who wait in ambush with water guns, water balloons or buckets of water to throw onto people emerging from their homes or cars.

- **Krishna Janmashtami** (August/September): This festival commemorates the birthday of the god Krishna. The best celebration can be seen in Mumbai where people form a human pyramid and climb on top of each other to reach curd-filled clay pots strung off high buildings. Celebrations in Mathura, Krishna's birthplace, are also grand affairs.

- **Ganesh Chaturti** (September): This festival honours the Hindu elephant-headed god Ganesh. During the first few days of the festival, huge Ganesh statues are installed in homes and on special podiums. At the end of the festival, the statues are paraded through the streets and finally submerged into the ocean, accompanied by singing and dancing. The biggest and grandest celebration takes place in Mumbai.

- **Navaratri and Dussehra** (September/October): The period of nine days before Dussehra is known as Navaratri (or "nine nights") when there are prayers to the nine forms of the Mother Goddess. The 10th day is Dussehra, which celebrates Rama's victory over the demon Ravana as told in the great epic the Ramayana. On the night of Dussehra, huge effigies of Ravana are

An Indian woman draws a *rangoli* at her doorstep as part of her Diwali preparations. Made from coloured rice, flour, sand and flowers, *rangoli* designs are passed down through generations.

burnt to mark the triumph of good over evil. Dussehra celebrations are more prominent in North India than in the south. In West Bengal, Navaratri and Dussehra are celebrated as Durga Puja, marking instead the victory of the Hindu goddess Durga over the evil buffalo demon Mahishasura. Bengali communities throughout India celebrate Durga Puja but the biggest celebrations are seen in Kolkata.

- **Diwali** (October/November): Diwali (Deepavali in the south) is also known as the "Festival of Lights" because all across India, candles and *diyas* (oil lamps) are lit to mark the victory of good over evil, brightness over darkness, truth over ignorance. As a continuation of

Lighting for Lakshmi

Diwali is associated with many myths and legends but my favourite one was told to me by Mrs Dayal (which is also a cautionary tale against ostentatious lighting):

A long time ago there lived a poor man and his daughters in a land governed by a king. One day, as the queen was taking a bath in the river, an eagle swooped down and snatched her jewelled necklace that was placed on the riverbank. The queen was distraught at losing her beautiful necklace. Seeing his wife's sadness, the king announced that whoever returned the necklace would be given any reward they desire up to half his kingdom. All the land searched for the eagle and the necklace but both could not be found.

The poor man's clever youngest daughter advised her father to find a dead snake and place it on the roof. A few days later the eagle flew over the man's house and upon seeing the snake, dropped the necklace to pick up the snake. With the necklace in their possession, the old man and all his daughters argued about how much gold they would ask from the king. But it was the youngest daughter chosen to accompany her father to the palace.

When the king asked the man what he wanted as his reward, the girl interjected and asked that only the palace and her father's house be allowed to light up every Diwali. Months later on the night of Diwali, the whole village was in darkness except for the brightly lit palace and the poor man's house lit by the light of one candle. Lakshmi, the goddess of wealth, feeling helpless in the dark, rushed to enter the palace but it was so bright that she turned away. Then she spied the humbly lit poor man's house that was more to her liking and she entered.

Year after year this happened and the poor man became richer and richer because of the annual visits of the goddess of wealth and the foresight of his clever young daughter.

the Dussehra narrative, it celebrates the triumphant return of Rama and his wife Sita to their kingdom of Ayodhya after the defeat of the demon Ravana. Diwali is a five-day long celebration, with the main celebration occurring on the third night, when the air is lit with the glow of oil lamps in and around virtually all homes amidst the noise and smoke from firecrackers and fireworks going off all the way till dawn. The lighted lamps are also meant to attract and welcome the goddess of wealth Lakshmi, who is said to roam the earth on Diwali blessing homes she visits. *Pujas* to the goddess are also conducted on this night.

Note that your domestic staff may ask for all five days off as some Indians consider it a new year celebration and would require the full five days for preparations, prayers and festivities. The five days of Diwali are Dhanteras, Choti Diwali, Diwali (public holiday), Padwa, and Bhai Duj. Each day has it own significance, traditions and prayers. Some may also request time to travel to their villages to celebrate with their families as they consider this the most important celebration in the year. Officially, there is only one day off (a public holiday) for Diwali.

You know when Diwali is coming when the air grows crisp and the tents go up for the greatest shopping experience in Delhi—Diwali *melas* (fairs). There are public and private *melas* (usually organised by associations and embassy schools), both equally festive and selling all manner of things including lights and Christmas ornaments. Diwali to Indians is like Christmas to Westerners. People prepare for it by cleaning and decorating their homes and buying new clothes, gold, jewellery, kitchen utensils and gifts for their families. New clothes are traditionally worn on Diwali.

The best way to spend Diwali is at an Indian home. It allows you to observe the traditions behind it and also the importance that Indians place on family. At the Dayals, we hung extra garlands of LED lights from our windows and around the trees in the garden to increase the chances of attracting the goddess of wealth. It is hard not to get swept up in the festive spirit. There is indeed something magical about sparks, firecrackers and the glow of thousands of oil lamps in the neighbourhood. You feel connected to an older, much larger story set across India, where for a day people are laying down their burdens to restore their hope in the triumph of all things good, in family and in prosperity finding them soon. For me, Diwali rekindles the warm memory of our Indian family—the Dayals, Santosh and Madhu—and the notion that love triumphs everything. I have always had a candle lit inside me for India and during Diwali; it multiplies a thousandfold to the burst of spectacular fireworks.

Seasonal/Harvest Festivals

These festivals mark the harvesting of crops and the change of seasons, which are considered auspicious times. The major harvest festivals are Pongal, Onam and Baisakhi.

- **Pongal** (14 January): This is Tamil Nadu's major harvest festival and is celebrated over four days. "*Pongal*" in Tamil means "to boil", and this festival is celebrated as a thanksgiving ceremony for the year's harvest. On the second day, a sweet rice pudding called *pongal* is boiled in earthern pots and offered to the sun god. On the third day, cattle are adorned with bells and worshipped.

- **Basant Panchami** (February): This marks the first day of spring and is mainly celebrated in North India. People wear yellow to symbolise the mustard blooms in the fields. In East India, this day is celebrated as Saraswati Puja to honour the goddess of learning and wisdom.

Before major festivals, flower vendors sprout up at street corners and garland the streets with their jasmine and marigold wares.

- **Baisakhi** (April): This is the harvest festival for North India and is better known as Punjab's harvest festival. It is also the Sikh New Year.
- **Onam** (August/September): Onam is the biggest festival in Kerala. This 10-day harvest festival welcomes home the mythical King Mahabali, who once ruled Kerala during its golden age. During this festival, Kerala's rich culture and heritage are on display with carnivals, fireworks, boat races and the traditional *Kathakali* dance performances unique to Kerala.

New Year's Days

New Year's Day (1 January) is not unique as it is one of many new years in India, depending on which calendars you use (Gregorian, lunar) and which state you live in. The Hindu New Year starts in April and is called by various names, such as Ugadi (Karnataka and Andhra Pradesh), Gudi Padwa (Maharashtra), Bohag Bihu (Assam). The Parsi New Year is in August, the Sikkimese one in December and the Islamic one (Muharram) varies in date. Another type of new year is the Indian financial new year which falls on Diwali (following another calendar called the Vikram Samvat) where merchants close old account books and open new ones with prayers to the goddess Lakshmi for success.

THE ARTS

Religion is found at the centre of almost every aspect of Indian life, including the arts. Sculpture, architecture, music, dance and theatre all reflect the religious imprint on the Indian artistic mind. To appreciate Indian art therefore requires an understanding of the role religion has played in the creative impulse since the beginnings of Indian culture till today.

Indian art traces its first beginnings in the artefacts and seals of the Harappan civilisation. The next phase began with the stone decorations of early religious monuments, chiefly Buddhist stupas and Hindu temples, which became more

A Madhubani artist shows off his painting. Originally painted on walls by women of the household, this traditional art from Bihar is still practised today.

elaborate and more profuse with sculpture over time. Indian sculpture too began with religious-inspired iconography, first in the depictions of the Buddha and later evolved into those of Hindu gods. Exuberance, sensuality and vivid tactile presence were the hallmarks of the early periods of Indian sculpture. In later developments, sculpture as well as other artistic fields began to follow a codified set of ideal canons of form that confined expression to well-laid-down rules. For example, architecture followed strict principles of proportion according to sacred prototypes. Music, dance and drama similarly adhered to principles spelt out in the 3rd-century treatise called the Natya Shastra, considered the most comprehensive ancient Hindu treatise and handbook on the performing arts.

Much of the art of the past drew its themes from Indian folklore, myths and India's two great epics—the Mahabharata

The Great Indian Epics

The Ramayana and the Mahabharata are the two great Indian epics that have had an enduring influence on Indian culture, art and philosophy since their said beginnings in 500 BC.

The Ramayana (or "journey of Rama") details the life of the hero Rama who was prevented from becoming the king of Ayodhya by his stepmother, who sent him together with his wife Sita and brother Lakshman into exile. The 10-headed demon king Ravana, having heard of Sita's beauty, abducted her and fled to his capital of Lanka. Rama, Lakshman and monkey god Hanuman pursued Ravana, eventually killing him to rescue Sita. The story extols the virtues of *dharma* (duty) and loyalty to family members as well as the karmic consequences of evil. The Ramayana has been expressed in art, poetry, dance, drama and sculpture not only in India, but also in Southeast Asia. Rama is also worshipped as the seventh avatar of the Hindu god Vishnu.

The Mahabharata is the longest poem in the world (eight times the Iliad and Odyssey combined) and tells the story of the political struggle between five Pandava brothers and their 100 cousins of the Kaurava clan during the Vedic age. Originally narrated by the sage Vyasa and written down by the elephant god Ganesh, the story builds to the pivotal battle at Kurukshetra. The heart of the epic is the Bhagavad Gita, the sermon spoken between the god Krishna and Pandava prince, Arjuna, before the battle. The Bhagavad Gita broadly discusses the concepts integral to Hindu ethics and morality and thus contains the philosophical foundations of the Hindu religion.

and Ramayana. These narratives continue to provide inspiration and guide the daily lives of millions of Indians today. In modern artistic expression, you can still detect that old spiritual muse, shaped by various techniques across time to meet the 21st century.

Indian music and dance are as old as its culture itself, with music believed to have originated with the Rig Veda (circa 5000 BC) as hymns and chants. Both continued as modes of worship in temples before taking on a more secular form with royal patronage. They have been the vehicles of Hindu mythology and religious philosophy for centuries, spread by singers and poet saints. Today, traditional music and dance are still appreciated, bringing the experience of thousands of years from the temples to the performance halls of our time.

Music

Indian classical music is based on melody (*raga*) and rhythm (*tala*) There are two main Indian classical styles: Hindustani and Carnatic.

- **Hindustani music** is often called the North Indian style of classical music. It consists of the *raga* (melodic line) and the *tala* (rhythmic cycle). There are over 100 *ragas*, with each assigned to represent a particular time of day and to evoke a particular mood. A performance would begin with the slow invocation of a *raga* and then the tempo is added and quickened to a rapid-paced climax. The performance would comprise a voice or one or several traditional musical instruments. In medieval times, Hindustani music gradually differentiated itself more from Carnatic music because of Muslim royal patronage, first from the Delhi Sultans and then by the Mughals, where it took on Persian elements. New *ragas*, *talas* and musical forms were invented with emphasis shifting from what was being performed to how it was being performed. Ravi Shankar, one of India's most famous sitar players, is credited for introducing Indian classical music to the West.

- The classical music of South India is called **Carnatic music** and it too is based on *ragas* and *talas*. It differs mainly in that it is almost entirely devotional in character and uses a different set of instruments.

Another category of music is devotional music, called *bhajan*, *kirtan* or *abhang*. Closer to folk music, it focuses less on form and more on creating a mystical and emotional experience when played during religious festivals and in temples.

Festivals

Music festivals are usually held in large cities, so there are plenty of opportunities to experience traditional performances. Chennai is the leading centre of Carnatic music. Concerts are held in small auditoriums called *sabhas* and a typical concert lasts for three hours. During the music and dance season in Chennai (15 December–15 January), as many as 500 concerts are held.

Dance

According to one legend, the art of dance was revealed through the graceful movements of the god Vishnu as he battled two demons. Seeing Vishnu's skilled movements, his consort Lakshmi persuaded him to disclose the secrets of dance to Brahma, who then imparted it to Shiva. In sculpture, Shiva is often depicted as the Nataraj (Lord of the Dance) performing the Tandava, a dance that symbolises the cosmic cycles of creation and destruction. The Nataraj form was developed in South India in the 9th and 10th centuries by artists during the Chola period through a series of bronze sculpture. By the 12th century, Shiva as the Nataraj achieved canonical stature.

The art of dance is rooted in the spiritual. It is said to evoke the oneness of god and creation through the dancer and her dance. It is characterised by graceful expression of eyes, hands, body postures and face according to the principles laid out in the Natya Shastra. There are 180 different styles of dance but the four well-known surviving forms are *bharatnatyam* (Tamil Nadu), *kathak* (North India), *odissi* (Odisha) and *kathakali* (Kerala). You can attend performances or pick a class to learn the basic moves. *Bharatnatyam* and *kathak* are relatively easier to pick up and adult classes are available. A word to the rickety-kneed: *Bharatnatyam* requires you to bend your knees for an insanely long time. For children, it is a matter of discipline to keep the knees in the bent pose but for adults, it borders on torture.

Bharatnatyam is the oldest dance and evolved from the temple dances of the *devadasis*, young girls dedicated to the temple from childhood. It is characterised by chiselled movements, expressive eyes and hands, and a distinctive bent-leg position.

Kathak originated from storytellers and assumed the form of courtly entertainment in the royal courts of North India. A whole class of dancing courtesans emerged and *kathak* eventually took on a Hindu-Muslim flavour. Both men and women can perform *kathak*, which is performed straight legged and with ankle bells to mark the rhythmic beat. Elaborate footwork and pirouettes characterise this dance form.

A *kathakali* performer in traditional costume.

Odissi dance developed in the temples of Odisha. It is curved, sensuous and graceful, and are characterised by highly sculptural poses, as if the temple sculpture were brought to life. The dance is mostly religious in nature and revolves around the stories of the god Krishna.

Kathakali ("story play") lies between dance and theatre and is unique to Kerala. Male actors enact legends or stories from the Mahabharata without speaking, relying only on facial movements and hand gestures to convey expressions and dialogues. The costumes are distinct for their huge voluminous skirts and large headgear. Faces are painted various colours: green to signify divine or heroic characters and black for demons.

There are also numerous folk dances, which are specific to regions and more spontaneous than the canonical classical dance forms. They are performed at religious and seasonal festivals or as entertainment. In the Deccan, women perform the *banjara*, dancing in a circle yodelling a monotonous tune. In Gujarat, men and women traditionally perform the *garba* dance during the nine-day Hindu festival of Navaratri.

Bollywood Dance

If you love Indian dance as much as I do and similarly do not have the flexibility of a five-year-old or the grace of a gazelle, then you can try *kathak* and *bharatnatyam*'s modern slutty teen sister—Bollywood dance. As long as you can shake your hips and shoulders vigorously, flick your hair and do imaginary household chores, you are ready to take on Bollywood. Feeding chickens, wiping windows, patting a dog whilst changing a light bulb; if you can imagine these, then you've got some moves down already. Do them whilst moving your shoulders up and down and you've mastered *bhangra*. Bollywood dance brings out the Indian *joie de vivre*, from the wobbly two-year-old to the grey-haired grandma, who may out-dance you at parties and festivals. A good sign that you've imbibed India is when you too break out in *bhangra* at the drop of a b-b-b-beat.

BOLLYWOOD AND INDIAN CINEMA
Bollywood

The Indian love for singing, dancing and drama come together in popular form through Bollywood. India's behemoth filmmaking industry, based in Mumbai, churns out more movies per year than Hollywood itself, from which it partly takes its name. Melodrama, over-acting, romance, comedy and violence, interspersed with songs and dance and multiple costume changes, characterise a typical Bollywood film. The aim is not realism or even logic and scientific laws, but escape

and fantasy to distract the masses from the real drama in their own lives. The price of a ticket can buy you three full hours (or more) of a world where good guys win, love and romance prevail and the gods come through without fail for the devoted. It is no wonder that Bollywood consistently outsells Hollywood in worldwide ticket sales year after year, offering the illusive pills of a dream life to those in dire need of a dream.

To get you up and running on this pinnacle of popular culture, here is a brief guide on what to expect in a Bollywood movie.

Plot

Do not get your hopes up here. At best, it will be as light as a *dosa* and at worst, completely illogical, which seems almost ironic for a country with the art for the narrative. Most of the time, the usual tired (yes, tired)-and-tested formula is applied: there's a boy, a girl, crying parents, a tragedy, villains with evil moustaches and a comic sidekick in the form of an idiot politician or lackey. They fight, they cry, they dance, they make up. Three hours later, all is well. Don't overthink it, don't even bother looking for it. Just enjoy the movie for its pure entertainment. If there is any plot, this is it: the movie can have box-office success if the actors are well known and the song and dance numbers are chart hits. As for the story, well, that's another story.

Characters

There is always a hero. And then there are the supporting characters who help him realise his herodom—the villain, the bad guys, the adoring heroine and his long-suffering mother. Bollywood's hero is strong, handsome, muscular and dance-inclined. He also loves his mom and cries when emotions get too much for his hefty handsome self. The bad guys never cry; they just laugh evilly. Do not be fooled by their evil black clothes, which do nothing but mock their terrible inability to kill or hurt the hero even if they have the numerical advantage, plus guns and other weapons.

Now cue the wind machine for Bollywood's heroine to make her entrance with her fan-swept flowing shampoo-ad hair. She is the putative virgin with the big doe eyes and beautiful body she is not aware of. She is sexually innocent until she is with the hero, virile enough to sweep her off her virtue-crusted pedestal and cause her (*sari*'s) fall. Sometimes she is portrayed as the "Westernised" antithesis to traditional Indian values (read: patriarchy) in her short skirts and big earrings. But once she dons a *sari*, she becomes the virtuous Indian woman (patriarchy heaves a sigh of relief). *Sari* on, all is well.

Song and Dance

A Bollywood film is not one without the sequences of song

and dance in spectacular locations. What once used to take place in fields and around coconut trees of rural India are now filmed against Icelandic glaciers, the Swiss Alps, in Spanish streets and other picture-perfect locales, adding to the escape of romance, the escape of travel.

Song-and-dance sequences, called "item numbers", play up the growing intimate relationship between the hero and heroine as she swings her hips into his heart. The playful dalliances of the two lovers are often chaperoned by an entourage of a hundred other dancers (perhaps a commentary on how hard it is to get alone time in India!). In a windy/rainy world of their own, they do what all lovers do—flirt, sing, dance, giggle, fall in love and change costumes every few minutes. No one said love was easy in India. But you and I know that once the music stops, so do the chances of staying together, the poor things. But we can always count on the predictably applied ending. Tears and a near-tragedy later, they reunite and all is well.

Bollywood Actors

They are the gods of the big screen. Love them or hate them, they will be the centre of popular culture and even more popular gossip, so you should at least arm yourself with some names. Amitabh Bachchan (known as Big B) is a Bollywood giant, as is Shah Rukh Khan (affectionately known as SRK). Other popular actors that have had a huge fan following for years are Hrithik Roshan (my favourite) and Salman Khan (known as Bhai). The indisputable and unchallenged Queen of Bollywood dance remains Madhuri Dixit. As with Hollywood actresses, Bollywood leading ladies seem to have a shorter shelf life than their male counterparts. But it has been India's actresses and not its actors that have broken through to Hollywood, such as Priyanka Chopra and Deepika Padukone, while remaining wildly popular at home as well. My personal bone to pick is that Indian actresses were once curvy, voluptuous sirens whose belly rolls proudly peeked under their *saris*. But the Bollywood heroine of today is 50 pounds lighter, a foot taller, a shade fairer and armed with a beauty pageant or model background. *Kya hua* (what happened)? All *was* well.

Tollywood, Kollywood and Art Films

The Indian film industry reflects the cultural, linguistic and social diversity of India. Bollywood is also often used mistakenly to mean Indian cinema, but it is only a part of the total film industry, which have centres in other regions and who produce regional films with their own fan base. Whilst Bollywood is mainly Hindi-based with a pan-Indian appeal, the two others are the Tamil (Kollywood) and Telugu film industries (Tollywood), which each having their own strong following. Although Bollywood films still dominate, things are starting to change, with Tollywood shaking Mumbai's traditional hold over Indian cinema. Tamil Nadu's Kollywood is also upping its standards and together the south is beginning to give Bollywood a further reason to shake.

India's art films, known as parallel cinema, have a large appreciative audience in the West, attributed to films by famous director Satyajit Ray (1921–1992), India's first internationally recognised filmmaker. Art films have less song-and-dance and more high-brow intellectualism, which means they don't make for profitable mainstream Indian cinema. You can watch them at cultural centres and film societies.

LITERATURE AND READING

Narrative has always been integral in transmitting Indian values and culture from ancient times. Stories, myths and legends have such a hold on the Indian mind that it comes as no wonder that India has produced some of the best writers and storytellers, with a populace known to be one of the world's most avid readers and appreciators of the written and spoken word.

If you love books, you are in the right place to collect them and to consume them. India is a bibliophile's paradise

ink

TRIGG

and books come a dime a dozen in the generous number of bookshops around the city. Going into one is not a matter of selecting the right book, but exercising restraint. Without it, you run the danger of cutting off social ties altogether and overloading your bookshelves to collapse. To get your head out of the books, there are also literature festivals to meet and mingle with the like-minded throughout India. The Jaipur Literature Festival is one of the most outstanding ones with acclaimed local and international writers invited as speaking guests in a charged atmosphere for bookworms to become social butterflies.

Literature Festivals
January
- Jaipur Literature Festival: *www.jaipurliteraturefestival.org*
- Lucknow Literary Festival:
  www.lucknowliteraryfestival.com
- Chennai Literary Festival: website unavailable

February

- Appejay Kolkata Literary Festival: *www.aklf.in*
- Delhi Literature Festival:
  www.newdelhiworldbookfair.gov.in
- Hyderabad Literary Festival: *www.hydlitfest.in*

November

- Tata Literature Live: The Mumbai Lit Fest:
  www.tatalitlive.in

December

- Bangalore Literature Festival:
  www.bangaloreliteraturefestival.org
- Goa Arts and Literary Festival: *www.goaartlitfest.com*
- Kochi International Book Festival:
  www. bookfestkochi.org

Famous Indian Writers

Bankim Chandra Chatterjee (1838–1894) is known as the father of the modern novel in India and greatly influenced generations after him. But it was Rabindranath Tagore who is credited as the most vital force in the cultural renaissance of Indian literature, representing its finest achievement. It is said that novels and short stories attained maturity in Tagore's gifted hands. In 1913, he won a Nobel Prize in literature, the first non-European to do so. Two of his works live on as the national anthems of India (Jana Gana Mana) and Bangladesh (Amar Shonar Bangla).

Bengal has also given the world the unlikeliest "Indian" author: George Orwell (1903–1950), who was born Eric Arthur Blaire to Anglo-Indian parents in Motihari.

The list of exceptional Indian authors can fill a hundred

more pages and a thousand more nights. Therefore there is much armchair satisfaction to be found in the discovery of the works of the Indian pen.

CHESS

A game believed to have originated in India is chess. It appeared around AD 600 as a game called Chaturanga and was later introduced into Persia and further adopted by the Arabs in the 8th century. The Arabs subsequently spread the game to Europe, where it evolved into its current form. Some scholars argue that chess originated in China. To date there are no firm theories to its origins, but there are legends surrounding its invention in India.

One such legend is the story of a king who loved to play games. He had played all the games in his kingdom and wanted a new game that was more challenging. One day he commissioned a mathematician to design a new one. After months of struggle, the mathematician came up with the game of Chaturanga, a game played on an 8×8 square board. The king loved this game so much that he offered to give the mathematician anything he wished for. The smart mathematician asked for one grain of rice for the first square, two grains for the second, four grains for the third, 16 for the fourth and so on until the 64th square was reached. "Is that all?" laughed the king. Then he ordered his servants to lay down the grains of rice as per the sequence. By the 30th square, all the grains of rice in the kingdom had been used. The king, realising that he was unable to fulfil the mathematician's wish, made him his top advisor in the kingdom. Since I'm no mathematician, I will leave it to you to calculate the grains that were needed for the 64th square.

CRICKET

The world's second largest country has just one nationally popular sport: cricket. Most outsiders will never fully understand the Indian obsession with the game that originated from other shores. But it is important to appreciate a sport that can bring the entire country to a halt and influence the mood of millions of people during match days.

India has reigned supreme on the world's cricket fields, as it does similarly so on any other field or street in India. It is played professionally in stadiums, recreationally in parks and socially at networking events, where cricket talk is a good way to find friends (or make enemies). So acquaint yourself with the rules of the game, terminology, matches and key players or better yet, get some hands-on experience.

Cricket players are idolised like movie stars or national heroes. In 2014, India awarded its highest civilian honour, the Bharat Ratna, to Sachin Tendulkar, a recently retired batsman.

Cricket has come a long way as the summer game for a

Cricket is so well loved that any place can turn into a cricket field.

small British and Indian elite. Now it is a populist, celebrity-heavy, politicised, billion-dollar industry and that, if anything, makes it a spectator sport of some interest. But I shall not be a spoilsport for those who love the players and their game.

NATURE

There are enough national parks and wildlife sanctuaries in India to fuel and fill your photo albums with India's indigenous birds and animals. India alone has seven natural UNESCO World Heritage Sites (see page 322) recognised for their rich biodiversity. Some of the more popular (and accessible) national parks are:

- **Corbett National Park, Uttarakhand:** India's first national park established in 1936 by legendary tiger hunter Jim Corbett is famous for its tigers. It is 260km from Delhi by road, which is the most popular way to get there. Otherwise air and train travel are also possible.

- **Rathambore National Park, Rajasthan:** This park is popular because of its proximity to Delhi and because it has luxury accommodation available for the less nature-inclined. The attraction is the tiger sightings, which are said to be fairly frequent, except during the time of Mr Dayal's visit. He came back thoroughly disappointed, with a consolation picture of a tiger snapped from a poster in his hotel lobby. No one can argue against his tiger sighting, even if it was a paper one.

- **Keoladeo National Park, Rajasthan:** Located 50km from Agra, this was once a duck shooting reserve for the maharajas. Today it is an important bird sanctuary renowned for its large congregation of non-migratory resident birds.

- **Kanha National Park, Madhya Pradesh:** The park was the setting for Rudyard Kipling's *The Jungle Book* and is home to tigers and *barasingha* (swamp deer) among others.
- **Kaziranga National Park, Assam:** Home to the largest population of one-horned rhinoceroses.
- **Sundarbans National Park, West Bengal:** The world's largest mangrove forest is also one of the top tourist places in the state and can be explored only by boat. It supports the single largest population of tigers.

NIGHTLIFE

India is not usually known for its nightlife because of curfews that require places to close early. Nonetheless, night owls still have an increasing number of watering holes to frequent, even if they have to start the fun earlier. Mumbai calls the (vodka) shots when it comes to the wide range of trendy new bars found in Bandra, South Mumbai and Colaba. Goa has a reputation as coastal party central with its range of bars and clubs. Bengaluru has a booming pub culture bar none.

Besides the bars and clubs, there is the "resto-bar", a restaurant and bar where you can grab a meal, dance and drink till curfew.

To party till dawn and not be subject to Cinderella-like timings, you will need to go to bars and clubs that operate in five-star hotels, which are exempt from the curfew. There you will find the affluent, who can afford to pay more for drinks for the chance to party longer and harder. Sometimes you may spot a Bollywood star well into the night. In Delhi, these are generally the safest night venues for foreign women looking to stay past the midnight hour.

Teetotallers have also plenty of options to enjoy live music, comedy and cultural performances in the major cities. Event information can be found online or in the local newspaper.

To Drink or Not to Drink

The age of legal consumption of alcohol varies according to the state but generally it is 21 years of age. In Delhi it is 25 and Goa, 18. In Mumbai, it is 25 for spirits, 21 for beer. Gujarat and Bihar are "dry states" which means alcohol is illegal without a permit. In Kerala, the sale of alcohol is restricted. Also note that many states have "dry days", on which the sale of alcohol is not permitted

CLUBS AND GYMS

Social Clubs

Many denizens of a certain vintage spend their weekends or evenings at Gymkhana clubs, cricket clubs and polo clubs, which retain their Raj-era atmosphere. The appeal of such clubs is timeless as symbols of social and political prestige and for its access to powerful networks. Membership is coveted even today, made particularly more valuable in some instances by its rarity.

The Dayals brought us a few times to the Delhi Gymkhana, where wicker chairs, a timber-clad ballroom for socials, and the genteel manners of its members all spoke of a charm that never quite left 1947. At the Delhi Gymkhana, it is said that permanent membership opens up upon the demise of another member (but it could also be due to a long waiting list and limited availability). My friend waited 17 years to get hers, and she showed off her card like a winning lottery ticket.

The good news for time-strapped foreigners is that these clubs have temporary memberships available for expatriates, but you have to be introduced by an existing member to qualify, and even then, under certain terms and conditions.

In Delhi, expatriates have the additional choices of embassy clubs, which may offer temporary membership to diplomats of other countries or non-diplomats who are citizens of that country. You should check these options out first to see if these clubs have the facilities and recreational activities that suit you.

I used to go to the American Club for zumba classes without having to become a member (but could not use any other facilities). I was also a member of the Italian Cultural Institute, where you can learn Italian and attend planned events but it was a less cultural, more culinary motive for me since the Institute also had one of the best Italian restaurants in town on its premises. My new-found tongue was confined to the menu.

Health Clubs and Gyms

You can find health clubs in five-star hotels, where being a member allows you access to the hotel pool, gym and other facilities. Although membership is expensive, many expatriates in Delhi see this as a reasonable trade-off for facilities that are clean and well maintained, especially for the pool. For gym facilities alone, there are alternatives places such as premium health club chains that offer the gym as well as additional services like personal training, and spa and beauty services. International gym chains are also present in India.

An alternative to getting your workout is to hit the parks. Delhi has plenty of great parks to take a walk in, such as Lodhi Gardens. The reasons why people opt out of this are pollution and, for the less populated parks, safety.

YOGA

India is the birthplace of yoga. Many Indians believe yoga is necessary to maintain good health and strength for a stronger and longer life. Therefore there is less of the stereotypical glamour of timber-floored studios and tight yoga pants of the West, and more of the serious focus on mind and body in relatively modest settings. The marked difference to me was how yoga seemed to be for everyone and not just the mystical, svelte and flexible. I have seen both the old and the obese slip effortlessly into a handstand and it opened my eyes (or maybe *chakra*) to how accessible yoga is in India.

There are ample classes to choose from, which teach the different forms of yoga, such as hatha yoga, ashtanga yoga and iyengar yoga. Lessons can be conducted in studios, homes and ashrams. I eventually chose to get private hatha yoga lessons at home (yes, you can!) because as a beginner I felt I needed personalised attention to get the basic poses right. My yoga guru Priyanka tailor-made the poses (*asanas*) for me to fit my flexibility level (none) and ailments (many) to

BREATHING 19...20...

generate the most benefit from the *asanas* in the comfort of my own home and sweat pants. Hence I saluted the sun twice a week and learnt how to let my stress leave with my breath in what I call the screwit-asan. Priyanka, the model for yogic patience, tolerated my creative terms and my downward dogged insistence on holding the *savasan* (corpse position) for far longer than needed. I called it restful meditation; she called it out as napping. Nothing gets past the seeker of love and light.

Those who are already further up on the transcendental ladder of yoga practitioners (yogis) may want to take the opportunity in India to further their practice by joining an ashram or a yoga school to train as a yoga instructor. Ashrams are usually located in far-off scenic locations with strong spiritual energy, creating an ideal setting for the traditional practice of yoga. Professional and even beginner courses are available and may span several weeks or months. Style and approaches vary, so it's best to do the research before joining an ashram. If you are a resident of India, you may also be entitled to local rates versus the "foreign" rates that are charged to foreigners who come to India to study yoga.

Yoga Vacations and Yoga Festivals

If you ask me to go on a holiday where I eat only *dal* and vegetables for a week and have to wake at 5am daily to greet the sun, I might not be so quick to call it a "holiday". But that is because I have yet to be enlightened enough to the spiritual and mental benefits of such a vacation. For some, this is the most ideal way to relax and breathe their troubles away; a yoga vacation in the mountains where the only itinerary is to meditate and stretch with other like-minded soul-searchers. Many ashrams do cater for these short getaways of quiet alone time.

If you prefer quiet alone time with hundreds of others, then consider a yoga festival. The International Yoga Festival is one of the biggest annual yoga gatherings in the world. It happens every March in Rishikesh, the small Himalayan holy town with the biggest yoga reputation. There are also other smaller yoga festivals throughout the country, which are good for yogis who prefer something more intimate.

Rishikesh

Rishikesh is one of the most popular destinations for yoga in India. Known as the "birthplace of yoga" and made famous by the Beatles, it is a holy town with temples, ashrams and yoga schools that cater to various styles of yoga and meditation. It is situated at the banks of the Ganges River and many believe that meditation here brings salvation. In 1968, the Beatles travelled to Rishikesh to attend meditation training. It was their interest in meditation and Indian culture that helped enlighten the West to Indian spirituality.

VOLUNTEERING

Volunteering is an excellent way of engaging with the local culture while contributing constructively. There are thousands of Indian and international NGOs (non-governmental organisations) operating in India, addressing a variety of issues from social and environmental causes to animal protection. You can narrow down the list by first enquiring at your own embassy or expatriate community if they are supporting any particular NGO or have affiliated volunteer programmes. You should also determine what cause(s) you want to get behind and the extent of commitment you are willing to make.

Other than your time, there are also charity organisations where you can donate money, food, old clothes, books, etc. In short, there are plenty of ways to contribute and many causes in need of people, funding and resources. You have an opportunity to change a life in India, so don't waste it. In so doing, you might find yourself changed as well. As Mahatma Gandhi more eloquently put it: "The best way to find yourself is to lose yourself in the service of others."

CHAPTER 8

LEARNING THE LANGUAGE

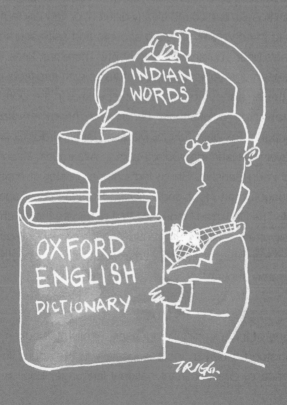

> If you talk to a man in a language he understands, that goes to his head. If you talk to him in his own language, that goes to his heart.

—Nelson Mandela

To be able to speak across India, you need to be well versed in India's 22 official languages and over 720 dialects. But if you are nowhere near polyglot-level, then you can settle for the country's two most widely spoken languages: Hindi (41%) and English. Ah, you say, I know one of them already! Prepare to be surprised. The English you speak and the English an Indian speaks can sound clearly different or vaguely familiar, helped in no way by differing accents and self-assurances of one's prior English-speaking ability. Therefore, keep your ears open and your mind even more so with this fact: India has the largest number of English speakers in the world.

Alongside English are Hindi and the other official languages: Bengali, Telugu, Marathi, Tamil, Urdu, Gujarati, Malayalam, Kannada, Odia, Punjabi, Assamese, Kashmiri, Sindhi and Sanskrit. South India has a greater diversity of languages than North India, which predominantly speaks Hindi. The Dravidian languages that dominate the south are usually state-specific, such as Kannada, which is spoken only in Karnataka. Hindi may be understood in the south but very rarely spoken.

ENGLISH AND INDIA

As one of India's official languages, English is spoken and understood widely in India, especially in the south. In the absence of one dominant national language, English has served as a linguistic bridge across diverse regional tongues. Hindi was the official language of the British Raj and continues to be the language for the educated elite and its aspirants, who see it as a mark of social status. It is also the most important language for national, political and commercial communication.

The country's educated elite are well versed in English, many having levels of proficiency far exceeding native English speakers from other countries. At the other end, those in rural India speak no more than a word. For the large middle, however, proficiency and fluency vary and your comprehension boils down to how well you interpret the heavy Indian accent and how clued in you are to the English most Indians speak today, the adopted and adapted result of the Queen's English having percolated 300 years through the Indian cultural filter.

Indian English

If you have problems understanding the English spoken in India, it is because Indian English is a language onto itself, with its own structure, vocabulary and pronunciations (and mispronunciations). It reflects the Indian middle class that thinks in "Indian" but speaks in English. The result is an entire lexicon of English phrases and words peculiar to India (aptly called Indianisms). For example, if someone wants to *prepone* a date, only those accustomed to the patois and the millions of Indians who have *preponed* things their entire life would know to move their schedule forward. Therefore to better communicate in English, you would need to learn English in this form. Yes, I too, dear reader, see the painful irony but it is more painful to miscommunicate, misunderstand and miss part of the fun that comes with learning things anew. You will soon find that Indianisms are endearing and effective ways of condensing long ideas, which will make you wonder by the end of your time in India why standard English should not adopt some of them.

Here are a few to start you off:

- *"Prepone"*: to bring forward, the opposite of postpone. It actually makes perfect sense. Standard English *has* adopted this one; it was added to the Oxford English Dictionary in 2010.

- **"Kindly adjust"**: This is the Indian version of "Sorry, please excuse the inconvenience I am causing, but I can't do anything much about it right now." It's what Indians say when forced to share an already packed train or elevator. But they will make room for one more no matter what.

- **"Your good name, please"**: This sounds pompous, but it is just the direct translation of the same Hindi question. Like prepone, it's an efficient and polite way of saying, "I'm sorry, I did not catch your name."

- **"Do the needful"**: This is the granddaddy of all Indianisms and is used mostly by and for bureaucrats. This short phrase means "I will not give you specific instructions but you are expected to understand since it's your job."

- **"Veg or non-veg"**: Since there are so many vegetarians in India (and indeed it is the default option in most restaurants), "non-veg" becomes an identity in itself. This very simple dichotomy is seen not only on food menus but also in matrimonial columns. "Veg "simply means "I'm vegetarian so just vegetables and no eggs or fish". "Non-veg" is "I eat anything". An extension of this is "eggetarian", a person who is vegetarian but eats eggs. "Non-veg jokes" means dirty jokes though.

- **"Timepass":** This is used to describe anything that implies passing time or wasting it on frivolous activities. "I went to the mall. Timepass." means "I went to the mall to kill some time because my next appointment was near there and going home was not an option."

- **"Expired":** If your driver tells you that his father has expired, offer condolences. It means that his father has died.

- **"Intimate":** When someone promises to intimate you later, do not take it as a declaration of future harassment. It simply means "inform".

- **"You people":** This is just a translation from Hindi, and is not meant to be divisive. It is similar to the plural "you" when referring to a group of people. You will often hear this expression when there is a need to distinguish between different groups of people, such as Indians and foreigners.

- **"Backside":** There's the front side and there's the backside. It makes sense, so stop giggling. In fact, you will find yourself using this very early into your stay because if you ask your driver to drop you at the back, he will respond, "Where, madam?"
"The back, please."
"Which side, madam?"
"Backside!" And there you go; your first Indianism is a cheeky little word that just crept up from behind.

Then there are also coined "English" words; those not found at all in standard English. These are formed either by literal translations from native tongues or by taking a noun and making it into verb by adding *-ing*. For example, one of my girlie pursuits is *crushing* on Bollywood actors (yes,

I admit it), which means to have a crush on or really like. Suffice to say, I also do not mind being pushed hard against them either. I also spend my days *cribbing*. Taken literally I could possibly make a good business out of baby cots but my *cribbing* comes in the unproductive form of complaining and whining. A very common sign outside fabric shops is "Suiting, shirting and panting". It would be nice if the tailor does work at exhausting speeds on your suit. Rather he will work, as all tailors do, *slowly-slowly*, which is the way Indians emphasise just-how-slowly he will work.

The love for *–ing* also manifests itself in verbs, namely the present continuous tense, which is the most often used tense. Like a linguistic *samsara* (cycle of life and death), Indians are trapped in a continuous grammatical state of doing. I am not liking this person. I am wanting to go to home. I'm not having the time. After three years, I too am knowing how to speak like this—until the past tense comes to save me.

In case you think Indian English is entirely new and everything-goes; it is in fact, at the same time entirely old and nothing-changes. It can be formal and stiff, as if it was written for a Victorian audience. Newspapers still use the word scribes for journalists, pachyderms for elephants, thespians for actors and other such words out of an old dictionary or Dickensian novel to report the best of times and the worst of times. Such is the tale of two Englishes in one city.

Pronounced Pronouncements

If there were indeed a national conspiracy to mispronounce things, it would certainly be in the word "development". I have yet to hear it pronounced correctly in India, since even new anchors get it wrong. Other words that also have a distinctive Indian mark are "v" and "w" words, where volcano is "wolcano" and white is" vhite". Perhaps it has to do with Hindi itself, where there is no distinction between w and v. I am still vondering vhy.

India in English

While having tiffin on the veranda of his bungalow, Narayan spilled chai on his pyjamas as he shouted at a coolie who ran through the garden and into the jungle like a frightened cheetah with what appeared to be loot wrapped in a shawl. After much hullabaloo, the thug was hauled back and it was discovered that Mrs Patel's missing bangles were indeed in his possession. It was either Narayan's kismet or karma for him to always be witness to trouble, having had more than a few coincidental brushes with dacoits from his terribly secret past.

There are 16 Indian (Hindi/Urdu) words in that paragraph about poor Narayan and his ruined morning. If you could fully understand it, it shows the reciprocal impact of India on the English language. Some of the words are like an Anglo-Indian linguistic memoir of the British Raj; words like veranda, jungle, bungalow, pyjama and cashmere were peculiar to India, and not Victorian Britain. Others were acquired through exposure to Indian culture. The early Indian immigrants to Britain brought with them curry, kebabs, samosa, chutney and the like. Similarly the Beatles suddenly made the world more aware of karma, avatar, guru, mantra, yoga and other aspects of Indian spirituality. There are yet other words whose Indian origin is less obvious, words such as shampoo, thug, punch, pariah, dinghy, lacquer and cot. You will find thousands more of such English words of Indian origin, and their etymology makes for a whole study in itself.

LEARNING INDIAN LANGUAGES

If your work or travel brings you to rural India, then you should learn the basics of the regional language as English is hardly ever spoken, much less understood in areas outside the main cities. If, however, your work or life in India is confined to the major cities where English is more widespread, there is indeed less of an incentive to learn. But I urge you to learn anyway.

Firstly, your interest in the language will always be viewed positively and appreciated by your Indian friends and colleagues as it shows, symbolically at least, that you respect their culture. Secondly, it can save you money. There is always the possibility of avoiding the foreigner price when you go out shopping. Indeed, that was my initial reason for wanting to learn Hindi. Nothing beats the look on the shopkeeper's face when he quotes you a ridiculous figure only to have you reply indignantly in Hindi. It shows you're local enough to know reasonable from rip-off. As with my case and face,

I could get away with being mistaken as *desi* (local). And I learnt to play that card well.

Even if your card says non-Indian, speaking in the local language is playing the game right as it is always appreciated and generally admired even if *namaste* and *dhanyavad* are all you can master. But much more than what you've bargained for is the immeasurable cultural insight that language will bring to you. It will open doors for you to speak with people you might not otherwise have had a chance to interact with and give you increasing confidence to step out of the bubble of familiarity and expand your experiences. Indians are very forgiving even if you speak their language badly. They may not correct you but they may laugh, and you may laugh, and the ice would be broken if it were not already melted in the unbearable heat of vulnerability. It will also demystify some of the why-and-say-WHAT?! of Indian English, the other tongue you will be learning whether consciously or not.

> To reap the most benefit out of your stay in India, learn its tongue because only then will you come to know its heart.

Having gone through the time and tedium of learning Hindi, I can tell you that it can be challenging at first. But courage, dear reader. The benefits far outweigh the homework. You do not need to aim for full proficiency, and indeed it is not required to get by. You can function just after a few lessons. My Hindi teacher Asha told me that if you speak perfect Hindi, many people might still not understand you because it is too "scholarly". So do as I did; leverage the fact that colloquial Hindi is a grammatical hodgepodge of Hindi peppered with English words, real or created.

If you are living in Delhi, Mumbai or Kolkata, you can still get away with learning just Hindi to be understood in these three cities. But if you are living in Chennai, Hyderabad or Bengaluru, then there is a higher chance you may need to learn the language specific to the state. It is Tamil for Chennai (Tamil Nadu), Telugu for Hyderabad (Telangana), Kannada for Bengaluru (Karnataka) and Malayalam for Kerala. Although seemingly diverse, they are all Dravidian languages and share similar structural aspects.

Hindi

Hindi is the main language used in the northern states of Rajasthan, Delhi, Haryana, Uttarakhand, Uttar Pradesh, Madhya Pradesh, Chhattisgarh, Himachal Pradesh, Jharkhand and Bihar. It is spoken in much of the north and central India alongside other languages such as Punjabi, Gujarati, Marathi and Bengali.

Hindi is easy to learn, especially if you already speak a Latin-based language. It has sentence structures similar to English, but unlike English, it has genders for its nouns (French and German speakers will find this aspect of Hindi similar to their own languages). The language also reflects India's obsession with hierarchy in the three different forms of "you": *aap* (polite), *tum* (informal), *tu* (very informal, denoting closeness such as between parent-child or lovers). Most Hindi learners stick with *aap*, erring on the side of universal politeness and even more universal laziness (since each form has its own verb conjugation, which you have to memorise).

Hindi is pronounced exactly the way it is written in the Romanised script. The Hindi script is called the Devanagari script and the jury is out on whether it is necessary to learn it since the Romanised script is sufficient to get by. I learnt Hindi in its totality, meaning to speak, read and write, and felt that knowing the script helped greatly with the pronunciations.

You also have the added advantage of being able to read street signs, road signs and other writings on the wall to help you navigate the cultural landscape.

In Delhi, you can learn Hindi at local language schools or through private tutors who give both individual and private group classes. Word of mouth is best because not all Hindi tutors are effective, many employing rote-learning techniques instead of explaining how the language works. I learnt Hindi (very effectively) at the American Embassy School in Delhi through the adult education programme offered in the evenings. I also found language books, such as *Teach Yourself Hindi* (with CD) very useful for pronunciation. Apply what you learnt right away so that you do not forget. I had the support of other "teachers" around me (because you can learn from *anyone*). Madhu and Santosh would practise with me while my *vegetablewala* made me practise by refusing to take my fruit and vegetable orders unless I said them in Hindi. I have since permanently substituted many English words for the shorter-by-a-syllable Hindi ones, such as *sabzi* (vegetables), *pyaz* (onion) and *aloo* (potato). This also includes other words where the Hindi equivalent is either more accurate or just more fun to say, such as *garmi* (uncomfortably hot) and *choto-mota* (small).

Voilà Wala!

This is a magic word that suddenly turns a non-living thing into a living, breathing entity. It broadly means "the one" and commonly refers to a seller or vendor. A *vegetablewala* is "the one who sells vegetables" and an *autowala* is "the one who drives an auto". *Wala* can also be combined with the name of a town or city to indicate where a person is from, such as *Delhiwala* (the one who is from Delhi). *Wala* can also be used to specify a certain thing. For example "I want *yehwala* (this one) and not the *chotawala* (the small one)." *Wala* is singular male, *wali* is singular female and *wale* is plural.

In Mumbai, there is a variety of colloquial Hindi called Bambaiya Hindi or sometimes Bhindi. It is a combination of mostly Marathi, Hindi and other Indian languages. Some Bollywood movies incorporate the Bambaiya patois. This, together with Urdu and catchphrases from other Indian dialects, make Bollywood movies challenging to follow for a Hindi beginner. The evening news, albeit less entertaining except for the shouting segments, is a much better way to test your language progress.

Even if you can't undertake a study of the language, you should master a few basic phrases to sound like you have. To jumpstart your learning/living, I've included some phrases in the Glossary. Even if you cannot get beyond *namaste*, over time colloquialisms will come to you as you immerse in the everyday. So *aaram se*, dear reader. This is another useful phrase, which means "chill, take your time, do it slowly" and can be used for a variety of situations to calm, assure or remind people to be careful.

As the *Karo* Flies

If you do not have the vocabulary for the Hindi verb, I've employed this simple and direct trick to turn it to colloquial Hindi. Just take the English verb and apply *karo* (Hindi for "do") to it. Call-*karo* (make a call), drive-*karo* (drive), *parcel*-karo (pack leftovers), wash-*karo* (wash). It does not work in all situations, but when it does, it gives wings to your basic Hindi and makes you sound more proficient than you really are. So go ahead and use -*karo* and watch your imaginative vocabulary and confidence take flight.

Sanskrit

Sanskrit is an official language in India but it is limited in its usage to religious ceremonies and instruction as it is considered a sacred language in Hindu, Jain and Buddhist traditions. People learn the language for its beauty and its connection to Indian tradition, thought and culture.

Tamil

Tamil is spoken in the south and is generally considered more challenging to learn because of the script and pronunciations as well as the relatively limited availability of language tutors and schools compared with Hindi in the north. The best approach is to ask around the international community. That being said, English is much more widely spoken in South India than in the north, and hence you can easily get by with English alone. Shopkeepers and even *autowalas* are fluent in English.

Note that you should avoid speaking Hindi in the south as there are residual sensitivities. In 1965, there were violent protests against Hindi being made the national language of India as it was seen by many Tamils as an act to make the south subordinate to the north. There is no national language to date.

CHAPTER 9

DOING BUSINESS IN INDIA

> ❛None can destroy iron, but its own rust can.
> Likewise, none can destroy a person,
> but his own mindset can.❜

— Ratan Tata

In 2016, India overtook China as the fastest growing major economy in the world and is predicted to be on a robust growth trajectory with stable annual growth rates and rising foreign exchange reserves. India also has the world's youngest population and a burgeoning middle class, making it attractive for consumer-focussed companies. This and India's growth potential and market size have led to more foreign companies setting up their facilities in India, helped along by various government initiatives, such as Make in India and Digital India. The Make in India initiative aims to boost the manufacturing sector while Digital India focuses on the creation of digital infrastructure, delivering services digitally and increasing digital literacy. There have also been landmark reforms such as a goods and sales tax to lure further foreign investment to the country.

Despite the great potential for business, India remains a tough place to do business. It still suffers from weak infrastructure and institutional inertia, although things have started to change since the election of the pro-market government of Narendra Modi in May 2014. Nevertheless it is necessary to go in well prepared and I have briefly outlined what to anticipate to get you started. To succeed in India, you will need to set realistic expectations, take a long-term view, and be positive, patient and resilient to reap the benefits from this awakening South Asian giant.

INDIAN WORKING CULTURE
Hierarchy in the Workplace

Indians have an automatic reverence for leaders, in large part due to the hierarchical nature of Indian society and the Indian family structure that provides its idiom. The boss is often seen as a benevolent patriarch who charts directions and solves problems. He is both admired and feared, or idealised in some instances. A consequence of this adulation is that subordinates are reluctant to voice opposing viewpoints out of deference and politeness. This deprives top leadership of critical feedback to improve management practices or worse, to avert disaster. If the office culture is as such, as a new boss you will need to consciously encourage open feedback to cultivate a discursive environment. This has to be consciously and consistently applied until you see a real breakthrough since your staff may just tell you what they *think* you want to hear (even if it looks like open feedback). It takes more than a few days to change deep-seated attitudes towards authority figures, and Indians value preserving relationships at all cost, even at the expense of painful truths.

Reverence to leaders occurs even in modern business organisations whose senior managers have been exposed to Western education and business practices. Likewise, you may be expected to know your boundaries as a subordinate if you report to an Indian boss. Reverence for authority figures happens psychologically across all levels and very often within the same person who gives it and demands it. I have observed Indian managers behave subserviently to their bosses in one instance, and roughly and authoritatively to their subordinates in the next.

A clear behavioural role between superior and subordinate seems to exist in the Indian mind, undergirded by a particular

No No

It is difficult to get a frank "no" in business (and in life) because Indians find it difficult to deny requests they are unable or unwilling to do in order to preserve relationships. This makes it all the more critical for foreigners to read the Indian synonyms for "no". This includes "Let's see", "I'll try", "maybe" and even the confusing and misleading "yes". Apart from verbal substitutes for "no", it is equally important to look out for other signals of "no", such as tentative tones and cautious body language. Too much faith in what is being said can lead you down a miserable path where you discover (usually too late) that your instructions were not followed. Too little faith conversely turns you into a micromanager and a cynic. The art lies in knowing how to read what is said and un-said correctly, which comes only with experience.

cultural attitude that hierarchy represents: power. Leaders are expected to show their power by taking charge and fronting and solving challenges. Subordinates can show a wide range of behavioural responses to such leaders, from admiration and reverence to more negative behaviours such as fear and sycophancy (known as *chamchagiri* — the art of flattery). When harnessed positively, the hold of power produces unquestioned loyalty to leader and organisation. However, note that as soon as a power shift occurs, allegiances also quickly follow.

Although Indian institutions are hierarchical, they are not so in all aspects. Social status and gender have less sway in the office where the concept of power outweighs most categorisations. Thus women in leadership positions command similar respect because of the power inherent in their authority.

Team and Work

The Indian sensitivity towards hierarchy shows itself more clearly when Indians gather to approach work as a group. Collaborative teamwork across levels of status and power can be difficult. Firstly, decisions tend to be pushed upwards towards the most senior member in the team. Secondly, because Indians do not like giving or receiving negative feedback, outcomes do not benefit from the rigour of group analysis.

The most debilitating effect is observed when "menial" work is involved. This is defined as any task perceived as beneath an individual's qualifications and social status. It can range from getting research data to getting a glass of water, and it can easily look to foreign eyes like passing the buck down the ladder until it falls on someone who believes it is his place and status to do it. It can lead to needless delays or even things *not* getting done especially where there are too many "leaders" delegating and too few doing. Close supervision therefore is required if you observe such team dynamics.

Within the office as a whole, hierarchical play becomes even more evident. "Menial" jobs are expected to be performed by those lower in the pecking order. For instance, as you walk out of the office for a meeting, you notice that the trash can is full. You announce, "Can someone clear that?" and then head out. Three hours later when you return, the trash can is still full of waste paper. It is not due to group deafness or laziness (well, maybe) but because your managers think that clearing trash is the job (and status) of the office peon. Some of them may even find it offensive to be asked to clear trash.

If you want a more collaborative, less hierarchical office culture, you must be the first to set the example. When your subordinates see that a person high on the hierarchy can clear the trash, get his own drink, photocopy his own papers, then there is more willingness to do the same for themselves and approach teamwork similarly. But if you want to play boss (i.e. be served) yet expect your subordinates to change their attitude, you will likely not have any transforming impact on the working culture. If your strategy is to let sleeping dogs lie, then leverage and manage the cultural norm well. Play your powerful boss card by clearly assigning the work to someone and hold that staff accountable for that particular deliverable so that there is no passing of buck... or blame.

MANAGING INDIAN STAFF

Indian employees respond well to the ideal leadership archetype—the authoritative but benevolent patriarch mentioned above. It sometimes requires you to maintain a high power distance whilst being altruistic, caring and generous at the same time.

Sometimes a result arising from playing the part is that some Indian employees may also expect empathy when it comes to absenteeism for family reasons, or even with extending personal loans. So you have to decide where to draw that "paternal" line. On the other hand, if you seek to build a flatter office culture, then you have to be mindful of how you maintain their needed sense of your authority when you narrow the power distance.

Indian staff are better managed with a more personal hand, rather than with detachment and being task-focussed. They respond better to people persons and bosses who participate in the office. Therefore it is important to celebrate festivals or special occasions together to build rapport. If you are heading a team, then this is also a good time to be generous.

Another important skill to learn is how to manage emotions because it is an emotional society and Indians tend to respond emotionally especially to what they perceive as criticism or negativity. The key is to know when to apply different management techniques to drive performance.

Fairness

Because Indians are sensitive to authority figures, you should always strive for fairness in the way you deal with your team members. It is said that one reason why the patriarch is so detached from his own children in the Indian joint family is due to the logic of wanting to appear fair in order to keep the joint family cohesive. Favouritism can cause factions to form, making teamwork even more challenging.

Quality of Work

You may find that the quality of work is not up to expectations, especially among untrained or lower-level staff, even graduates. It is usually due to the lack of exposure, or even educational background where there could be marked differences between those from public and private schools (and those who claimed they went to school). If you are working in an environment that demands no-compromise, such as in pharmaceuticals and manufacturing, or one where you deem the general quality of work is sub-par, then it is worth investing your time in tight supervision to change attitudes or improve overall competence.

To discourage the blame game, enforcing individual accountability and calling out shoddy work (behind closed doors) are important and necessary. It is equally important to manage your own expectations based on the capabilities of your team—for their sanity and yours. Nobody would like to work with a bitter ball of frustration, but people do appreciate a boss that pushes them to improve themselves within realistic reach.

Micromanaging

Foreign managers often feel that they have to micromanage in India. One reason is that employees may not have the awareness of certain criticalities in the task or project assigned to them. Therefore managers are often required to sit down with the staff and go through the details together, making it feel like micromanaging. You should make an assessment whether it is a competence or training issue. If it's the latter, then see it as an investment of your time to build employee capability, which will ensure smoother delivery of results in the long term.

Lateness

If your office is operating on "Indian Standard Time" (i.e. perpetually late), then you may want to enforce your expectations on punctuality. However, you also need to temper this with the fact that traffic is often the cause of occasional lateness (not habitual lateness), especially during the monsoon season when a boat may be more effective than a car in getting to work.

Hiring and Firing

There are many people in India, but too few of the ones that companies would ideally like to hire. There is indeed rising competition for good talent, especially in the middle and senior levels. To fill senior positions, tap on your networks for references. For other positions, it is best to enlist the help of recruitment companies because they would save you precious time narrowing down candidates and spotting fake degree qualifications. An ad in the papers or job website will likely generate huge numbers (this is India!) of unsuitable applications. Because of the ease of getting fake certificates nowadays or the high amount of exaggeration on resumes, you could administer a written test or ask them to prepare a short presentation to test their said capabilities. Do not be fooled by seemingly polished appearances.

Hiring is fairly easy but dismissing workers is not. Strong labour unions and labour laws that highly favour employees make it difficult to retrench or dismiss someone. Therefore take the time to choose your people wisely.

BUSINESS ETIQUETTE

Meetings

Meeting are usually scheduled in the late morning or early afternoon. They should be arranged at least a month prior, and because they may be cancelled at the last minute, it is wise to call and confirm before you leave the office. Allow extra time for transport delays and aim to be punctual. Although many people operate on "Indian Standard Time", the person you might be meeting may not. Furthermore, punctuality is appreciated even if it may not be practised. Meetings can take place over lunch and even dinner (but never breakfast, unless you are in the financial sector where this is more common).

Depending on company practice, taking minutes for critical meetings is useful, especially those where key decisions were discussed. Minutes serve as a written log about verbal

agreements made and can help address any confusion downstream. Minutes can be sent to the other party for agreement a few days after the meeting along with any follow-ups to be made.

Greetings

Indians love titles such as Doctor, Professor and the likes. If someone does not have a professional title, use the honorific titles of "Sir" or "Madam". Do not use first names unless invited to do so. Business cards are usually exchanged after the introductions. Cards should be received with the right hand or both hands. Present your business card with the details facing the recipient.

Business Attire

Business attire is conservative. Men should wear business suits and women should dress conservatively in suits or dresses. The weather often determines clothing and summer attire may be more casual. Nonetheless, dressing up for the first meeting is a sign of respect, regardless of the temperature outside.

THE ART AND TUMBLE OF GETTING TO YES!

Yes is the handshake, *yes* is the completion of a project and *yes* is the jubilation of overcoming the odds. Getting there, however, is less than euphoric. Therefore, it is good to prepare yourself for doing business in India. Read up, research and seek advice from others before you take the plunge, or you can find yourself in deep water or in over your head.

Indians prefer to do business with those they know and those they can trust and respect. Therefore, expect much small talk for the first meeting about topics such as your family and impressions of India, which will be used to feel you out. If there is a mutual acquaintance that can facilitate an introduction, it will hasten the process of getting to "yes" as you can leverage the known relationship.

The time between the introductions and a "yes" can be long, frustrating and tedious, especially when dealing with the government. It is often fraught with unpredictability where it can go one way today and another tomorrow (this is where minutes are useful). Be patient, be flexible and be prepared that nothing in India goes according to plan at first. Even if you pray for it each day, progress does not happen in a neat, predictable straight line, but rather in squiggles, circles and spirals. Do not lose your temper or your mind at this acrobatic way of working as you can very quickly undermine your hard-earned efforts in building those key relationships.

Part of the reason behind delays is that Indians are non-confrontational, so if you do not know how to read their signs then you will find yourself wasting time chasing red herrings and jumping through hoops. Another reason for the twists and turns is the approach to decision making itself that allows for and embraces the concept of relativity. A decision made in one context holds true for that context but if the circumstances were to change, then it stands to reason that the decision should be revaluated in light of the new variables. Therefore, learn to deal with the curve balls. Be open to advice from your peers, hired consultants and Indian colleagues to minimise the scrapes and bruises.

The Decision Maker

Decisions are usually reached by the person(s) with the highest authority, so identify and focus on getting to the highest authority as early as possible for greater effectiveness. This may involve asking directly to be connected, through recommendations or working through the hierarchy. Industry networking events are effective channels.

If you have been only communicating with a subordinate, ask him to help introduce you to the boss but keep him involved as he too would like to be credited for any positive outcome arising from it. It is also important to get his support before such an introduction.

THE BUSINESS ENVIRONMENT

Some people say there are two Indias when doing business. The first is the old India of government-owed companies that are slow and heavy with bureaucracy and long negotiations. The other is the new nimble businesses with international experience and easy access to decision makers. You have to learn how to deal with both and the business environment common to them.

Complexity

Expect complexity. This is the advice and the lesson that many foreigners deduce along the way as they experience the ups and downs and workarounds of doing business (as well as living) in India. Therefore, leaders need to get involved early to anticipate and solve problems before they become irrecoverable disasters.

It is also important to find ways to deal with roadblocks. You will need reliable local partners who are familiar with the operating environment in India and a slew of consultants and locally relevant advisors to tackle issues such as distribution, taxes, property ownership, labour laws and state-specific laws.

Bureaucracy

Bureaucracy and red tape can get the better of many companies trying to do business in India. Complicated and obscure laws can delay or worse, derail efforts, and many companies can easily get mired in legal entanglements even before they get off the ground. The best way to approach bureaucracy is not on your own. Hire good professional Indian consultants and intermediaries who are familiar with the national and state systems (and better yet, the people behind them) to ensure your company fully complies with the laws of India. Even then, someone somewhere can pull up an obscure law and pull the carpet from under you before you have time to react. Assume that everything that could go wrong will. And therefore the quality of your advisors is extremely important.

Corruption

Oftentimes bureaucracy and corruption are known to go hand in hand and indeed, a little hand giving hand is not seen as anything out of the ordinary in India, where things can get so bogged down indeterminately with officialdom that it literally pays to make things go faster. This does not happen only in the hallowed halls of bureaucrats but anywhere where people want shortcuts, to incentivise speed or favour or to turn a blind eye. Many foreign firms try to stay away from bribery (which is illegal), but many do not always succeed. They will do so, albeit reluctantly, if it becomes a requirement for business success. Planning ahead and anticipating problems can help minimise the need for a bribe.

Be on the lookout also for signs of corruption right under your nose in your own company. For example, a supervisor is regularly paid off to receive inferior quality materials from a supplier, thus affecting the quality of your products. Areas where major corruption tend to occur are in procurement and large purchase contracts, getting licences and matters related to real estate and land ownership.

Corruption can also take the form of nepotism. There is a cultural tendency to look out for family and friends, and that could mean an employee offering contracts or jobs to family members who are less qualified than other candidates. Employing robust internal governance may weed out existing problems and prevent reoccurrence.

Gifts

In India, it is customary to send gifts to business partners and officials during Diwali or other festivals as part of relationship building. Gifts are usually sweets or nuts and dried fruit but a gift that is substantial can be a hint for reciprocal obligations.

Disruptions

Power outages and *bandhs* (strikes) can be quite common so businesses have to work around them and adapt. Although they disrupt efficiency, they can be managed. Disruptions can also come from monsoon weather and family emergencies.

Delays

"Indian Standard Time" also seems to apply to projects. As much as you have a deadline to meet, the project will move at the speed that circumstances dictate. You can minimise delays by proper planning and close supervision, but expect delays to happen regardless. Therefore, establish a realistic time frame for results.

Last words of advice:

- Build your relationships and cultural knowledge because you cannot win India over without knowing Indians better.
- Be resilient because India can be a trying market. Therefore build a network of trusted people, both local and foreign, to help when things get difficult.
- Be open-minded because you cannot change the ways things are but you can find ways to work around them.
- Be patient because it is critical to success. The market is complicated with unimaginable delays, so adopt a long-term view. Take comfort that everyone else encounters challenges too.
- Be persistent. If you fail, dust yourself off and keep trying, knowing that you are building a set of work and life skills that will add immeasurable value to your work experience.

CHAPTER 10

AT A GLANCE

> ‘The only people who see the whole picture are the ones that step out of the frame.’
>
> **—Salman Rushdie**

Official Name
Republic of India (short: India)

Indian Name
Bharatiya Ganarajya (short: Bharat)

National Anthem
"Jana-Gana-Mana" (Thou Art the Ruler of the Minds of All People), composed by Rabindranath Tagore

Flag
Three equal horizontal bands of saffron, white and green, with a blue *chakra* (24-spoked wheel) centred in the white band. Saffron represents courage, sacrifice, and the spirit of renunciation; white signifies purity and truth; green stands for faith and fertility. The *chakra* symbolises the wheel of life.

National Emblem
The Lion Capital of Ashoka

Timezone
GMT +5.5 hours

Dialling Code
+91

Electricity
220–240 volts, 50Hz

Measurements
Metric system

Area
Ranked 7th largest in the world at 3,287,263 square km

Climate
Tropical (south) and temperate (north). The monsoon season runs from July to September.

Currency
Indian Rupee (INR or Rs). One rupee is divided into 100 paise. Currency notes: 5, 10, 20, 50, 100, 500 and 2,000.

Coins (commonly used)
50 paise and 1, 2, 5 rupee coins

Government Type
Federal parliamentary republic

Capital
New Delhi

Administrative Divisions
29 states and 7 Union Territories* (Andaman and Nicobar Islands*, Andhra Pradesh, Arunachal Pradesh, Assam, Bihar, Chandigarh*, Chhattisgarh, Dadra and Nagar Haveli*, Daman and Diu*, Delhi*, Goa, Gujarat, Haryana, Himachal Pradesh, Jammu and Kashmir, Jharkhand, Karnataka, Kerala,

Lakshadweep*, Madhya Pradesh, Maharashtra, Manipur, Meghalaya, Mizoram, Nagaland, Odisha, Puducherry*, Punjab, Rajasthan, Sikkim, Tamil Nadu, Telangana, Tripura, Uttar Pradesh, Uttarakhand, West Bengal)

Population
Ranked 2nd in the world at 1.2 billion (July 2016 est.)

Population of Major Cities
New Delhi 25.703 million; Mumbai 21.043 million; Kolkata 11.766 million; Bengaluru 10.087 million; Chennai 9.62 million; Hyderabad 8.944 million (2015)

Languages
According to the Eighth Schedule to the Constitution, there are 22 official languages. The five most widely spoken are: Hindi 41%, Bengali 8.1%, Telugu 7.2%, Marathi 7%, Tamil 5.9%. English enjoys the status of a subsidiary official language and is the language for national, political and commercial communication.

Religions
Hindu 79.8%, Muslim 14.2%, Christian 2.3%, Sikh 1.7%, other and unspecified 2% (2011 est.)

Literacy
71.2% (total population)

Population below Poverty Line
29.8% (2010 est.)

FAMOUS INDIANS

India has produced many famous personalities that have excelled in their field and made their mark on the global stage. Their lives have inspired a whole generation of Indians and continue to inspire millions more in India as well as around the world.

Political Leaders

Mahatma Gandhi (1869–1948)

Popularly honoured as the "father of the nation", Gandhi was the foremost political leader of the Indian independence movement, which sought the overthrow of British rule. Gandhi inspired millions with his philosophy of non-violence as well as his unwavering commitment to independence and alleviating the plight of women and the "untouchable" caste.

Jawaharlal Nehru (1889–1964)

Widely regarded as the "architect of modern India", Nehru steered India through the difficult period following independence as its first Prime Minister.

Dr B. R. Ambedkar (1891–1956)

Popularly known as the "architect of the Indian Constitution", Babasaheb (as he was called) was a political activist and social reformer who inspired the Dalit Buddhist Movement and campaigned for greater equality for the "untouchable" caste and women.

Literary Greats

Kalidasa (4th–5th century)

Kalidasa is considered the greatest poet and dramatist in the Sanskrit language.

Rabindranath Tagore (1861–1941)

Considered to be one of the biggest literary figures after Kalidasa in the cultural history of India, Tagore was the first Indian to be awarded the Nobel Prize for Literature in 1913.

Sports Heroes
Sachin Tendulkar (1973–)

Tendulkar is regarded as one of the world's greatest batsmen. In 2014, Tendulkar was conferred the Bharat Ratna, India's highest civilian award. He is the first sportsperson, as well as the youngest Indian to receive the award.

Entertainment Legends
Satyajit Ray (1921–1992)

Ray is India's first internationally recognised film maker. He was honoured with the Oscar's Lifetime Achievement award and the Bharat Ratna, India's highest civilian award, in 1992.

Amitabh Bachchan (1942–)

Bachchan (affectionately known as Big B) is considered a stalwart of Indian cinema and one of the biggest stars Bollywood has ever seen. Known for his deep baritone voice, he is respected and adored in India.

Rajinikanth (1950–)

Shivaji Rao Gaekwad, known by his stage name Rajinikanth, is the megahero of the Tamil film industry. Like Bachchan, Rajinikanth is considered a living legend of Indian cinema and has helped popularised regional cinema worldwide.

A.R. Rahman (1966 –)

Singer-composer Allah Rakha Rahman is the first Indian to

win an Oscar (actually two Oscars—for original score and original song) for Danny Boyle's *Slumdog Millionaire* in 2009.

Industry Giants

Jamsetji Tata (1839–1904)

Regarded as the "father of Indian industry", Tata was an Indian pioneer and industrialist, who founded the Tata Group, India's biggest conglomerate company. He is the story behind the building of the Taj Mahal Palace Hotel in Mumbai.

Science and Academia Trailblazers

Srinivasa Ramanujan (1887–1920)

A self-taught mathematician from Tamil Nadu, Ramanujan made extraordinary contributions to the development of number theory, infinite series and continued fractions. His life is portrayed in the biopic *The Man Who Knew Infinity* (2016).

Sir Chandrasekhara Venkata Raman (1888–1970)

Chandrasekhar was influential in the growth of science in India. In 1930, he won the Nobel Prize for Physics for his discovery that when light traverses a transparent material, some of the light that is deflected changes in wavelength. This phenomenon is now called Raman scattering. His nephew, astrophysicist Subrahmanyan Chandrasekhar (1910–1995), won the 1983 Nobel Prize for Physics for key discoveries that led to the currently accepted theory on the later evolutionary stages of massive stars.

Amartya Sen (1933–)

Sen is an Indian economist who was awarded the Nobel Prize for Economics in 1988. He has worked on social choice theory and contributed to the field of development economics.

UNESCO WORLD HERITAGE SITES

There are 35 World Heritage Sites in India out of which 27 are cultural, seven are natural and one mixed*.

State	Cultural Heritage Sites
Delhi	Qutb Minar (12th century), Humayun's Tomb (1572), Red Fort Complex (1648)
Uttar Pradesh	Agra Fort (16th century), Fatehpur Sikri (16th century), Taj Mahal (17th century)
Chandigarh	The Architectural Work of Le Corbusier (20th century)
Rajasthan	Hill forts of Rajasthan (7th–16th centuries), Jantar Mantar at Jaipur (1727)
Gujarat	The Queen's Stepwell (11th century), Champaner-Pavagadh Archaeological Park
Bihar	Mahabodhi Temple Complex at Bodh Gaya (3rd century BC), Nalanda (5th–12th centuries)
Madhya Pradesh	Buddhist Monuments at Sanchi (2nd century BC), Rock Shelters of Bhimbetka, Khajuraho Group of Monuments (AD 950–AD 1050)
Maharashtra	Ajanta Caves (2nd century BC–AD 6th century), Ellora Caves (AD 600–AD 1000), Elephanta Caves (5th–8th centuries), Chhatrapati Shivaji Terminus (1887)

State	Cultural Heritage Sites
Goa	Churches and Convents of Goa (16th–18th centuries)
Odisha	Sun Temple at Konark (13th century)
Karnataka	Group of Monuments at Pattadakal (8th century), Group of Monuments at Hampi (14th–16th centuries)
Tamil Nadu	Group of Monuments at Mahabalipuram (7th–8th centuries), Great Living Chola Temples (11th–12th centuries),
West Bengal, Tamil Nadu and Himachal Pradesh	Mountain Railways of India: Darjeeling Himalayan Railway (West Bengal), Nilgiri Mountain Railway (Tamil Nadu), Kalka-Shimla Railway (Himachal Pradesh)

State	Natural Heritage Sites
Himachal Pradesh	Great Himalayan National Park Conservation Area
Uttarakhand	Nanda Devi and Valley of Flowers National Parks
Rajasthan	Keoladeo National Park
West Bengal	Sundarbans National Park
Sikkim	*Khangchendzonga National Park
Assam	Kaziranga National Park, Manas Wildlife Sanctuary
Others	Western Ghats

CITY RANKINGS

Mercer's Quality of Living 2016 ranks 230 cities based on a variety of factors including political, economic, environmental, personal safety, health, education, transportation and other public service factors. The survey also identifies the personal safety ranking for cities. South Indian cities emerged at the top for quality of life and personal safety among cities in India. Considerable population increases in Mumbai and New Delhi in recent decades are cited to have exacerbated existing problems, such as access to clean water, air pollution and traffic congestion.

Quality of Living 2016
Hyderabad (139th in global ranking)
Pune (144th)
Bengaluru (145th)
Chennai (150th)
Mumbai (152nd)
New Delhi (154th)

Cost of Living 2016
Mumbai
New Delhi
Chennai
Bengaluru
Kolkata

Personal Safety 2016
Chennai
Hyderabad
Bengaluru
Pune
Kolkata

CULTURE QUIZ

SCENARIO 1

A month into his employment, your driver asks you for a loan of Rs6,000 for medical treatment for his ill wife. What do you do?

Ⓐ Draw a hard line and tell him that you do not lend money, but give your reasons for doing so.

Ⓑ Lend the full amount and agree upon a repayment schedule.

Ⓒ Give a portion or up to the full amount and let him know this is a one-off goodwill bonus.

Comments

The most common response is **Ⓑ** Servants generally expect their bosses to take care of them in time of crises because many live hand-to-mouth each month with little to no savings. However, since he has only been working for a month, it is hard to determine if his request is genuine. Lend the money in good faith, and pursue the repayment actively. If he lapses and continues to ask for loans, then you have grounds to go for **Ⓐ** next time. For longer-serving staff who have performed well, **Ⓒ** builds a lot of goodwill and loyalty. For smaller loan amounts, you can consider asking him to work for it by giving him extra jobs to do or more overtime work.

SCENARIO 2

Your toilet is choked and you call the plumber to fix it. He tells you that he will be at your house tomorrow at noon. You shift back your hair appointment to a safe time of 4pm. It's 3.30pm and there's still no sign of him. What do you do?

Ⓐ Continue waiting because flies are starting to colonise.

Ⓑ Leave the house and head to the salon because you know, hair.

Ⓒ Call another plumber and risk this scenario being replayed.

Comments

All three options are possible. Depending on the severity of the situation, all of us at many points during our stay in India will have to decide if or when to cut our losses. Do not expect punctuality; people will come when they come and there could be a number of reasons—the plumber was tied up with another job, he misunderstood you, traffic or he just needed an extra long *chai* break. He may even show up unannounced the following day (more common than you think!). If you call someone else whilst waiting for him and he does finally show, he will not feel offended if you decline his services. As a gesture, you may want to reimburse him for his conveyance (the common word for "transport"). You can also try to call him to check if he is on the way or has forgotten. If he says he's five minutes away, expect him in about an hour. The key lesson here is that it is critical to build your own list of reliable resources before stuff happens. Get recommendations from friends, preferably from a local.

SCENARIO 3

A friend invites you to dinner because she wants to introduce you to her uncle whom she thinks you would love to meet. At the dinner, the uncle brings up a business proposal and asks if you would like to get on board. Caught off-guard, what do you say?

A You politely decline.

B You change the topic. Aren't killer whales amazing?

C You agree to explore but feel bad because you were not really interested.

Comments

Most people would choose **C** out of courtesy, but there is a larger lesson here on the cultural notion of commitment. You are not expected to commit on the spot and even if you do, you will not be held to that commitment. In India decisions are context-sensitive, which means that a decision reflects its surrounding circumstances at that point in time. Should there be changes to the context, Indians understand that positions would likewise need to be recalibrated. In this case, you can confidently agree to explore and wait for the uncle's call to see if *he* was committed to the follow-up.

SCENARIO 4

Your gardener has invited you to his house for his son's birthday and you agree to go. You arrive at his one-room dwelling in a rough side of town and his wife offers you a cup of water. Do you:

A politely decline?

B take it and pretend to drink?

C drink it and pray?

Comments

If you are unsure of the water source, then it is better to decline than get sick from contaminated water, unless hypocrisy is easier to stomach. Blame it on yourself being a foreigner in a self-deprecating way and people will empathise; say "My stomach is not as strong as yours." If you really must drink, either out of compunction or thirst, then ask for black tea (north) or filtered coffee (south) because at the very least, you know the water has been boiled. Additionally, invitations like these are common, and your staff consider your presence an honour. But if you want to avoid tricky food and drink situations, you can decline the invite and send a gift.

SCENARIO 5

You have already been waiting for an hour to get a permit in a queue that has barely moved. You have observed at least three men who came after you leave happily with their permits, if but a few hundred rupees poorer. How do you react?

A Angrily ask to speak to the supervisor.

B Check your wallet then slip away to pad up someone else's.

C Continue to wait; you've learnt patience anyway.

Comments

All the options are possible depending on where you stand on the issue of corruption. Bribes are commonplace in India's bureaucratic culture, and paying bribes is seen as a necessary part of getting things done to save time and hassle or to obtain an advantage over others. It can happen along the entire management chain, so even the supervisor may be in on the take. Therefore, yelling at him will serve no purpose other than to draw attention to yourself and to instigate him to make things more frustrating for you (by paperwork). Bribes are commonly seen as a way of life and indeed *chai-pani* (literally tea-water, the euphemism for a small bribe) can smoothen the process provided you know how to do it and the right person to target. But if you prefer to not perpetuate this culture, then it requires patience or a third party. You can *still* get things done on your own without any greasing; it just takes that much longer.

DOS AND DON'TS

DOS

- Make an effort to learn Hindi (if staying in the north).
- Dress modestly especially when visiting a temple, mosque or *gurudwara*.
- Treat elders with respect.
- Ask about each other's family in a conversation.
- Learn the Indian headshake as another way of communicating.
- Bargain at markets and learn to sense when someone is trying to rip you off.
- Insist that the meter be used for auto-rickshaw rides and taxis.
- Ignore Indian men scratching or touching their privates in public.
- Be patient when simple tasks become excessively tedious.
- Develop the cultural love for dancing.
- Expect the unexpected and keep an open mind.

DON'TS

- Use your left hand to eat, handover food, money, gifts or touch someone.
- Accept green-tinted drinks of milk or sweets from strangers during Holi. *Bhang* (marijuana) is traditionally consumed during Holi.
- Speak Hindi in South India. Use English.
- Expect people to follow the rules. Flexibility is an established way of life.

- Make comments about the caste system as this topic is considered socially and politically sensitive.
- Criticise India; only Indians can acceptably do that.
- Ever hit or deride cows. The cow is always right in every instance, even if it is languishing on the road and creating a traffic nightmare.
- Expect people to be punctual or things to go by your schedule.
- Point your feet at people as the feet are considered unclean.
- Show affection in public.
- Accept torn currency as it is hard to pass it on in the next transaction.
- Be surprised that many Indian households prefer washing men (*dhobis*) to washing machines whereby clothes are collected and then returned a few days later cleaned and pressed.
- Lose your temper at the *babu* because he can make things exceedingly more difficult than it is.
- Feel offended if strangers ask you intrusive questions.
- Become a cynic.

GLOSSARY

GREETINGS

English	Hindi	Tamil
Hello	*Namaste*	*Vanakkam*
My name is …	*Mera nam … hai*	*En peru…*
How are you?	*Aap kaise hain*	*Yeppadi irukkireergal*
I am from …	*Main … se hum*	*Naan … irundhu varean*
Thank you	*Dhanyavad/Shukriya*	*Nandri*

COMMON EXPRESSIONS

English	Hindi	Tamil
I don't understand	*Main nahi samajti*	*Yanakku puriyavillai*
Excuse me	*Maaf kijiye*	*Mannikka vendum*
It does not matter	*Koi baat nahin*	*Onnum prachanai illai*
Let's go	*Chalo*	*Vaa pogalam*
What is this?	*Yeh kya hai?*	*Enna ithu?*
See you soon	*Phir milenge*	*Meendum santhippam*
Good/Really?/ I understand	*Accha**	*Nallathu nijamavaa? Enakku puriyuthu*
Okay/it's fine	*Thik Hai*	*Sari paravaillai*
Crazy!	*Pagal!*	*Kirukku!*

*one word in Hindi, separate phrases in Tamil

AT HOME

English	Hindi	Tamil
It's delicious	*Bahut swaadisht hai*	*Suvaiyaaga irukku*
I am full	*Pet bhar gaya*	*Vayiru nirambi irukku*
My stomach is upset	*Mera pet kharab hai*	*Vayiru sari yillae*
I am sleepy	*Mujhe neend aa rahee hai*	*Enakku thookama irukku*

AT A RESTAURANT

English	Hindi	Tamil
Is this very spicy?	*Bahut mirchi hai kya?*	Ithu *romba kaarama?*
Bill, please	Bill *cahiye*	Bill *kodunga*
Doggy-bag this	*Parcel karo*	*Ithu pack pannunga*

SHOPPING

English	Hindi	Tamil
How much?	*Kitna ka hai?*	*Ithu evalavu?*
Give me a discount	Discount *kar lo*	*Korachi kodunga*
Too expensive	*Bahut mehenga hai*	*Romba vilai*
Show me that, please	*Woh dikhayenge*	*Athai kaattungal*
Show me some more	*Aur dikhayenge*	*Innum kaattungal*
Do you have other colours?	*Isme aur rang hai kya?*	*Vera niram irukka?*
Is the colour fast (will not bleed)?	*Rang pakka hai kya?*	Colour *poguma?*
I don't want it	*Nahin cahiye*	*Enakku vendaam*

ON THE ROAD

English	Hindi	Tamil
Thief! Help!	*Chor*! *Bachao*!	*Thirudan*! *Kaapatrungal*!
Please confirm my ticket	*Mera* ticket confirm *karo*	*En* ticket confirm *pannunga*
Where is the bathroom?	Bathroom kahaan *hai*?	*Kalivarai enge*?
How far?	*Kitna door*?	*Evvalavu dhooram*?

WEDDINGS AND FUNERALS

English	Hindi	Tamil
Congratulations!	*Badhai ho*!	*Paaraattukkal*
The bride is beautiful	*Ladki bahut sundar hai*	*Punnu romba azhaga irukka*
(I am) very sorry	*Bahut afsos hua*	*Mannikkanum*

COMMON ACRONYMS

For a culture known for prolixity, Indians do love their acronyms. Here are some of the more common ones you'll encounter:

AC   : air conditioner
AIR   : All India Radio (state-owned radio stations)
CBSE : Central Board of Secondary Education
CM   : Chief Minister
FIR   : First Information Report (what you fill out to report a crime)
FRRO : Foreigner's Regional Registration Office
GOI   : Government of India
IAS   : Indian Administrative Service
IIT   : Indian Institute of Technology
IPL   : Indian Premier League
ISD   : International Subscriber Dialling (international calls)
NGO : Non-government organisation
NRI   : Non-Resident Indian
PAN   : Permanent Account Number (a taxpayer identification number)
PIO   : People of Indian Origin
RBI   : Reserve Bank of India
STD   : Subscriber Trunk Dialling
TTE   : Ticket Taker Examiner (used for Indian railways)

RESOURCE GUIDE

EMERGENCY NUMBERS*

Police   : 100
Fire   : 101
Ambulance   : 102
Disaster Management : 108
Women's Helpline   : 181

* Note: From 1 January 2017, the single emergency number 112
  has been operational throughout India.

HOSPITALS AND MEDICAL FACILITIES

There are various private and public hospitals. As public ones usually do not meet standards expatriates might be accustomed to, most opt for reputed private facilities, which are known for their standards and have English-speaking staff. India's reputation as a growing medical tourism destination has also ensured that private facilities maintain international standards. Although medical treatment in India is relatively affordable, it is always best to have health insurance.

A common problem is the lack of transparency and the limitation in coverage. Expatriates with pre-existing health conditions may want to consider getting additional coverage through international health insurance companies. Expatriates under corporate employment contracts are generally offered health insurance as part of the relocation package.

New Delhi
- **Apollo Indraprastha Hospital:** www.apollohospdelhi.com
- **Fortis Hospital:** www.fortishealthcare.com

- **Max Super Speciality Hospital:** www.maxhealthcare.in
- **Primus Super Speciality Hospital:**
  www.primushospital.com

Mumbai
- **Bombay Hospital:** www.bombayhospital.com
- **P.D. Hinduja Hospital:** www.hindujahospital.com
- **Wockhardt Hospitals:** www.wockhardthospitals.com
- **Asian Heart Institute:** www.asianheartinstitute.org

Bengaluru
- **Bangalore Hospital:** www.bangalorehospital.co.in
- **Greenview Medical Centre:** www.gvhcol.com
- **Mallya Hospital:** www.mallyahospital.net
- **Vikram Hospital:** www.vikramhospital.com

INTERNATIONAL SCHOOLS

There are a variety of international and private schools available in the major cities. Here, I have listed a sampling of the more popular international schools in New Delhi, Mumbai, Bengaluru and Chennai.

New Delhi
- **American Embassy School:** www.aes.ac.in
- **British School:** www.british-school.org
- **Japanese School:** www.ndjs.org
- **German School:** www.dsnd.de/en
- **Lycee Francais de Delhi:** www.lfdelhi.org
- **Amity International School:** www.amity.edu
- **DPS International School:** www.dpsi.ac.in
- **Pathways (Gurgaon):** www.pathways.in

Mumbai

- **Dhirubhai Ambani International School:** www.da-is.org
- **Bombay International School:** www.bisschool.com
- **American School of Bombay:** www.asbindia.org
- **Singapore International School:** www.sisindia.net
- **DSB International School:** www.dsbindia.com

Bengaluru

- **The Canadian International School:**
  www.canadianinternationalschool.com
- **Ebenezer International School Bangalore:**
  www.eisbangalore.com
- **Greenwood High International School:**
  www.greenwoodhigh.edu.in
- **Indus International School:** www.indusschool.com
- **Inventure Academy:** www.inventureacademy.com
- **The International School Bangalore (TISB):** ww.tisb.
  org
- **Stonehill International School:**
  www.stonehillinternationalschool.org
- **Trio World Academy:** www.trioworldacademy.com

Chennai

- **American International School:** www.aischennai.org
- **British International School:** www.britishschool.co.in

Expatriate Clubs and Social Networking Sites

The major cities have fairly large expatriate communities, which is reflected in the growing number of expatriate clubs. These are good platforms to connect and interact as well as to get advice. Some like InterNations and MeetUp are available in almost all the major Indian cities, whilst others are city-specific. Since I have more experience with New Delhi, I am better able to safely recommend more clubs for this city.

- **InterNations** (www.internations.org) is a global social community that unites expatriates in 300 countries worldwide. It has communities in Bengaluru, Chennai, Kolkata, Mumbai, New Delhi and Gurgaon.
- **MeetUp** (www.meetup.com) enables you to make contact with other people in your city and arrange events based on shared interests.

New Delhi

- **Delhi Commonwealth Women's Association** (open to all nationalities): www.dcwaindia.com
- **Delhi Expat Club:** www.delhexpatclub.com
- **Delhi Network:** www.delhinetwork.org
- **Global Girls Group**, a women-only expatriate group based in Delhi, that organises social activities for its now 500 members. Founded by my friend Ankita Gupta, this is a great and safe way to make new friends. For more information and to register, go to the Facebook page of the Global Girls Group.
- **Gurgaon Connection**: www.gurgaonconnection.com
- **Yuni-Net (Delhi)**: This is a Delhi-based web group (Yahoo) that shares practical advice such as where to find second-hand furniture, small appliances, apartment shares, piano teachers, etc. You have to apply to be a member first so as to ensure that all members are legitimate expatriates. The website is at www.beta.groups.yahoo.com/neo/groups/yuninet-delhi

Nationality-specific

- **American Women's Association:** www.awadelhi.com
- **Japanese Association:** www.delhinihonjinkai.in
- **Nederlandse Vereniging:** Send an email to nederlandinindia@yahoo.com
- **New Zealand Association:** www.anzadelhi.org
- **Nordic Women's Association:** www.wix.com/delhiindia/noradelhi

Mumbai

- **The American Women's Club of Bombay (AWC):** www.awcmumbai.com
- **Mumbai Connexions:** www.mumbaiconnexions.com

Chennai

- **Overseas Women's Club:** www.chennaiowc.com

Bengaluru

- **Overseas Women's Club:** www.owcbangalore.org

Hyderabad

- **Twin-Cities Expatriates Association:** www.hytea.org

Travel by Train

For railway enquiries and to book tickets, go to www.indianraail.gov.in

For advice on how to prepare for an Indian train journey, see:

- www.seat61.com/India.htm#classes
- www.tripadvisor.in/Travel-g293860-c63603/India:Travelling.By.Trains.Booking.Tickets.html

FURTHER READING

History and Politics

- *India: A Concise History*. Francis Watson. Thames & Hudson, 2002.
- *The Legacy of India*. G.T Garrat. Black and White, 2005.
- *The Discovery of India.* Jawaharlal Nehru. Penguin Books, 2008
- *Timeline of India.* Gordan Kerr. Canary Press, 2011.
- *India after Gandhi.* Ramachandra Guha. Macmillan, 2007.
- *India From Midnight to Millennium & Beyond.* Shashi Tharoor. Penguin Books, 2012
- *Teardrop on the Cheek of Time: The Story of the Taj Mahal.* Diana & Michael Preston. Corgi Books, 2007
- *Emperors of the Peacock Throne.* Abraham Eraly. Penguin Books, 2000
- *South Asian Politics.* Edited by Neil DeVotta, Routledge, 2016

Flora and Fauna

- *Birds of India*. Krys Kazmierczak. OM Field Guides, 2000
  A comprehensive illustrated guide to over 1,300 bird species found in India, Sri Lanka, Pakistan, Nepal, Bhutan and the Maldives.
- *Trees of Delhi*. Pradip Krishen. DK, 2006
  The best field guide to trees in Delhi.

People and Culture

- *Cultural History of India*. Basham. Oxford University Press, 2014.

- *The Indians*. Sudhir Kakar & Katharina Kakar. Penguin Books, 2014.
- *Being Indian*. Pavan K Varma. Penguin India, 2005.
- *India's Culture*. B.P Singh. Oxford University Press, 1998
- *A Book of India*. B.N. Pandey. Rupa India, 2004.
- *Hinduism*. Rasamandala Das. Hermes House, 2012.
   A good primer to the religion.
- *Eating India*. Chitrita Banerji. Penguin Books, 2007.
- *The Argumentative Indian*. Amartya Sen. Penguin Books, 2005.
- *Indian Essentials*. (various contributors). Penguin Books, 2010.

Language

- *Teach Yourself Beginner's Hindi*. Rupert Snell. McGraw Hill, 2003.
- *Hindi-English Bilingual Visual Dictionary*. DK Publishing, 2008.

Doing Business

- *India Business Checklist*. Rupa K. Bose. John Wiley & Sons, 2009.
- *Doing Business in India*. R. Kumar, A. Sethi. Palgrave Macmillan, 2005.
   An insightful read on how Western managers can bridge the cultural gaps and complexities of India's business environment through case studies of European and American companies' business experiences in India.
- *Jugaad Innovation*. Navi Radjou, Jaideep Prabhu, Simone Ahuja. Random House India, 2012.

Fiction

- *A Passage to India*. E.M. Forster. Penguin Books, 2005.

  A story that reveals the uneasy times of pre-Independence India. This book won the James Tait Black Memorial Prize for fiction.

- *Kim*. Rudyard Kipling. Rupa Publications, 2013 (first published in 1901).

  A story about the adventures of a young Irish boy in British colonial India. Kipling won the Nobel Prize in Literature in 1907.

- *Midnight's Children*. Salman Rushdie. Vintage, 2013.

  This is an epic novel set at the point of India's Independence. It won the Man Booker Prize for Fiction (1991), "the Booker of Bookers" in 1993 and the James Tait Black Memorial Prize for Fiction in 2008, among others.

- *The God of Small Things*. Arundhati Roy. Random House, 2008 (first published in 1997).

  A story of an affluent Indian family in Kerala forever changed by one fateful day. It won the Man Booker Prize in 1997.

- *City of Joy*. Dominic Lapierre. Grand Central Publishing, 1988.

  An American doctor experiences a spiritual rebirth in an impoverished section of Kolkata, referred to as the "City of Joy" after this novel. It was adapted into film in 1992.

- *The Inheritance of Loss*. Kiran Desai. Grove Press, 2006.

  Set in the Himalayas, the story explores notions of nationhood, class and modernity through its characters. It won the Man Booker Prize in 2006.

- *The White Tiger*. Arvind Adiga. Free Press, 2008.

  Winner of the 2008 Man Booker Prize, the story centres around a poor Indian villager whose ambition leads him to explore the contradictions of India's social order.

- *Interpreter of Maladies*. Jhumpa Lahiri. Mariner Books, 1999.

  A collection of short stories with deft cultural insight on Indian traditions in a modern world, this book won the Pulitzer Prize for Fiction in 2000.

Fiction By Author

- William Dalrymple (1965–) is a writer and historian whose books weave excellent scholarship within arresting narratives. I recommend Dalrymple's *City of Djinns* (1993), *White Mughals* (2002), *The Last Mughal* (2006), and *The Age of Kali* (1998).

- R. K. Narayan (1906–2001) is among the best known and most widely read Indian English-language novelists. Many of his works capture Indian traits and are set in the fictional South Indian town of Malgudi. I recommend *Swami and Friends* (1935) and *The Guide* (1958), which won him the National Prize of the Indian Literary Academy, India's highest literary honour.

- Ruskin Bond (1934–) is an award-winning Indian author of British descent. Considered to be an icon among Indian writers and children's authors, his stories chronicle contemporary India. He was awarded the Sahitya Akademi Award for English writing in 1993, the Padma Shri in 1999 and the Delhi government's Lifetime Achievement Award in 2012. I recommend *The Best of Ruskin Bond* (2000).

- Rabindranath Tagore (1861–1941) wrote novels, stories, essays, songs and dramas. His best-known works are *Gitanjali* (*Song Offerings*, 1910), *Gora* (*Fair-Faced*, 1910), and *Ghare-Baire* (*The Home and the World*, 1916).

ABOUT THE
AUTHOR

Lynelle Seow is convinced that she must have been Indian in her previous life, given her interest in all things Indian. In this life, she is a Singaporean who has dreams of being a Bollywood dancer despite the reality of two left feet and an incredible lack of coordination. She holds a Master of Architecture, but prefers to build castles in the air and bridges to other cultures. She has lived and worked in Singapore, the United States, the Philippines and India as various avatars: architect, editor, branding-marketing professional, and volunteer English teacher. She is married to Benjamin Yap and they have eight plants together. She lived in India for what seemed to be a short lifetime and currently resides in Singapore.

INDEX

Titles in the CultureShock! series:

For more information about any of these titles, please contact any of our Marshall Cavendish offices around the world (listed on page ii) or visit our website at:

www.marshallcavendish.com/genref